The 1935 Riots in St Vincent

The 1935 Riots in St Vincent

From Riots to Adult Suffrage

ADRIAN FRASER

THE UNIVERSITY OF THE WEST INDIES PRESS
Jamaica • Barbados • Trinidad and Tobago

The University of the West Indies Press
7A Gibraltar Hall Road, Mona
Kingston 7, Jamaica
www.uwipress.com

A catalogue record of this book is available from the
National Library of Jamaica.

ISBN: 978-976-640-597-7 (print)
978-976-640-598-4 (Kindle)
978-976-640-599-1 (ePub)

Cover illustration by Josette Norris
Cover and book design by Robert Harris
Set in Minion Pro 10.5/14.2 x 27
Printed in the United States of America

To my granddaughter, Malia Fraser

CONTENTS

ILLUSTRATIONS

TABLES

ACKNOWLEDGEMENTS

THE PRODUCTION OF THIS BOOK OWES A LOT to the contribution made by several individuals, organizations and institutions. Special thanks have to be given to my friends Randolph Cato and Candy Veira. Randolph arranged for me to meet his father, Clement Cato, who was a policeman stationed at the courthouse on the day of the riots. His information was extremely useful in understanding what took place at the court yard on that day. Clement Cato also suggested that I speak to Lucas Layne, who was one of two policemen based at Georgetown during that time. Layne put me in contact with Baha Lawrence, a young taxi driver in 1935, who died as an amputee in March 2016 at the age of 101. Candy Veira not only arranged for but also participated in interviews with Osment Williams, who was wounded during the riots at Camden Park, and Kathleen Sardine, niece of John DeSouza, whose shop and home were stoned. Robert Ogarro invited me to his home to meet Norman Williams and Ronald Paris, who were not participants but observers of the proceedings at the court yard. Interviews with all of these persons were valuable in providing information that was not documented elsewhere. This was particularly so for Georgetown, where the only data available was provided by a police patrol that visited after the disturbances had finished. The information provided by Layne and Cato was extremely useful since they had been actively involved in trying to control the rioters. Lawrence recounted his experiences as taxi driver at Sion Hill.

A sabbatical and study leave granted by the University of the West Indies allowed me to visit the newspaper library at Colingdale and the Public Records Office at Kews Gardens in London. My initial research started at the St Vincent and the Grenadines National Archives when it was still in the process of being organized. Youlou Griffith, the archivist, was able to point me to available documents even before they were fully documented. Once the National Archives was finally established in a new building, its staff offered great assistance. Special thanks have to be given to Jeon Adams and to Cashena Foster, who were very supportive in accommodating my many requests and who checked occasionally to ensure that everything was in order. I am making a special appeal here for financial assistance to the National Archives. The microfilm machine there, I am convinced, was the first ever built. Using it was frustrating because it would work for ten minutes and stop for five. Having to be subjected to that exercise constantly was torturous. There were other inadequacies, but, despite the shortcomings, the staff gave me strong support, at times even allowing me access to material that was tattered.

Staff at the libraries of the University of the West Indies campuses at Mona, Cave Hill and St Augustine were very supportive. Pat Baptiste, librarian at the University of the West Indies Open Campus in St Vincent and the Grenadines, helped me to access information from campus libraries at Cave Hill and St Augustine. The National Archives in Port of Spain allowed me access to the *Port of Spain Gazette*, which had done extensive coverage of the riots.

The National Trust, through Osei Morris, made photographs of the court-house available to me, which enabled artist Josette Norris to create the design that forms the cover of this book. Josette has to be singled out for appreciation for the effort she put into the illustration for the book cover. G.P. McIntosh provided me with a photograph of George McIntosh, and other members of their family, particularly Frankie McIntosh, supported me and offered personal information not available elsewhere. Neil Jackson helped to improve the scanning of a street plan of Kingstown on 21 October 1935. A small monetary contribution from the Eastern Caribbean Group of Companies, through its general manager, Ken Boyea, helped to defray the cost of shipping documents from the Public Records Office.

Professors Bridget Brereton and Woodville Marshall's comments on the first draft guided me tremendously, but they bear no responsibility for any shortcomings in the final product.

My family had to put up with my many distractions and frequent absences. To my granddaughter Malia – who, seemingly intrigued by my long stays at the computer, often kept me company, requesting, in return, that I print her artwork for her – I have dedicated this book.

ABBREVIATIONS

CLC   Caribbean Labour Congress
HMSO   His (or Her) Majesty's Stationery Office
MP   Minute Papers
RGA   Representative Government Association
SVA   St Vincent Archives
SWMA St Vincent Workingmen's Cooperative Association

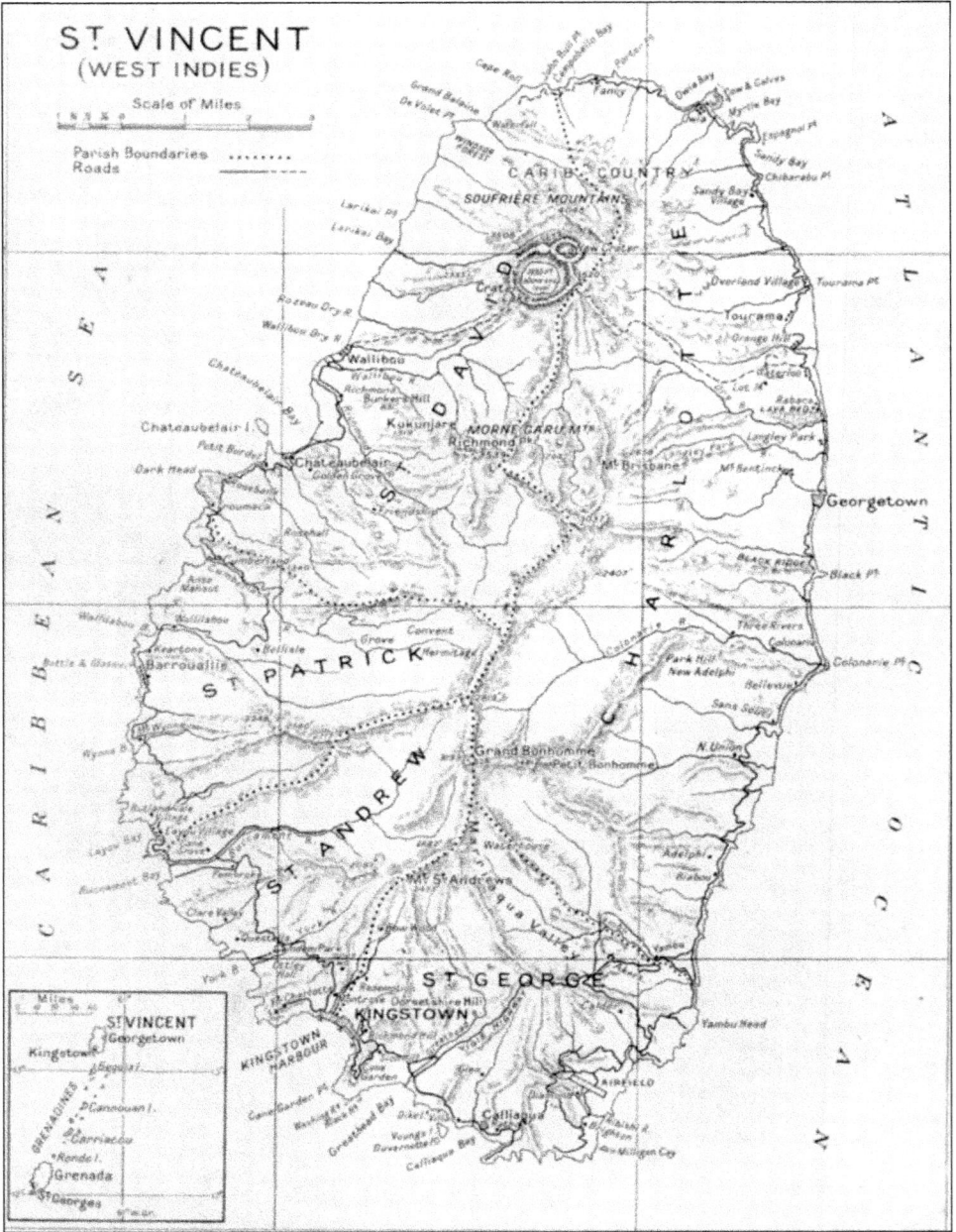

Figure 1. Map of St Vincent

INTRODUCTION

THE 1935 RIOTS IN ST VINCENT HAVE, UP to now, not been given any in-depth treatment.[1] It has had cursory treatment in works by O. Nigel Bolland and Richard
Hart that dealt with the spate of rebellions in the Caribbean in the 1930s. It has
also been the subject of brief articles and commentary in other works, including term papers and university theses.[2] This work sets out to correct this gap
in the literature. Writers on the disturbances of the 1930s, whether we choose
to describe them as riots, uprisings, rebellions or simply as disturbances, have
tended to lump them together, thus concealing the nature of their differences
and obscuring the depth of their analysis.[3] This book is, to some extent, an
adaptation and expansion of chapters 4 and 5 of my PhD dissertation.[4]

Although the socioeconomic conditions prevailing in the colonies in the
1930s were quite similar, there were differences, as shown at least in the case of
St Vincent, that helped to shape the political economy. This in turn would have
influenced the content and nature of the disturbances. Some of the disturbances were little more than strikes, but undoubtedly they had certain common
features throughout the region, with some aspects more pronounced in one
country than in another, based on a number of different factors. This examination of the St Vincent riots will help to strengthen the analysis and broaden
our understanding of the disturbances of the 1930s.

In most of the Caribbean countries identified with having rebellions in
the 1930s, the following features predominated. Efforts had been made, prior
to the 1930s, to organize and mobilize workers, in some cases with incipient
or quasi-formed unions or other organizations catering to the needs of workers. These were more pronounced in Jamaica, Trinidad and British Guiana,
where workers had been exposed for some time to a degree of organization
and consciousness-building. But other islands had similar organizations: the
Barbados Workingmen's Association, the St Kitts Workers League, the Labourers and Unemployed Association of Belize, and the Antigua Workingmen's
Association. Despite some working-class agitation in St Lucia on 6 November

1935, there were no working peoples' organizations. In any event, St Lucia, like Antigua and the Bahamas, was not subjected to any major disturbance. In St Lucia, Governor Selwyn Grier, with the experience of St Vincent behind him, moved quickly to prevent any unrest there turning into riots. The HMS *Challenger*, which was asked earlier to assist in St Vincent, arrived in St Lucia on 3 November, prior to the strike of 4 November.[5] Although, generally, the riots might have been more stimulated by the economic conditions of the 1930s than by the mobilization of workers, it is nevertheless true that the prior organization and mobilization of the working people would have influenced responses to the economic crisis that affected the region.

Strikes were also central to most of the disturbances. In fact, many of the disturbances began with strikes, which often turned into riots because of the reaction of the planters and of the police who were called to their assistance. In a number of cases, strikes followed the disturbances. These strikes occurred mainly on the plantations, at the docks and, in the case of the Bahamas, at the salt pans. Bolland describes the pattern that manifested itself throughout the region: "We see a frequent pattern in these rebellions, a local and quite specific labour dispute, having to do with rates of pay or methods of payment or an abusive overseer, or not enough work to go around, become a source of confrontation with management who promptly sought the backing of the police."[6]

The predominance of sugar as a Caribbean export crop has led to the literature being preoccupied with conditions on the sugar plantations because of the centrality of strikes in the disturbances. Considering the St Vincent case, where strikes were absent and sugar plantations were not as dominant as in most other Caribbean countries, the analysis needs to be expanded to incorporate the dynamics impacting on the regional economic scene. References are made to the loading of coal in St Lucia, banana production in Jamaica and the strike at the salt pans in the Bahamas. There is little reference, however, to the fact that St Vincent was not a sugar monocrop economy and that its two major crops, arrowroot and Sea Island cotton, were crops with whose cultivation the peasants were heavily involved making them significant players in the export economy.

To better understand the nature of the disturbances in St Vincent, it is necessary to identify the factors that gave a different shape to the country's political economy. This will explain why the disturbances manifested themselves the way they did.

Bolland makes the important point that "a comparative regional analysis of the labour rebellions between 1934 and 1939 is therefore essential for the further understanding of the whole historical process".[7] What this work does is to provide a thorough analysis of the 1935 riots in St Vincent, informed not only by government documents but also by newspapers and interviews with participants in the riots and also with observers. It carries the story beyond 1935 to the introduction of adult suffrage in 1951 and shows how the riots impacted on the political economy and shaped the move to adult suffrage.

CHAPTER I

ST VINCENT IN 1935

THE ST VINCENT RIOTS OF 21 AND 22 October 1935 that followed disturbances in St Kitts earlier in the year placed St Vincent among the first group of Caribbean colonies to have experienced riots and disturbances in the 1930s.[1] This chapter looks at St Vincent in the period before the riots, with a brief description of the capital, Kingstown, where the riots started.

St Vincent was administratively part of the four British Windward Islands, with a governor based in Grenada and administrators in charge in the other islands during his absence.[2] The colony included a number of smaller islands called the Grenadines, some inhabited and others not. It covered 150 square miles, 133 on the mainland of St Vincent and 17 in the Grenadines; the Grenadine islands comprised Bequia (the largest, at 7 square miles), Union Island (4), Canouan (2.6), Mustique (2), Mayreau (1) and Balliceaux (0.7). The population in 1935 was estimated at 55,219, an increase of 7,258 from that indicated in the 1931 census.

Kingstown, the capital and main town, had a population, at the time of the 1931 census, of 4,269, with Barrouallie, boasting a population of 1,267, being the only other town to reach 1,000. When the outer suburbs were taken into account, Kingstown reached a population of 6,408, Georgetown 1,824 and Barrouallie 1,692. St Vincent was to a large extent a one-town colony, with Kingstown being the commercial and administrative centre, the other towns being largely rural settlements.

Kingstown was built around three main streets running slightly north-west to south-east, parallel to the seashore and to each other. Bay Street, nearest to the seashore, contained many of the mercantile houses, the factory and warehouse of the Arrowroot Association, and the police barracks. In Middle Street were the principal dry goods stores and groceries and the Kingstown Club, which the elite of the country frequented. Back Street, which combined Granby, Halifax, Grenville and Tyrell streets running from east to west, held the main residences, public buildings and churches.[3] Along Back Street was the public library, whose upper floor, referred to as the Carnegie Hall, was often the venue for public lectures and different forms of entertainment. Lectures and discussions on the Italo-Abyssyninan War were held there. It was also the place where Marcus Garvey addressed Vincentians when he visited in 1937. Also on that street were Barclays Bank, the St Vincent Agricultural Bank and one of the country's two cotton factories.

The centre of the town was dominated by a square that had been built by the French during their short period of control from 1779–83. It constituted the market area, commonly referred to as the market square. The square was located between Bedford Street on the western side, which ran perpendicular to the three main streets, and a canal on the eastern side that ran across and intersected the main streets. The canal divided the Bay and Middle streets into lower and upper sections. At the southern end of the market square was the town hall.

The courthouse, with the magistrate court on its ground floor and the legislative council on the upper floor, was also located in the centre of the town. The courthouse was to the north of the market square and was separated from it by Back Street. Corea's Dry Goods Store was located at the intersection of Middle Street and Bedford Street, and Corea's Liquor Store at that of Bedford and Lower Bay streets. The police barracks was situated at the intersection of Upper Bay Street and Hillsboro Street, which ran roughly parallel to the canal on the eastern side. The yard of the courthouse, the market square, Corea's Dry Goods and Liquor Stores and the police barracks became the focus of activities at the beginning of the riots on 21 October.[4]

The 1931 census listed seventy villages in St Vincent. These emerged first from neighbouring estates on land that was either rented or purchased by former slaves following emancipation in 1838 and, later, from land settlement areas provided by government land settlement schemes. Georgetown, which was twenty-two miles away from Kingstown, was the country's second town. Its location near the Carib country estates and being home to the lone sugar factory made it a centre of activity. Motorable road from Kingstown to the windward coast reached only as far as Georgetown.

LAND SETTLEMENT AND THE ECONOMY

St Vincent was the first of the British colonies to have accepted the recommendation of the 1897 West India Royal Commission for the establishment of government-sponsored land settlement schemes. The report of the commission presented a gloomy and pessimistic view of the future of sugar cultivation and recommended the establishment of the labouring population of the Caribbean as small farmers. St Vincent was singled out as a special case. The report stated: "It seems to us that whether the sugar industry is maintained or disappears, it is absolutely essential in the interest of the native population that the settlement on the land should be facilitated; in no other way does it seem to us to be possible to maintain even the most moderate degree of prosperity in St Vincent."[5]

Starting in 1899, following the destructive hurricane of 1898, estates were acquired in the leeward parishes of St Patrick and St David, of Richmond Hill in St Georges and of New Adelphi and Park Hill in the Charlotte parish. Following the initial acquisition of land and the establishment of the scheme, accommodation had to be made to settle refugees from a volcanic eruption in 1902. By 1910, the scheme had been extended to Union Island in the Grenadines. The total acreage acquired by then was 7,060 acres. The purchase of the Belair estate in 1912 was the last such scheme until the establishment of the Three Rivers scheme in 1932. Despite the absence of land settlement schemes in the intervening period, workers had been able to acquire some land by rent or purchase through the Crown Lands Scheme that had started in 1891 and from private land owners. This, however, came nowhere near to satisfying the demand for land (see table 1).[6]

Numerous petitions to the government seeking land through another land settlement programme were made over the years, particularly following the 1932 Three Rivers Land Settlement Scheme. It was seen as essential to the economic well-being of the people and the country – really, as a solution to the country's economic problems.[7] It was a surprise to C.Y. Shephard of the Imperial College of Tropical Agriculture in Trinidad that, up to 1931, the government had not undertaken any land settlement since 1914.[8] G.A. Jones, agricultural commissioner for the Caribbean colonies, had voiced the view, on a visit to St Vincent in 1932, that those persons who had acquired land had a real stake in the country and were developing into most useful citizens.

A land settlement committee was set up in 1931 to examine the suitability of lands for peasant settlements and to determine how they were to be acquired.

Table 1. Land Acquired through Land Settlement Schemes

Estates	Acreage	Year Acquired	Settlement	Parish
Convent	200	1899	Cumberland Valley	St Patrick
Spring	381			
Grove	315			
Belleisle and New Works	228			
Hermitage	400			
Troumaca	195	1899	Linley Valley	St David
Rose Bank	285			
Belmont	273			
Rose Hall	717			
Richmond Hill	285	1899	Richmond Hill	St Georges
New Adelphi	505	1899		Charlotte
Park Hill	796			
Clare Valley	394	1901	St Andrews	
Questelles	239			
Union Island	2,600	1910		Grenadines
Sandy Bay	89	1911		Charlotte
Lammies	87	1911		St Patrick
Belair	400	1912		St Georges
Three Rivers	722	1932		Charlotte

Source: Report of Gurney, Grenada, West Indies, 14 November 1898; Agricultural Superintendent's report, Thompson to Chamberlain, no. 287 1898/99, 4 November 1899, SVA; Colonial Reports – Miscellaneous, no. 90, St Vincent: Report on the Administration of the Roads and Land Settlement Fund from 1 January 1911 to 31 March 1914, SVA.

The *Times* in its edition of 15 April 1931 echoed the growing demand for an extension of land settlement, indicating that it is, "without doubt, of immense interest to the people".[9] The committee recommended the purchase of several estates. The one with which the government decided to proceed was the Three Rivers estate, which was acquired in 1932.[10]

The establishment of the Three Rivers Land Settlement Scheme, after an absence of land settlement for twenty years, raised hopes that the government was about to embark on another period of land settlement. In July 1935, based on the constant call for land as expressed by the newspapers, Administrator Grimble intimated the government's need to monitor the financial progress of the Three Rivers scheme as an explanation for not moving further on land settlement. But, clearly, his explanation flew in the face of the fact that previous schemes had not been financially unsuccessful.

His second reason was more acceptable. In reference to the leeward region, where the greatest necessity for land existed, he indicated that owners in that region were unwilling to sell their land.[11] G.A. Jones, in a letter to the governor and responding to the administrator's of 22 July, highlighted the leeward parishes of St Patrick. He noted that "the people are suffering from want of work on these estates and from the fact that they have no land to cultivate other than certain inaccessible mountain gardens". He argued that "the future prosperity of St Vincent like the other islands in the West Indies will depend to a large extent on the facilities placed at the disposal of the agricultural workers to become owners of their own holdings".[12]

Of a population of 12,700 in the leeward parishes, 7,000 were landless, although some of the landless included professional people and others such as schoolmasters, artisans and clerks. Working the land, nonetheless, constituted the main livelihood for most families. The local estate owners, although only three "per thousandth" of the population, owned 70 per cent of the cultivable land. In a confidential document, Administrator Grimble indicated to Governor Grier the seriousness of the situation:

> The disadvantages of so uneven a distribution have been keenly felt of recent years. During the period of financial depression, employment has been reduced to the lowest limit and the labourer without land for the cultivation of market produce or even provision for his family has suffered extreme hardship. A considerable increase of the incidence of praedial larceny has been the natural result of these conditions; the beginnings of social unrest in the leeward region are observable.[13]

In the leeward estates of St Patrick and St David, land hunger was indeed most acute. Fourteen persons owned 2,108 acres. The remaining 5,563 acres were owned by a single planter. Apart from the control of a substantial portion by a single individual, the situation was made worse by the fact that more than one-third of the cultivable area was kept uncultivated, creating severe social and economic hardships. Grimble noted, too, that the single owner was a dispenser of "feudal like charities" and had a strong hold over the workers. It was under those circumstances difficult to undertake land settlement without his cooperation. Grimble did suggest, however, that if they did not get the consent of the owner in question, there should be adequate justification for its acquisition.[14]

But the demand for land did not only come from parishes in the leeward region. There were petitions from different parts of the colony, including the Grenadines. The *Times* found it necessary to support a petition from the Island of Bequia for the purchase of an estate that was advertised for sale in February 1935: "The life in these small islands of the Grenadines is most precious as everyone knows and no opportunity should be allowed to slip which may be made use of in bettering their conditions. . . . We commend the request of these people to the Government and hope that they will receive the consideration they deserve."[15]

As can be seen from statistics for 1933 (see table 2), the ownership of land was quite uneven, with eighty-eight holdings of over one hundred acres each occupying over 60 per cent of the land.

Although land settlement was considered critical to the economic development of the colony, it also had a social dimension. This had been recognized since the establishment of the early land settlement schemes, where efforts were made to encourage the rural working population to live on lands distributed. It was based on the recognition that "the school, church, shop and cricket pitch were much appreciated village amenities".[16] Cricket was encouraged on the estates, something that seems to have been common to other West Indian colonies. It certainly acted as a social bond between workers and management.[17] There was, in fact, a great interest in cricket in 1935 at the national level and on

Table 2. Land Ownership Statistics for 1933

Category	Holdings	Total Acreage
Under 10 acres	4,907	11,756 acres; 3,884 house spots (i.e., parcels of land 50–60 square feet each)
11–50 acres	233	4,655 acres
51–100 acres	30	2,135 acres
101–1,000 acres	84	29,773 acres
Over 1,000 acres	4	5,703 acres

Source: *Times*, 23 February 1935.

the estates. An incident that took place a month after the riots demonstrated the significant role that cricket was playing. In November 1935, a few weeks after the October riots, two hundred workers of the Mount Bentinck estate and residents of the Mount Bentinck village turned out to welcome home from holidays abroad Allan Richards, proprietor of the estate on which their cricket field was located. They were enthusiastic in their welcome, shouting "God save Master Allan". What was significant though strange about this was that it was a time of growing tension and conflict on the estates, following the disturbances of 21 and 22 October.

It is true that Richards's relationship with his workers was exemplary. In its issue of 19 December 1935, the *Times*, a critic of the planter class, recommended Richards as a suitable candidate for the 1936 general elections. It argued that "if there is an estate owner whose consideration for labour has become proverbial it is Mr. Richards". But the real significance of this unusual relationship can be recognized from a message read to him that complained that the workers' cricket field had been taken away during his absence. They were begging him for another spot.[18] Cricket was indeed an essential part of estate and village life. Rupert John captures this: "In those days, a village team would travel to various parts of the island to play against other teams. . . . The return of the . . . team was greeted by great enthusiasm and song. In fact, as the successful team approached their home village, they would be heard singing songs announcing their victory over the other team."[19]

THE ECONOMY

Two visitors to St Vincent in 1935 were in full praise of the beauty and development of the colony. In the *Times* of 21 February, one writer who labelled himself a "visitor" declared that, in the last eight years, St Vincent was the most improved West Indian island. It is not clear what led him to, or even entitled him to, arrive at that conclusion. He had, however, spent two months in the country eight years previously and was so impressed with its development on his return that he waxed poetical. The harbour buildings that needed repairs eight years before were "properly repaired and dancing a bright array of painted colours under the influence of a truly tropical sunlight". He identified features that impressed him: good streets; new buildings that reflected the architecture "in vogue in the West Indies"; the Edinboro Castle Club, the best of its kind in the West Indies; the modernized transport system; the Mount Bentinck sugar plant and the most up-to-date rum distillery. Indeed, he was surprised by the absence of promotion to lure visitors to the country.

In its issue of 31 August 1935, the *Vincentian* carried an article captioned "St Vincent" by another visitor, who was impressed with the "charming scenic beauty" that "can hardly be surpassed anywhere". He was fascinated, too, by the cleanliness of the streets, the sea bathing resorts, the town's potential as a health resort, the cotton factory, the fort and the "hospitality and courtesy" of Vincentians, who, he felt, could well give a lesson in those areas to many.

Both visitors who were so impressed with the country focused, naturally, on the physical landscape and the friendliness of the people. In terms of an understanding of St Vincent in 1935, their comments were to that extent super-ficial. Other commentators, residents of the country, looking at it from the perspectives of persons living there, portrayed a different picture. In the *Times'* first issue of 1935, D.A. Niles's poem "Depression" speaks to the impact of the worldwide depression on the colony and its people. He sets it in an international context:

All over this civilised world today
Depression, Depression is what people say
If this continues, Tis better to die
For to live in this world one
Always would cry.

Then he ends his poem:

Its time, Its time, Its time
Depression has caused enough crimes
When shall we be rid of this turbulent pest
Oh Lord! Let depression go back to its nest.[20]

Niles, a Vincentian, was reflecting on the reality of life in the 1930s. The news-papers, without knowingly doing so, detailed aspects of what Niles might have been hinting at. In its 3 October issue, the *Times*, commenting on the matter of trade, stated: "Business circles have said that there is at present an almost incredible dullness in trade, the cry comes from every hand." But then the paper leaves room for some optimism: "Perhaps it is darkest just before the dawn."

Even the governor was prepared to express his concern. In an address at a meeting with members of the Representative Government Association (RGA), he painted a gloomy picture: "This colony is very near the Rocks. I want this little colony of St Vincent to keep away from these rocks. It is only fair that if we can keep our financial ship off the rocks we should do so."[21]

The governor was no disinterested observer. He wanted to reduce expectations and stave off criticisms which, for a long time, had associated the weak economic situation with the nature of Crown colony government. The purpose of the visit of the Closer Union Commission in 1933 was to examine the possibility of a closer union between Trinidad and the Windward and Leeward Islands. Their investigation suggested to them that there was more concern about the future prospects of the colony and its financial state than about "closer union".

The poor economic state of the colony was blamed on the administration by persons who made submissions to the commission. It was, for some time, a commonly held belief that if the people had had a greater say in their affairs, the economic situation would not have been as desperate as it was then. In the colony's second town, Georgetown, there were complaints by merchants and shopkeepers that "there was little money in circulation", leading to the bad state of affairs they were experiencing.[22]

The poor economic situation was reflected in the lack of employment, dreadful conditions of work and depressed standard of living. Not only was employment hard to get but it was irregular, the labouring class having, at most, probably less than six months' employment during the year. It was worst on the leeward coast, with workers having only three or four months' employment per year, at most. Agricultural labourers received eight pence to a shilling for five to six hours' work, getting even lower on some parts of the leeward coast.[23]

The context that shaped the features of the Vincentian economy was somewhat different from many of the other colonies of the English-speaking Caribbean. The report of the Agricultural Department for 1935 made the point that "planters in St Vincent are indeed fortunate in being able to grow a variety of crops and also in having a number of annual crops so that it is possible (within limits) to change from one crop to another according to the prevailing market conditions".[24]

Two things stand out when looking at the Vincentian economy of that period. First, sugar had lost its original dominance. In fact, it lived a marginal existence, with fluctuating fortunes. It was virtually a dead crop by 1913, when only 250 pounds were exported. It had fallen on rough times in the immediate aftermath of the two disasters, the 1898 hurricane and volcanic eruption of 1902, that had struck St Vincent at the turn of the century. By the end of the first decade of the twentieth century, it was limited to particular areas, with its only value lying in its being a rotation crop for cotton and arrowroot and in preserving the soil that was being exhausted by cotton planting.[25] Sugar export had a brief revival during the war years and, by 1934, had reached an annual value of £5,979. Its highest point, however, was in 1928, when it realized a value of £14,193. But, in 1928, it represented only 9 per cent of domestic exports, compared to 95 per cent for Barbados, 97 for Antigua, 86 for St Kitts, 20 for Trinidad, 45 for St Lucia and 19 for Jamaica.[26]

The West Indian Sugar Commission of 1930 was not scheduled to visit St Vincent since it was not a major producer of sugar. There were, however, applications for assistance in procuring equipment for a newly established sugar factory and for a new factory producing mainly syrup. The commission, therefore, visited. The planters later began to give much more attention to the production of syrup than to sugar, the value of its export doubling that of sugar in 1934. In that year, 1,680,000 pounds of sugar, valued at £5,979, was produced. The production of syrup on the other hand, reached 269,233 gallons, valued at £11,218.[27] By 1935, there was only one small factory manufacturing sugar and rum.

A replacement for sugar was desperately needed, for even during the last years of its nineteenth-century existence, it had employed few workers, with the result that there was large unemployment. The two crops to which the country turned were Sea Island cotton and arrowroot. Arrowroot had been exported since 1830, although its cultivation started long before this. While the slaves had been initially responsible for its cultivation, after emancipation the estates started producing it for commercial purposes and took it up particularly in a period when the price of sugar was low. The nature of its production, particularly the need for little care, suited the slaves and the newly emancipated who were attached to estate labour. It could be grown on hilly areas and on estate backlands, the kind of lands available to former slaves. The failing sugar industry in the latter part of the nineteenth century drove the planters to a greater concentration on the production of arrowroot, thus influencing the price and making it more difficult for the peasants.

With the collapse of the sugar industry at the end of the nineteenth century, arrowroot presented itself as an alternative crop, particularly when St Vincent became its major producer in the world. The cultivation of arrowroot was aided by the colony's "very pure water", giving it "an almost monopolistic natural advantage", all of this a product of its geological structure.[28]

The other crop that served as a replacement for sugar was cotton, a crop that used to be grown before British control of the region. Concentration on sugar detracted from its cultivation, which was continued primarily in the islands of the Grenadines. There, a variety known as Marie Galante was grown.[29] The call by the 1897 West India Royal Commission for greater diversification led the Imperial Department of Agriculture of the West Indies to encourage the production of cotton, a task it shared with the British Cotton Growing Association.[30] The introduction of a new variety, Sea Island cotton, in 1902 came after experimentation in St Lucia. In 1903, with financial assistance from the Volcanic Eruption Relief Funds, a factory was built.[31]

With the planting of arrowroot and Sea Island cotton, the diversification away from sugar began, to the extent that those two crops dominated the exports of St Vincent until the 1950s, when bananas became the premier crop. Arrowroot and Sea Island cotton fluctuated in their dominance of exports. What was of significance to the St Vincent economic landscape was the heavy involvement of peasants in the export of those two crops. The high price of cotton by 1910 attracted, particularly, those who were allottees of the land settlement schemes.[32]

Sea Island cotton thus oscillated with arrowroot for premier export status. The *Times* of 7 December 1946 highlighted what was more clearly seen by then, that "the Sea Island cotton industry forms an essential part of the economics of this country. Apart from the lint which is exported, the cotton seed oil and the meal have been so widely used that the loss of this industry will hurt the colony very hard." (See table 3.)

The 1935 annual report on the social and economic progress of the people of St Vincent indicated the extent of plantation and peasant production of those crops (see table 4). The figures listed for arrowroot are somewhat misleading, for the estate production figures include portions of peasant cultivation retained as payment for processing their crops. There was also a practice of peasants selling their entire crop to the estate to have the benefit of immediate payment.[33] Some peasants preferred this manner of operating to taking their starch to the Arrowroot Association, where they got an advance but had to wait over a year for full settlement. "Peasants in some areas received loans from factory owners and decided to sell them all their produce."[34]

What stood out, too, about the agricultural production of this period was the fluctuation in acreage planted in the two major crops and hence the impact on prices, and vice versa. The *Vincentian*, in a comment on the arrowroot industry in its 28 September 1935 issue, noted: "The tendency toward over production

Table 3. Quantity and Value of Exports, 1933–1935

Crop/Animal	Quantities exported			Values exported £		
	1933	1934	1935	1933	1934	1935
Arrowroot Starch (lb)	4,589,435	6,526,003	6,609,856	55, 510	75,044	76,668
Sugar (ton)	850	750	725	8, 162	5,979	6, 406
Syrup & Molasses (gal.)	278,528	269, 233	148, 357	11, 624	11, 218	6, 182
Rum, proof (gal.)	9,832	5,761	5,468	1,475	908	641
Cotton – Sea Island (lb)	160, 792	204,519	205,549	8,107	9,346	9,947
Cotton – Marie Galante (lb)	78,508	53,907	38,604	1,619	1,123	804
Copra (lb)	2,149,641	2,015,675	840,602	8,978	6,551	3,418
Coconut (no.)	17,713	979,988	3,391,582	38	2,538	10,215
Cocoa (lb)	100,230	94,758	97,242	1,141	894	915
Banana (stem)	431	458	5,837	37	46	475
Cassava Starch (lb)	681,761	480,587	778,059	3,110	3,081	4,124
Groundnut (lb)	47,334	12,048	15,282	292	83	98
Nutmeg (lb)	27,342	21,544	30,240	342	269	378
Mace (lb)	6,015	5,044	6,796	301	210	283
Maize (lb)	1,884	34,350	4,261	8	109	25
Pea (lb)	120,658	60,274	100,872	754	377	624
Lime (no.)	596,629	1,183,281	695,570	219	198	166
Plantain (stem)	–	–	–	181	484	295
Sweet Potato (150-lb bag)	7,909	9,868	9,150	2,186	3,152	2,294
Yam (lb)	–	–	–	83	160	168
Tannia (lb)	–	–	–	519	607	477
Animal						
Goat (no.)	2,642	2,372	2,114	873	633	758
Poultry (no.)	–	–	–	820	770	687
Pig (no.)	2,637	2,174	2,390	3,422	3,705	3,954
Sheep (no.)	756	800	958	408	438	485
Ass (no.)	150	103	45	206	127	85
Horse (no.)	7	9	2	223	233	55
Cattle (no.)	70	19	22	391	108	135

Source: *Annual Report of the Agricultural Department,* 1935, 1; Frederick Walker, "Economic Progress of St Vincent since 1927", *Economic Geography* 13, no. 3 (1937): 225–33.

Table 4. Agricultural Produce by Peasants and Plantations in 1935

Crop	Estimated percentage produced by plantations	Estimated percentage produced by peasants	Percentage exported
Cotton – Sea Island (lb)	44	56	100
Cotton – Marie Galante (lb)	20	80	100
Cacao (lb)	70	30	60
Arrowroot (lb)	75	25	98
Cassava (lb)	67	33	75
Sugar (ton)	100	–	50
Syrup (gal.)	80	20	73
Copra (lb)	98	2	100
Maize (lb)	25	75	33
Groundnut (lb)	60	40	50
Pea and Bean (lb)	65	35	50
Sweet Potato (lb)	20	80	25
Plantain (stem)	10	90	16
Tannia (lb)	10	90	30
Yam (lb)	10	90	40
Miscellaneous vegetables (lb)	10	90	25
Banana (stem)	64	36	65
Tomato (lb)	1	99	25
Orange (no.)	45	55	50
Grapefruit (no.)	40	60	20
Coconut (no.)	90	10	90
Lime (no.)	22	78	57
Mace (lb)	60	40	99
Nutmeg (lb)	60	40	99
Ginger (lb)	5	95	56

Source: *Colonial Office Annual Reports*; *Agricultural Department Annual Report, 1935.*

due to the pardonable eagerness on the part of many a grower to grasp every opportunity for relieving himself of that benefit effect of the economic crisis is now shifted to some extent to Sea Island cotton."

A summary of the work of the Imperial Department of Agriculture (1898–1907) reflected a pattern which continued up to the 1930s. On the issue of arrow-root as the premier industry, it noted: "St Vincent has more than supplied the market demand, and it is hoped that the greatly increased area planted in cotton will tend to reduce the area planted in this crop and enable remunerative prices for the starch to be obtained."

The smaller-scale cultivation of individual peasants gave them an advantage over the estates in their flexibility and ability to shift from one crop to another. They were thus able to adjust much more easily than the estates to changes in price and demand. The acreage of arrowroot, 3,700, planted in 1935 was influenced, to some extent, "by a revival in the Sea Island cotton market. As good cotton land is usually good arrowroot land an improvement in the cotton market in 1936 would probably further decrease the arrowroot acreage especially where land is owned by peasants."[35]

Fluctuations in the number of acres planted in major crops in any year depended on price and demand. The number of what can be called minor crops that were exported and the extent of peasant involvement was significant. But the word "minor" is, in this context, a misnomer, for it relates mainly to "their contribution to total national exports and does not reflect their significance to small cultivators" that extended beyond the "statistical computation".[36]

The value of all agricultural produce and animals listed as having been exported in 1935 was £130,762. Table 3 indicates the extent of exportation and value. While, individually, the minor crops in particular years pale into insignificance when compared with the major crops, they still had a significant impact on what was a small economy. They were important because of the extent of small-grower involvement in their production. Likewise, livestock, although not a major contributor to the colony's economy, also made a significant contribution to peasants and labourers. They were sold in the regional market. Frederick Walker stated that "almost any day one may see boat loads of grunting animals being transported to the inter-island schooners and sloops in the Kingstown harbour".[37]

Cultivators who owned fewer than ten acres of land were likely to be persons who combined work on their land with employment on estates or elsewhere. Labourers on estates were provided with land on which they produced part of their subsistence, of which they sold any surpluses.[38] There were also agricultural labourers who did not live on the estates but owned or rented Crown lands elsewhere. Therefore, in the "ten and under" category, there was little distinction between a labourer and a peasant cultivator. Most cultivators in St Vincent, large and small, were involved in the market economy.[39]

The major crops were cotton (Sea Island and Marie Galante), arrowroot, sugar and its by-products. Other listed produce were classified as minor. Small cultivators produced 30 per cent of cacao, 33 of cassava, 40 of groundnuts and 90 of vegetables. They dominated in the smaller minor crops of maize, sweet potatoes, plantains, tannias, yams, vegetables, tomatoes, grapefruit and what are classified as miscellaneous (see table 4). Most of these crops were sold in regional markets, particularly in Barbados, Trinidad and, to a lesser extent, Grenada. Ground provisions had been exported to Barbados since 1842.[40] From 1897, livestock was also a part of the export trade.[41] At play was St Vincent's proximity to Grenada, Trinidad and Barbados, with regular traffic by boat between the mainland and the Grenadines facilitating traffic to Trinidad and Grenada.

The production and export of tomatoes, peas, mangoes and other fruit and vegetables to Canada and Bermuda were stimulated by the creation of the Fruit and Vegetable Bureau in 1929.[42] Other produce, such as avocado, peas, limes and oranges, were later added to the list of goods shipped by the bureau before its closure in July 1935. Another fruit that came into the picture later was the banana. An agreement to sell all bananas for export, during the period 1936–40, to the Canada Banana Company was made by the Cooperative Banana Association that was formed in 1934. The plantations were the ones that first ventured into its production, putting 234 acres into this crop while the peasants looked cautiously at developments.[43] By June 1935, 340 acres had been planted.[44] The first shipment was made on 31 July 1935, when 114 stems were exported on the *Lady Nelson* to the Canadian market.[45]

When the worldwide economic depression began to impact heavily on the country during the early years of the 1930s, employment on the estates was even more drastically reduced. During these harsh economic times, the workers of St Vincent focused more attention on the acquisition of land than on estate labour. It must be remembered that the cotton and arrowroot estates did not create as large a demand for labour as obtained with the sugar industry in its period as the premier crop. It is therefore easy to understand why the main focus of the agricultural workers was on ownership and access to land. There were opportunities for peasants and labourers with the kinds of crops that were being exported.

SOCIAL ASPECTS: EDUCATION, SOCIETY AND RELIGION

The 1945 report of the West India Royal Commission (also known as the Moyne Commission) noted that "social progress in the West Indies was slow and chequered".[46] It paid particular attention to social services, identifying the conditions that existed and the needs arising from those conditions. The commission visited St Vincent in January 1939, as part of their investigations into colonies affected by disturbances. The report would have reflected the situation pretty much as it was in 1935, since little had changed. Housing throughout the West Indies, in its view, left much to be desired. The members of the commission visited areas in each colony where housing conditions were identified as being poor. They also inspected model buildings, examined efforts to deal with slum clearance and rehousing, and entertained oral evidence on housing. The 1936 *Annual Colonial Report* for St Vincent and the 1939 Orde Brown report on labour conditions had already pointed to the poor state of housing in St Vincent: "Timber and board are difficult to obtain. The majority of peasants and labourers cannot afford to buy those materials. A certain amount of rough timber is obtained illegally from government owned mountain land. Most plantation owners demand payment for timber taken from their lands and even for grass and cane trash required for roofing."[47]

Orde Brown emphasized the fact that housing was bad and drew attention to the extent of overcrowding. Houses on estate lands were extremely small and poorly constructed and maintained. Peasant-owned houses were not much better, as their standard was also described as being low.[48]

In the rural areas and slum sections of the town, in particular, a yard accommodated more than one house. The yard, according to Roger Abrahams, perpetuated and allowed for the continuation of the "forces of tradition, order and continuity within the community".[49] But it represented much more than this; it was the centre of community gossip and the place where news from Kingstown, the capital, was relayed.

The overcrowding and poor state of housing facilitated the development and spread of disease. The Moyne Commission reported that "the generally insanitary environment gives rise to malaria, worm infection and bowel diseases; leaking roofs, rotten flooring and lack of light encourage the spread of tuberculosis, respiratory diseases, worm infections, jigger lesions and rat borne diseases; overcrowding, which is usually accompanied by imperfect ventilation, is an important agent in contributing to high incidence of yaws, tuberculosis, venereal diseases and to a certain extent, leprosy".[50]

St Vincent was, however, singled out as "decidedly healthy". "Diseases such as malaria which were found elsewhere were not present. The diseases prevalent were tuberculosis, venereal diseases and affections of the digestive system."[51]

As with other things, the Moyne Commission was critical of the state of education. It pointed to shortage of accommodation for schoolchildren. Accommodation, when available, was in disrepair, badly planned and with poor ventilation. Furthermore, "curricula are on the whole ill-adapted to the needs of the large mass of the population and adhere far too closely to models which have become out of date in the British practice from which they were blindly copied".[52]

An active teachers' association existed. It saw education not as an isolated entity but as being part of other developments in society. This can be seen from its presentation to the governor in 1935 and, later, to the Royal Commission.[53] The teachers' association was very much involved in efforts to form a West Indies and British Guiana Teachers Association and had two of its members, B.R. James and C.W. Prescod, elected as members of the bigger association.[54]

Religious denominations were still actively involved in the educational system. They provided for and were responsible for the maintenance of twenty-four primary schools, thirteen held by the Methodists, nine by the Anglicans and two by the Roman Catholics.[55] Of a population of 55,219, the number of students on roll was 10,432, with 4,331 placed in government schools, 2,883 in Methodist schools, 2,546 in Anglican schools and 672 in Roman Catholic schools.

Despite the small professional class, an active literary and intellectual atmosphere was in existence. Newspapers carried regular information about the achievements of blacks in Africa and the diaspora. The Italo-Abyssinian War was regularly featured and became the subject of debates. A St Vincent literary association existed and had regular lectures and discussions. In April, there was a lecture on Mathew Arnold and, in June, a discussion on "What is St Vincent's greatest need at this present moment". Four newspapers, three of them weeklies, were in existence at the beginning of 1935 – the *Investigator*, the *Times*, the *Vincentian* and the *Speaker*, but the *Speaker* ceased publication in July 1935.[56]

C.V.D. Hadley, in an article written in 1949 entitled "Personality Patterns, Social Class and Aggression in the British West Indies", attempted to identify the social structure in St Vincent. He highlighted three different groupings that constituted its structure: first, the proletariat, which he described as persons engaged in agricultural field labour, fishing and other occupations that earned wages on a daily or weekly basis. This label, he argued, applies to the "vast majority" of villagers in the West Indies. In the level above that group on the social ladder was the "un-established emergent or lower middle class". This group included elementary school teachers, junior posts in business and the civil service, and small landed proprietors. Then there was the "established upper middle class". In this category were members of professions, those holding senior posts in the civil service or in business, and "whole families usually have behind them at least one or two generations of such status".[57]

It is not the intention here to be caught up with fine definitions of class and social groupings but to work along with Hadley's definitions and assumptions in a bid to understand Vincentian society in 1935. In his view, one of the weaknesses of the social structure here was "the paucity of the middle class as a whole with a preponderance among such middle class families as do exist, of families of the emergent type and a relatively small number of families of the upper or established middle class type".[58]

This was taken up by others. Representatives of the St Vincent Clergymen's Fellowship in their appearance before the West India Royal Commission argued that there was a marked absence of a middle class in St Vincent. The *Times*, responding to that view, suggested that what was lacking was "the establishment of an independent, thriving middle class".[59]

Although one cannot be precise because of the nature of the classifications in the 1931 census and the broad categorizing provided by Hadley, from the census it seems that the proletariat grouping would have numbered about 14,895, the unestablished, emergent or lower middle class 4,321 and the upper middle class 1,359.[60]

RELIGION

The 1931 census had classifications for seven categories of religious denominations. These included the Roman Catholics, Anglicans and Methodists who had been functioning in St Vincent during the period of slavery and onwards. Then there was the broad category of Presbyterians, and then "other denominations", non-Christians and not-described. Not identified were the Church of Scotland, which had been established in St Vincent since 1839, the Gospel Hall religion, from 1903, and the Salvation Army, from 1905. The category of "other denominations" included sects such as the Plymouth-Brethren, Adventists and the Shakers.[61]

The religion that will be highlighted in this discussion is the Shakers, a name that was given to it by its detractors.[62] It was indigenous to the colony, but its origin is still a matter of conjecture. Sheena Boa,[63] based on a study of correspondence from Methodist missionaries in St Vincent to their head office in England, put its origin at 1846 on the Calder estate. It is likely that it existed on the estates during the period of slavery but only became known to the European population after emancipation, when former slaves began to move away from the estates into villages that they were beginning to create.

Boa notes that the religion attracted mainly disaffected members of the society. The members, mostly from the working class, were obviously more comfortable and at ease with a religion run by persons of their own social class that allowed a display of strong emotions. It also gave disaffected members of society the opportunity to meet and worship without the interference of Europeans and without having to meet the European standard of dress that was expected in the established churches. Members, given the hostility towards their religion even before 1912, were nominally baptized as Weslyans (Methodists), and the original group at the Calder estate worshipped at the Methodist church. The Methodists were, however, concerned about their "use of convulsions" and noisy prayer meetings, and the worshippers were expelled from the Methodist Church, one group in 1849 and another in 1851.[64]

As their numbers grew and spread throughout the island, the established churches called for the prohibition of their religious practice. Indigenous religions and organizations had always presented the colonial authorities and elites with challenges and concerns, and this became more formidable after emancipation, when the former slaves began to form their own organizations. Anglican minister S.F. Branch, in a memorandum to the 1897 Royal Commission, hinted at this:

> We have an excitable, suspicious and still ignorant labouring population, drifting away from the old clerical control as shown by the numerous new friendly societies, all self-managed and not as heretofore directed by ministers of religion, and in the recent self constituted religious societies. The labourer, by his lay, friendly and religious societies and his revolt from the healthy control of clergy of the Church

and Ministers of Weslyan body shows he is testing the pleasure of thinking and determining for himself.[65]

The growth of the Shaker religion was also a concern for other churches and officials in the colony, with Chief Justice Sharpe in 1851 even calling them "fanatics" and recommending their arrest if they "scoff at Christian religions".[66] On the minds of the officials, too, were allegations that some of the leaders of the 1862 riots that occurred on the northern estates were members of the Shaker religion. The religion continued to attract increasing numbers and became established in different areas of the country.

It had, however, been confined "to out of the way places . . . as its followers endeavoured if anything to avoid publicity".[67] In October 1901, an article appeared in the *Sentry* that inflamed passions and added to the fears held by sections of the public. The atmosphere was being carefully prepared to declare the religion illegal. This came at a meeting of the legislative council on 8 July 1912 when Administrator Murray introduced a bill to render the practice illegal, referring to the religion as barbaric.[68] The *Times* and *Sentry* complimented the administrator, referring to the religious practice as "demoralising and [a] burlesque of Christian worship"[69] and as "a relic of barbarism, a blot on our civilisation and a stain on the pages of the history of the colony".[70] The ordinance, entitled "An Ordinance to render illegal the practice of Shakerism as indulged in the Colony of St Vincent", was forwarded to England on 12 October 1912 and was cited as the Shakerism Prohibition Ordinance. "Any magistrate adjudicating a case brought under the Ordinance was to have the final say as to whether the customs and practices constituted Shakerism."[71]

Prosecutions followed, as people were arrested for violating the law. On 17 February 1913, six persons were charged at Questelles, five were convicted, one woman receiving a reprimand. The ringleader, a man, was fined thirty shillings or one month's hard labour if in default. Two other men were fined one pound each or fourteen days hard labour if in default. All fined were given one week to pay their fines.[72] In 1920, there were nine convictions; in 1921, nineteen persons were charged fines amounting to £210; in 1923, twenty-three were convicted; eighteen in 1925 and twenty-two in 1927. There were no convictions in 1924, 1928, 1929 and 1932. In 1933, however, there were thirty-five convictions and an amazing ninety-four in 1934.[73]

The riots of 21 and 22 October brought a new dimension to the Shakers' struggle, which was taken up by the new legislators who emerged from 1937, following small constitutional changes.

POLITICS AND THE POLITICAL ENVIRONMENT

Before adult suffrage, the ownership of land was a central part of the franchise that determined who were qualified to vote in national elections or make themselves available as candidates.[74] At the 1925 elections, under a new constitution that restored electoral registration and ended the pure Crown colony system of government, there were only 671 registered electors. The council was made up then of the governor and, in his absence, the administrator and four *ex officio* members – one nominated and three elected. The official section of the council was in the majority. To be qualified as an elector under the franchise, the individual had to be a man of twenty-one years, or a woman of thirty, and a British subject residing for at least two years or domiciled in the colony at the time of registration. One needed to also have at least one of the following qualifications – a net income of at least £30 per annum; to be the owner of real property in the island, valued at least £150 "above all charges and encumbrances"; or to be paying rent of at least £12 per annum in respect of real property in the island. In any event, as Ann Spackman stated, the "real power remained with the bureaucrats who were in control of departmental administration and in the person of the Governor who was ultimately responsible, to the Imperial government for policy decisions".[75]

St Vincent, in 1935, was eleven years into the new constitution of 1924. A small social and economic elite controlled what level of internal power existed, the government still being irresponsible by nature of the colonial political dynamics that advanced the interests of the colonial power rather than that of the people of the colonies. This bred contempt from the population, which hardened during the harsh economic times of the 1930s. The six elected representatives that served since 1925 could not claim to represent the bulk of the people. In fact, as late as 1939, the Moyne Commission took note of the high franchise qualifications relative to average incomes. The commission was of the view that it was a deliberate effort to restrict the electorate "to the comparatively well-to-do".[76] Of the persons elected to serve, with the reintroduction of elected government, Walter McGregor Grant and Alexander Murdoch Fraser had been nominated members under the old nominated council. Grant was a merchant auctioneer and insurance agent; Fraser, a plantation owner of Scottish descent, was born in St Vincent but spent five years at school in Scotland;[77] and the new man, Joseph Milton Gray, a merchant and landed proprietor, was born of a "poor labouring woman" and "transient Scotsman".[78]

There was, before 1935, some tinkering with the constitution. In 1931, an amendment to the 1924 constitution provided for the governor, three *ex officio* members, one nominated official, one nominated "un-official" and three elected members to constitute the legislative council. The change allowed for one nominated "un-official" to replace one of the *ex officio* members. For the 1931 elections, the Kingstown electoral district had 297 registered electors, with 247 voting. For the Leeward District, the number of registered electors was seventy-seven, but there was no election since there was only one candidate. In the Windward district, the number of registered electors was ninety-seven and the number that voted was eighty-two.[79]

Members of the RGA sought to achieve a further extension of the franchise and became even more critical of Crown colony government.[80] A commission that was set up to examine the possibility of a closer union of several of the West Indian colonies prompted the convening of an unofficial conference of West Indians in Dominica in 1932. Indeed, in the struggle prior to 1924 to achieve elected representation, West Indian political activists began to maintain closer contact through efforts to establish regional labour associations and through RGAs, as in the case of Grenada, Trinidad and St Vincent. The issue of political union was on the agenda for the smaller colonies of the Windward and Leeward Islands.

The Closer Union Commission, in its report, noted that the legislative council had an equal number of official and unofficial members, with the governor having a casting vote. It admitted that "the Governor may and on rare occasions does, by the use of the official bloc and his casting vote, carry measures against the possible unanimous vote of the unofficial members". It felt that what was important was that the executive must govern. It recommended a system that would allow the unofficial members to be in a permanent majority, but with the governor retaining, in the last resort, the right to exercise his traditional power.[81]

The unofficial conference held in Dominica in October 1932 was critical of Crown colony government, which, the delegates argued, neglected the poorer sections of the community and was responsible for the colonies' economic failures. They also expressed the view that all adults who paid direct taxes should be entitled to vote and that the franchise, with regard to property and income qualifications, should be lowered. Even at that stage, some expressed the desire for adult franchise within the context of a federation. At that meeting, St Vincent was represented by two members of the RGA, newspaper editors R.M.

Anderson and Ebenezer Duncan. This expression of closer regional cooperation continued, since it was believed that it was going to be easier to have an
extended franchise and a more progressive constitution under some form of
political union. The *Times*, in a commentary on the unofficial conference in its
3 May 1934 edition, suggested that it had written a new page in the history of
the British West Indies as far as the Leewards and Windwards were concerned.

News of Italy's invasion of Abyssinia in 1935 that was carried in the newspapers and on the cable boards helped to heighten political consciousness.
Meetings took place to protest Italy's action. Those meetings were organized
and chaired by members of the RGA. On occasions, Albert T. Marryshow of
Grenada visited and lectured on the issue. At a meeting on 16 October, despite
the short notice, the Carnegie Hall was crowded. The *Times* of 17 October 1935
reported, "The address on the whole made an indelible impression on the hear-
ers and the loud cheering and clapping testified to the appreciation of sympathy
with all what was said."

Heightened political interest was also reflected in the keen attention given
to the town board elections. The *Vincentian* of 4 January 1934 noted, "This fact
plainly shows that we are coming more alive to the fact that it is essentially
important for every citizen of the community to be vitally interested in the
affairs of his country." The town board was a form of local government that
had existed since 1897. While the governor would annually appoint persons
whom he considered fit to be town wardens for the small towns,[82] Kingstown,
on the other hand, exercised a form of local government. Under that system,
the Kingstown Board was partly elected and partly nominated. The board
was authorized to provide services relating to the maintenance and lighting
of streets, to the provision of water, and maintaining cemeteries and play-
grounds.[83] The Kingstown Board was something of a political nursery for Vincentian politicians who became active in the 1930s. The Kingstown Board in
1932 included W.M. Grant as a nominated member and Antonio H. DaSilva,
who had already been part of the colonial legislature.

The role of the governor was central under the existing constitution; Gordon Lewis describes him as "the local powerful agent of a powerful Colonial
Office".[84] A new governor, Sir Selwyn Grier, assumed governorship of the
Windward Islands in February 1935. Dissatisfaction with the St Vincent administrator was so strong that there were high expectations of the new governor.
Clement DeBique, writing in the *Times* of 21 February 1935, welcomed him
to the country, claiming that he had come to them at the right moment, a

time when the island was moving down the road "to perdition". The island, he claimed, needed "a brave and strong man with a fertile brain to direct affairs from above".

The *Times* was in the forefront of criticisms of the administrator and the kind of government that existed in 1935. In its editorial of 7 March, it suggested that it would be good for the governor to get first-hand information about the functioning of the government. It also wondered about his impression of the legislative council. It did not think the council could be held in high regard by the governor after his contact with the Grenada legislature. The opportunity was taken to comment on the state of the legislature. "We long for the day when this Council will no longer consist of mutes who complacently nod assent but will be comprised of thinking Councillors who will debate warmly and strongly in true parliamentary manner according to their convictions."

The criticisms of the government were not new but had intensified through the early part of the 1930s. The political activists and labour leaders tended to focus, among other things, on education. Albert T. Marryshow, in a speech to the RGA in 1933, singled out the education system for attack. He said that it was "part of a conspiracy to make you a subservient being, a cog in a conscienceless machine with no stimulus for creative work, with no racial individuality, no sense of justice, no appetite for duty, no love of freedom".[85]

The attacks on the administrator intensified. In the same 7 March issue of the *Times*, an article entitled "De Omnibus Rebus" by Quiz referred to the many recent "government appointments and disappointments". According to Quiz, "Dame Rumour stated at one time that we were to lose our administrator. This did not seem to give the public such a terrible blow." On 14 March, under the caption "Making a Mess of Government", DeBique argued that if the governor were to investigate affairs in the country he would find "gross irregularities" with the administrator, "heads and heels involved". On 18 April, the issue of "Bungling in Local Government" was highlighted. The issue of 6 June carried an item captioned "Grimble the administrator Must Go". It stated, "Let us, however, hope for the good of our island's progress and prosperity that St Vincent would at no distant time be relieved of Mr. Grimble whose early career and intensive researches among uncivilised people have fashioned him for the government of backward people only." The reference to uncivilized people had to do with his previous position in the Gilbert and Ellice Islands in the Pacific.

In the 13 June issue, the call was again made for Grimble to go: "Grimble Must Go – He believes native labour must be exploited". He was accused of not believing in paying native workers a reasonable wage, a reference made to some difficulties at the Electricity Supply Authority. The 20 June paper again made another call for Grimble to go, stating that his administration was "un-British" and had no sympathy for the poor. The 26 September issue listed specific matters that, in the paper's view, reflected his maladministration. At a time when the focus of attention was on increased representation in the legislative council through a lowering of the franchise, the assumption by some was that Crown colony government was not inherently bad. The major problem was with the style and administration of its functionaries. Grimble, therefore, as administrator, received the bulk of their criticisms, and there was hope that the new governor would be able to fix things.

In light of the report of the Closer Union Commission and debates by the 1932 "Unofficial Conference", some pressure was being applied in individual colonies for further constitutional development. The recommendations made for St Vincent were for an increase of the number of elected members in the legislature from three to five, with nominated "un-officials" to be increased to three, and official members, including the administrator (or president), to be reduced to three.[86] The *Investigator* of 17 August 1935 applauded the recommendation to increase the measure of popular representation in the legislature, arguing that it was "indisputable evidence that the Colonial Office recognizes the increasing growth of political consciousness in the community". The qualification for electors involved one important change. Under the previous constitutional arrangements, women, even if they possessed the relevant income and property qualifications, had to be thirty years of age or older to exercise the franchise. With the new constitution, they were required to be over twenty-one years of age.[87]

A number of things were coming together: frustration about the weak economic situation that was blamed on the type of government and the lack of involvement of a broader cross-section of the population and, consequently, the continuation of the domination of the legislature by a narrow class of people. The nominated unofficial member in the legislature in 1935 and the three elected members were all wealthy persons. Alex Fraser was an estate owner who controlled two estates with a total of 1,017 acres of land; A. DaSilva was described as a wealthy merchant, and Fred Corea as the largest merchant in the colony as well as an estate owner of 298 acres with controlling interest in other estates. A.M. Punnett was the nominated unofficial member. He had three estates and his relatives had control of seven other estates.[88]

It is of some significance that the spark that triggered the 1935 riots was ignited by a meeting of the legislative council on 21 October 1935. The context was, in this respect, different from that in a number of other colonies that faced disturbances in the 1930s, where the major issue centred on conditions related to work on the estates.

CHAPTER 2

THE OCTOBER 1935 RIOTS

ONE OF THE ARGUMENTS RAISED IN THIS BOOK is that a study of the St Vincent riots will deepen our understanding of the rebellions of the 1930s. It was suggested at the end of the last chapter that the context that gave rise to the St Vincent riots was somewhat different from that of the other colonies that experienced rebellions. Central to this is the fact that the riots started in the yard of the courthouse during a meeting of the legislative council and not over labour disputes in a plantation setting or at the docks or in the oil fields.[1] They therefore demand careful attention.

The events that sparked the riots can be traced back to an 18 October meeting of the legislative council, presided over by the governor of the Windward Islands, Sir Selwyn Grier. Two revenue-generating bills were read for the first time. They were the Licences (Amendment) Ordinance 1935 and the Customs Duties (Amendment no. 4) Ordinance 1935. The governor accepted full responsibility for the measures, since St Vincent needed "to be able to budget for necessary developments and to build up the rapidly shrinking Reserve funds for the colony". It was, he argued, "the duty of the Government to face the situation fairly and to place the colony's finances in reasonably sound order". The colonial secretary[2] was to present data "to show the pressing necessity that existed for creating new sources of revenue and would explain the general principles upon which the measures to be introduced had been founded".

The legislature was told that vital improvements were not carried out earlier for lack of funds but could no longer be delayed. Among matters needing urgent attention were a casualty hospital for the Grenadines, the need to move the hospital at Chateaubelair to more spacious quarters and bridges to be repaired on the Windward coast. These required new revenue amounting to £3,535 to meet those needs.[3] The governor had made previous attempts to alert the people of St Vincent to the country's critical financial situation. On his way from Grenada, he made a visit to the islands of the Grenadines and raised the issue of the sad state of the country's finances. At Union Island, he had pointed to England's critical position "and asked the people to help in the way of taxation". In Canouan, he dwelt again with the island's finances, "whence he touched on the people's law abiding behaviour as he was informed and agreed with one of his predecessors when he said that 'the people wore a smiling face'".[4]

But even before this, at a meeting of the finance committee on 2 May 1935, Administrator Grimble drew to the committee's attention concerns raised by the secretary of state about "the depletion of the Reserve Fund and Surplus Assets", the excess in expenditure in 1934 under certain heads and "the desirability in general of not incurring any Supplementary Expenditure during the year unless compensating savings could be foreseen".[5] Later, in an address to the St Vincent RGA, the governor once again highlighted the critical financial situation of the colony. The colony, he said, had been running at a financial loss for the last four years and found itself near to the rocks. St Lucia was on the rocks already, and he was not prepared to see the same for St Vincent. He declared:

> We can do what we can with the small resources at our disposal, but everything ought to be put on sound financial footing. If we have to raise loans in St Vincent we must meet our obligations in the future and not bring discredit on the West Indies. When schemes break down it is not only damaging to the colony of St Vincent but to other colonies too. I cannot afford to run the risk of that happening.[6]

It was against this background that the governor attempted to introduce taxation measures at a meeting of the legislative council on 18 October. Among the measures introduced was the adoption of higher rates of import duties on what he described as a strictly limited number of articles. The governor spelled out the details and gave justification for the measures, anticipating, no doubt, a negative reaction to their introduction:

> The articles selected to bear the increased duties were among those which can be classified as luxurious. They are beer and ale, spirits, tobacco, cigarettes and matches. Particular care has been taken to avoid increases which will affect the poor, for example, no addition has been made to the duty on such imports as bags,

snacks, sewing machines, illuminating oil and common soap. Nor has any increase been made in the case of staves, barrels and puncheons since any advance of duties on such imports would have the effect of an additional tax on exports.

The other measure involved the reduction of import duties on motor vehicles but with higher rates of licensing fees for those vehicles. He explained, "The policy implied is a sound one, in as much as it is clearly more logical to encourage the importation of motor vehicles by reducing the duty thereon and at the same time, to increase the license fees to a scale compatible with the actual wear and tear which they inflict upon local roads."[7]

The bills were read for the first time following two motions to that effect. The legislative council was to continue its sitting on Monday, 21 October, to bring the measures into law. It was likely that no representatives of the working people would have attended the session and listened to or been impressed with the colonial secretary's explanation for the implementation of those measures. On the following Saturday, 19 October, it appeared, based on news that was being circulated, that even before the measures became law there were increased prices on a number of commodities, including some not affected by the import duties. The price of matches went to one box a penny, but they had previously been sold at three boxes for a penny. The information about increased prices on a variety of commodities reached the governor on the weekend. He stated later that, apart from the increased price of matches, there was no basis for those rumours.[8]

There were, however, discussions in different circles about the proposed measures and their possible impact. A number of working people who had concerns about the reputed rise in prices approached sympathetic members of the RGA. George McIntosh, who "stood out as the champion of the cause of the poorer class", was the one they moved to, since they found him very approachable and considered him one who was always prepared to listen to their cries.[9] He was the son of a Scottish father and black mother whose occupation was listed as a cook. He was a pharmacist and political activist, being one of the founding members of the RGA. He became a member of the Kingstown Board in 1923.[10] His drugstore was located near the vegetable market and was frequently visited by peasants and members of the working class, especially on Saturdays, their market day, when they came to sell their goods and buy necessities for home. McIntosh, it was reported, kept a blackboard in front of his store, on which he not only carried news on matters of local interest but also made comments. On that Saturday, according to one witness, his comments were about the possible effects of the fiscal measures, expressing the view that the island was going on the rocks.[11] Some persons, it appeared, had contacted McIntosh on Sunday. Given these developments, the resumption of the meeting of the legislative council on Monday, 21 October, when discussions on the proposed measures were to have resumed, would have generated much interest.[12]

Monday, 21 October, opened "bright and sunny".[13] The legislative council, with the governor still presiding, met at its usual meeting place, the upper floor of the courthouse building at 10:00 a.m. The first order of the day involved the presentation of the badge of Officer of the Civil Division of the Order of the British Empire to J.H. Otway, the colonial treasurer. Following notice of a motion regarding postage stamps by the member for Kingstown, the two amendments that were introduced the previous Friday were read for a second time. The Licences (Amendment) Ordinance was dealt with by the council in committee and passed without change. It was during discussion about possible amendments to the Customs Duties (Amendment no. 4) Ordinance that the proceedings of the house were interrupted.[14]

The first indication to members of the legislative council that there was anything amiss came at around 11:30 a.m., when noises were heard coming from the yard of the courthouse. This was at first not taken seriously since the court was meeting on the bottom floor and the noise was thought to be associated with proceedings there. Crowds had gathered in the court yard. McIntosh, who had been among a very small group of spectators at the council meeting, appears to have left the meeting of the legislative council shortly after. He got on to his bicycle and was met by persons who seemed determined to confront the governor. He was reported to have urged them to go to the governor not with any noise but with a letter. He went back to his drugstore accompanied by some members of the crowd, where, in collaboration with A.C. DeBique, also a member of the RGA, he addressed a letter to the governor.[15] In the letter that was taken to the governor at about 12:20 p.m., a request was made for an interview in order to represent the concerns of different people.

McIntosh's note to the governor in the letter he presented was as follows: "A number of working men have approached me asking me to interview your Excellency. Would Your Excellency be good enough to grant an interview today? If your Excellency is disposed to so grant the interview I shall be pleased if you will mention the hour most suitable when I shall be pleased to wait on Your Excellency." The letter also included a list of topics to be discussed – Customs

Amendment Law, Minimum Wage Bill, Workingmen's Compensation Law.[16] The governor indicated verbally that he was prepared to meet McIntosh with any delegation at 5:00 p.m. at the Carnegie Library Building. The governor was to indicate later that there was nothing in McIntosh's letter to indicate urgency.[17]

The crowd at the courthouse had increased in numbers. Among the early crowd gathered in the yard of the courthouse were about fifteen women, reportedly armed with small sticks.[18] The crowd grew to an estimated three hundred, the majority being women, some of whom, according to reports, had stones, sledgehammers, cutlasses and knives.[19] In the crowd were persons who were initially attracted by the commotion and went to see what was happening. There were others who were not originally a part of the crowd but joined it and even assumed leadership roles. Some of them were associated with a club in Paul's Lot called the Ranch which was used for gambling, drinking and political discussions. This group included Martin Durham, Samuel "Sheriff" Lewis and Donald Peters, all of whom received gaol sentences for their part in the riots.[20] "Sheriff" Lewis, who was said to have issued instructions to some persons in the crowd, was nicknamed "Haile Selassie". This name he got at a meeting called to highlight the struggle of the Ethiopians. That meeting was addressed by Albert T. Marryshow of Grenada. Following Marryshow's call for support of the Ethiopian "brothers", "Sheriff" reported that he stood up and declared, "From now on I am no more Sheriff, call me Haile Selasse."[21]

As the noise became more pronounced, the governor adjourned the legislative council meeting at about 12:35 p.m. to go down to the court yard in an effort to disperse the crowd. He was accompanied by his aide-de-camp and members of the council. When the crowd heard the governor's response to McIntosh's letter, they became extremely angry, since they felt that, at the later time given for the appointment, he would have been returning to Grenada, where he was based. They feared too that if the matter was not dealt with at that point they were unlikely to get it addressed later that day. As the governor stood on the stairs leading from the legislative council, the noise intensified, with the crowd determined to see him immediately. He was met with shouts of "We can't stand any more duties on our food and clothes!", "We want work!", "We are hungry!", "Something will happen in this town today if we are not satisfied!"

The governor's attempt to speak was drowned out by noise coming from the angry crowd. His efforts to be heard were fruitless until McIntosh, who was in the crowd, rang a bell that he borrowed from the registrar's office. He was assisted by other members of the RGA, Ebenezer Duncan, Clement DeBique and St Clair Bonadie, who had joined him.[22] This calmed the crowd for a brief period, and the governor tried to explain that additional duties were placed only on commodities used by the wealthy. The noise continued and he could hardly be heard. He indicated that he was moving into one of the rooms of the courthouse and asked that representatives join him there.[23] Colonial Secretary Grimble reported:

> As it was useless to attempt further pacification from the steps and the Police in parade kit could not control the mob, through which they were scattered, His Excellency decided at about 1:00 p.m. to make a further effort to address the whole mass of people in the Court Room immediately behind him. He was obliged to retire foot by foot facing the mob, into the building. . . . The room was filled by the people who remained for some minutes as clamorous as before, still brandishing their weapons.[24]

The governor, though continually interrupted, tried to reiterate his argument that the new taxation affected luxuries and not the poor man's commodities. He explained that if the price of necessities had suddenly been raised in the local shops, the matter would engage his particular attention, because no increased duties under the new tariff could justify any shopkeeper raising the price of necessities. The governor pledged that, if there was genuine unemployment, road work would be found on the windward road within the next fortnight. He then repeated his desire to meet with their representatives at the Carnegie Library at 5:00 p.m.

He then left the courthouse, at the prompting of McIntosh, whose son had come into the courtroom and indicated to him that the crowd had damaged the telegraph office.[25] As the governor reported, "I found myself again surrounded by a crowd of people who appeared to be in an even more excited condition than before."[26] The *Times* reported on the situation that then prevailed: "Sticks and other weapons were brandished over the heads of the Governor and Administrator as they, with diplomatic tact tried to mitigate the high feelings of the mob. The Attorney General was given two cuffs by one who alleged that he was kicked by him."[27]

Meanwhile, about one hundred persons had broken into the neighbouring prison. Among those who led the move to the prison and ordered the warder to open the gates was "Sheriff" Lewis, who used the name "Haile Selassie" in doing so.[28] This was prompted by the untimely arrival of a gang of prisoners who were on their way back to the prison with a stone cart "on which there was a load of stones and a sledge hammer". The sledgehammer was seized and the warder and prisoners driven off.[29] Warder Johnson was seriously wounded by a blow to his head, while Chief Warder Joshua received three blows on his left hand. Material damage was done to the prison office. Items, including tables and clocks, were broken, keys taken away and glass windows smashed.[30]

When the attack was made on the prison, all of the prisoners were not present. Apart from those who had just returned to the prison compound, ten were engaged in cutting grass at Government House. When Warder Quammie, who was in charge of the gang there, heard the news of the riots and the release of prisoners, he ordered the prisoners under his charge to the Government House stables and told them to put down their implements, which he then locked in the engine room. Following instructions conveyed by Mrs Grimble, wife of the administrator, he left with the men for the prison. On their way, the prisoners were encouraged to attack the warder and join the released prisoners, but three of them were able to persuade the rest not to.[31]

The situation had by then got completely out of control at the yard of the courthouse. Doors and windows of the courthouse were smashed, along with cars belonging to official and unofficial members of the council.[32] Among the cars attacked was that of the governor, which carried the official flag. Fred Hazell, a prominent merchant and lieutenant in the volunteer force, received two cuts in his bid to silence the crowd. Further injury was prevented by the fact that a few members of the crowd, who had recognized him, came to his rescue. He had to go to the hospital to attend to a wound in his head but was later able to rejoin the other volunteers.[33] He returned with a rifle, which he held as a lieutenant in the volunteer corps.[34] During the melee in the yard of the courthouse, he was said to have been responsible for the death by gunfire of one John Bull, who, it is alleged, had attacked him. Governor Grier, in one of his reports to Secretary of State Malcolm MacDonald, indicated that Hazell was attacked by "one of the ring leaders armed with a knife and was compelled to shoot him".[35] What happened precisely is difficult to discern, but it was believed that John Bull was the person responsible for wounding Hazell in his head.

The cable office located at the corner of Hilsboro and Halifax streets, opposite the courthouse, was attacked quite early. Cable wires were cut and the office broken into, but the equipment was spared from damage. Later, however, the governor's aide-de-camp, Lieutenant Commander C.D. Milbourne, accompanied by Bell, manager of the cable office, had to go to the cable hut near the beach at Arnos Vale, some two miles away, after having been requested to send a cable to Grenada to seek the services of the HMS *Challenger* that was stationed there. Through the use of a hand-transmitting set, they were able to request the assistance of the HMS *Challenger*. Since the matter was urgent, protocol was dispensed with and the request was sent directly to Grenada rather than through the commander-in-chief in Bermuda. On their way back to Kingstown, their car was attacked by a crowd armed with clubs and cutlasses. During the confrontation, one of the attackers was shot.[36] The cable reached the commander-in-chief through the Grenadian colonial secretary at 3:00 p.m. Apart from the services of the *Challenger*, the colonial secretary was urged to send members of the Grenadian police force that could be spared. Nine constables were sent, with a sergeant in charge.[37]

The situation demanded urgent attention, but the size of the police force available became an issue. There were fifty-one members of the police force, thirty-two stationed in Kingstown, three in the Grenadines, fourteen at the outstations on the mainland and two were on leave. Before the trouble started at the courthouse, there were five non-commissioned officers and men serving as guards at the council chamber, three were in attendance as guards at the courthouse, and three were engaged as witnesses in matters before the court. Of the others based in Kingstown, five were on patrol, five on duty at the police barracks; three were off-duty and eight resting.[38] While the governor was trying to be heard in the courtroom, some of the police in attendance were sent to the police barracks to obtain arms. They were attacked on their way, and the sergeant, who was seriously injured, was put out of action. Six armed police returned, but damage had already been done to the prisons and courthouse. Their attempts to close the gates of the court yard only further infuriated the crowd.[39]

A second contingent of three policemen that attempted to go to the court yard shortly after was mobbed by the crowd at the market square. One constable, Dennie, was isolated from the rest, beaten and trampled in the road, suffering severe injuries. Anderson, a second constable, was knocked over and fell in a neighbouring drain, while the third, Clement Cato, returned to the police barracks after being clubbed and wounded with a cutlass, getting one of his fingers broken in the process.[40] At about 1:50 p.m., the chief justice read the Riot Act from the steps of the courthouse after being asked to do so by the governor. While the Riot Act was being read, the chief of police was injured by a stone thrown at him from behind. A large section of the crowd had by then

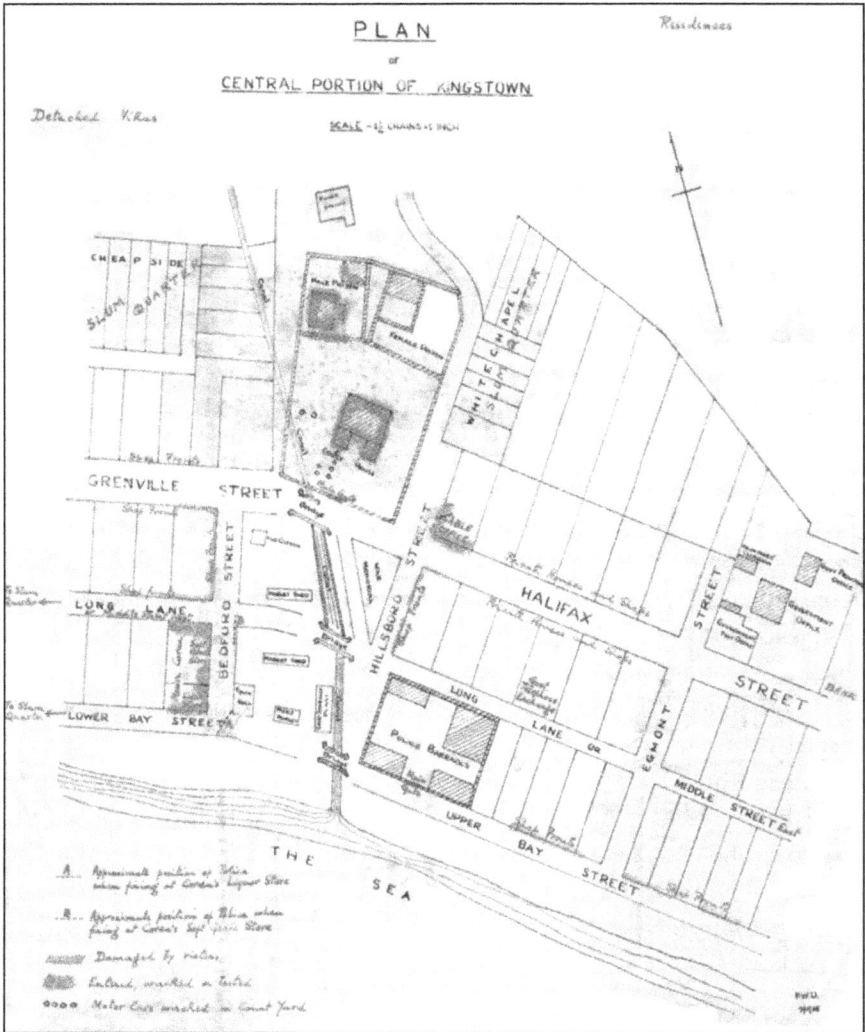

Figure 2. Plan of central portion of Kingstown

been moving towards the market square in the direction of the business places of Fred Corea, a merchant and member of the legislative council.

Members of the crowd that had moved towards the market square proceeded to attack and loot Corea's liquor and dry goods stores that were located along Bedford Street between Middle Street and Bay Street (see figure 2). Corea was perceived as one of the architects of the measures introduced in the legislative

council, a fact that explains the fury with which they attacked his premises.[41]
Evidence about the looting of other stores in Kingstown is very sketchy.[42]

A third detachment of policemen moved to the marketplace, where they
joined the colonial secretary. Their attention was focused on stopping the looting of the business places of Corea. The colonial secretary estimated that there
were four or five hundred people present, three hundred of them being actually
involved in looting. Six armed police remained stationed at the court yard,
while two who were unarmed guarded the governor.

Other available members of the police establishment stationed themselves
on Bay Street some thirty yards away from the activity. Shots were fired in
the air, forcing the main body into the adjoining soft goods store. "Bales and
boxes of merchandise were being carried out of the building and passed down
the Middle Street away from the scene of disturbance."[43] Following instructions from the colonial secretary, shots were fired, first at the top of doors and
windows of the soft goods store and then into the crowd. This succeeded in
scattering them, but one man, who was hit by a bullet, lay dead at the Middle
Street entrance to the store. It was widely believed that he was not involved in
the rioting but had just come out of a neighbouring rum shop belonging to C.R.
Williams. Fourteen others were wounded and hospitalized, two of them dying
a few days later. Among the dead was a pregnant lady, who was also reported
not to have been involved in the looting.[44]

One resident, in a letter to a relative in Trinidad, described what she saw:

> We had a time of it here. None of us have ever experienced the like of it before. The
> town was in confusion on Monday. Corea's Dry Goods and Grocery business were
> broken into and cleaned out. You should have seen the people passing the streets
> with bolts of cloth as if they had bought them. . . . The people were armed with
> sticks and stones and I am afraid after the ship leaves they may do something worse.
> I heard a man passing saying the next thing will be fire, so I suppose we will have
> to look out. The people went to the Governor but in the wrong way and now they
> are all in for it, there are a good many arrested. St Vincent has been so peaceful all
> these years. I never thought I would have experienced a riot.[45]

The fact that there were casualties seemed to have had some impact on the
crowd, many of whom hurriedly moved away, leaving the area deserted. A
number of policemen remained, to prevent any further disturbances there. A
large crowd, however, continued to congregate around the area of the courthouse. The colonial secretary, who had moved back to the court yard, reminded

those present that the Riot Act had already been read and that serious consequences would follow if they did not disperse. Some left, but the majority remained, flourishing their clubs and knives, "with threats against the white race". He later made mention of one woman who appeared with several men, shouting, "We lick all you white men up tonight." A few stones were also thrown. At around 3:00 p.m., a shot was heard from Middle Street, where the officer in charge killed another man. The crowd began to move away from the court yard and market place[46] at about 3:40 p.m., and calmness was beginning to prevail in the area.[47]

McIntosh later reflected on his role and that of members of the RGA. He stated in the *Times*:

> Let us take a retrospective view of what was done on this never-to-be-forgotten memorable day of October 1935 in St Vincent. A number of working people hear that government is passing a law increasing the duties on certain commodities. On Saturday, their market day, they approach the shops and stores and are told that the prices on these commodities have gone up. Suffering want on the Sunday they . . . determine to speak to the Governor who is again meeting his Council on the Monday to carry on legislation imposing increased taxation. They are unaware of how to do it themselves; they therefore approach certain persons who they know would be sympathetic towards them, and these persons try to help them by making an appointment with the Governor whom they were never privileged to meet before.
>
> Anxious as they were, their mentality leads them to believe that if immediate action were [sic] not taken no help could be forthcoming; hence when the governor postpones the time for meeting them from 10:00 a.m. to 5:00 p.m.[48] they grew suspicious; they were anxious and so they became agitated; they clamoured to see the Governor at once. He met them and in some unfortunate way they got to understand from the words spoken to them by the governor that Mr. Corea was responsible for their trouble and so amid their cries of "We want work"! "We want food" they rushed to the two nearest business places of Mr. Corea and broke them open.[49]

At the police barracks, special constables and members of the volunteer force were being sworn in for special duties by the chief justice. Policemen were put to guard the armoury, power station and cable office and to patrol the market square and surrounding areas.[50] The promised meeting at the Carnegie Public Library was the next sign of activity. The governor was joined by McIntosh. He spoke from the balcony of the public library, while the crowd, which he estimated at about one hundred but which was probably about two

hundred, listened in the street. Again, their cries were about unemployment
and low wages. The administrator, in his report, was at pains to point out that
those were the only two complaints that were then being voiced.

The governor, who seemed not to have been convinced about the reality of
unemployment, indicated that if there was indeed genuine unemployment he
was prepared to start additional work on the windward side of the island. Later,
he returned to the police barracks accompanied by Administrator Grimble,[51]
while McIntosh and other members of the RGA continued to address the crowd
to prevent them following the governor and administrator. McIntosh asked
the crowd to be satisfied with the promises made by the governor, but when he
asked them to sing the national anthem, some in the crowd said they would
rather sing "Haile Selassie".[52]

OUTSKIRTS AND SUBURBS

The Area of North River Road (Kingstown)

Reports were received at police headquarters about disturbances on the out-
skirts of Kingstown.[53] The *Times* was later to report that the rioters "had spread
their sphere of activity into the suburban districts and invaded the homes of the
most wealthy people, treating them with the utmost scorn and disrespect".[54] The
reports indicated that a group of persons armed with cutlasses and sticks was
seen in the area between North River Road and Level Gardens. This, it has to be
noted, was in the vicinity of the residence of Fred Hazell, who had been implicated in the shooting of John Bull.[55] A small contingent of police and volunteers
led by Lt H.J. Hughes, which included police constables Roberts and Paynter,
was despatched to the area. Their first encounter was with an armed party of
six men at North River Road. After a gunshot was fired in the air by Hughes's
patrol, they dropped their cutlasses and sticks and ran to a river nearby. Some
men who were hiding in the bush on the hill near Bishop's House were chased
by the patrol party and ran in the direction of McKie's Hill in the vicinity of
the Girl Guides Hut. Two of them sought refuge in a neighbouring house and
were later captured, but not before inflicting a wound on Roberts, who had to
be taken to the hospital, where he was detained.[56]

Cane Garden

A telephone message to police headquarters from Henry Hayward, a planter and resident of Cane Garden, about one mile from the police headquarters in Kingstown, alerted the authorities that homes were being looted and damaged in that area. At about 5:30 p.m., a party led by Lance Corporal A. Baynes was sent by lorry to investigate the situation and to try to put a stop to what was alleged to be taking place there. The homes which were subjected to attacks were those of Frank Child, estate manager; Gordon Gunn, merchant; planter Hayward; Bell, manager of the cable station; and a Mrs Bunyon. Mrs Child and Mrs Gunn were actually on their way to Kingstown in a bid to escape the rioters in their area. The truck transporting the police and members of the volunteer corps was stoned by a crowd of about thirty men armed with sticks and cutlasses. The investigating party was able to prevent an attack on the home of Gordon Gunn, but other houses had already been damaged, among them that of Bell, which appeared to have suffered most. Hayward's telephone was smashed and pieces of glassware and furniture damaged.

Hayward indicated that he had offered the rioters five dollars and asked them to go home but they threatened to kill him and his housekeeper. A Canadian Press (Canapress) news report, in describing the reaction of Hayward, stated that "he attempted to give money to ease their rage". This action by Hayward perhaps spoke more about himself, the state of society at that time and the motivation of the rioters than about anything else. In contrast, O.W. Forde, planter and lawyer, whose home was near Hayward's, was saved from any attack because it was being protected by a group of workers whom he had brought from his estate in Arnos Vale. Forde, a member of the RGA, was one of the lawyers who defended McIntosh when he was arrested later for allegedly being the mastermind behind the riots. The party from police headquarters was able to rescue the housekeepers of Bell and Hayward, who were hiding in the houses where they worked. One man who was wounded by a gunshot during the encounters at Cane Garden was identified as Martin Durham, who was presumed to be the leader of the gang of rioters operating in that area.[57]

There was also some disturbance at Sion Hill, an area adjoining Cane Garden. Baha Lawrence, who worked as a chauffeur at a taxi service belonging to Donald McDonald, spoke about his experience on that day. His employer, who was white, attempted to pass through Sion Hill, in an effort to transport two women from Villa to Kingstown, but was turned back by a crowd that had gathered there. When a call came, later, from Punnett, the owner of the Diamond estate, who wanted to get back to his estate from the Windsor house in Kingstown, where he was then located, Lawrence was sent to chauffeur him. Punnett sat in the back of the car and was covered with a blanket. When the crowd at Sion Hill recognized Lawrence, a black man, they allowed him to pass on his way to Diamond. He had also been asked by his employer to bring back to Kingstown the two ladies who had earlier sought his services. At Sion Hill, the passengers in the car were recognized, and the crowd rushed to the car, at which point, Lawrence was forced to accelerate and speed away, accompanied by sticks and cutlasses that were fired at the car.[58]

Following these attacks on the homes and persons of those of European descent, some of their children were taken to the police barracks, where they spent a few days. The situation in Kingstown remained relatively quiet for the rest of the night of 21 October. It was certainly so when HMS *Challenger* arrived from Grenada at about midnight, following the receipt of a cable from St Vincent at 3:00 p.m. It included among its party nine constables and a sergeant from Grenada who were sent to assist the police in St Vincent. A contingent of two officers and twenty-six ratings was landed at about 12:15 a.m. and proceeded to patrol the town before going to the police barracks, where, at 3:00 a.m., they took over guard duties, freeing up local police and volunteers for other duties.[59]

Disturbances at Georgetown and Byrea

One of the areas outside Kingstown where there was serious unrest was in the north-eastern area of St Vincent, at Byrea and Georgetown, twenty and twenty-two miles respectively from Kingstown. News of the riots in Kingstown reached Georgetown on the Monday afternoon at about five o'clock, when the passenger bus arrived from Kingstown. This created some excitement as people gathered around the bus to hear the news. The police became somewhat alarmed when a man from Georgetown, who should have been at the gaol in Kingstown, disembarked from the bus and indicated that the prisoners were let out.[60]

The police in Georgetown, Corporal John Bailey and Constable Lucas Layne, decided to forestall any trouble by reading the Riot Act. Following this, at about 6:30 p.m., they were able to disarm a small group of men carrying sticks and cutlasses and to place a few of them in prison cells. The next indication of any kind of disturbance was at about 8:00 p.m., when five women travelling north to Georgetown from the area of the Grand Sable estate informed the police that

Child, the manager of the Grand Sable estate, had been knocked down by a stone. A decision was taken that their priority was to protect Georgetown. District constable Charlie Jones, however, left to go to Grand Sable to investigate the incident. On his way, he was confronted by a crowd which, upon hearing his mission, beat him and threw him into a neighbouring cotton field.[61]

A crowd estimated to be about two hundred had gathered at the Mount Bentinck estate shop, but reluctantly dispersed when police constable Layne, who was sent to the area, informed them that the Riot Act had been read and that such an assembly of people was not allowed. At that time, crowds were gathered in Georgetown and, joined by some people from Mount Bentinck, went on a rampage, attacking the police station, the post office, the church and the home of merchant Ottway. An attempt by the district medical officer, Dr Gallwey, to go to Child's assistance was blocked by the crowd, and he was urged to go back. After having been temporarily stopped at about 8:30 p.m. by the Georgetown police, disturbances resumed at about 10:00 p.m. when persons from Byrea and from the Grand Sable area moved there, smashing street lamps and shop fronts.

The absence of telephone communication with Georgetown from about 3:30 p.m. onwards had aroused suspicion by the authorities in Kingstown that there might have been trouble in that area. The governor received news at about 8:00 p.m. that there was, indeed, trouble in Georgetown, but it was difficult to attend to it until the arrival of the HMS *Challenger*, which supplemented their local forces and allowed them to send a patrol to Georgetown. A fourteen-man patrol of special constables, volunteers and members of the police force, led by Captain Alban Da Santos, an officer of the volunteer force, was sent to that area at about 1:55 a.m. Several stops were made along the way to enquire about the situation in those areas. At Biabou, there had been a slight disturbance earlier, but everything was back to normal. At Sans Souci, at the gap leading to the Sans Souci house where the manager of the estate lived, they found the first evidence of disturbances. Telephone wires were found on the ground and had to be cleared to allow them to pass through. Dublin, the manager, who was asleep, was awakened, but he was not aware of any trouble, not even that his telephone lines were cut.

They were informed at the Colonaire police station that there had been some disturbance earlier at Park Hill (which was serviced by the Colonaire police) and two arrests had been made. At Byrea, they were confronted by a more serious situation. Telephone lines and poles were placed across the road, and in one particular area, three trunks of coconut trees were found lying across the road. Further along their way to Georgetown, they found numerous obstacles strewn across the road. At Grand Sable estate, Child, the manager, who had been struck earlier, was found with a bandaged head. He reported that the incident had taken place at about 7:30 p.m., but he had only been able to have his wound attended to shortly before their arrival, since the district medical officer had been prevented from getting to him before.

Other obstacles were encountered before they arrived at the Georgetown police station, where the corporal in charge, Corporal Bailey, reported on the situation and informed them that he had made several arrests. On the arrival of the fourteen-man patrol at the Orange Hill estate, things were quiet and reports were that the situation had been that way for the whole previous evening. At the Mount Bentinck estate, which they reached at about 6:30 a.m., there were no reports of any serious disorder, but the angry expressions on the faces of workers who had reported for work suggested that all was not right. The workers reluctantly responded to the call for them to go either to work or back home. At the estate shop, a large crowd had gathered, and one man was arrested based on information given to the patrol. The crowd was also informed of the consequences of staying around, since the Riot Act had been read. The patrol put on a show of force by marching to the police station with fixed bayonets, in an effort to impress the crowd with the seriousness of the situation. They continued to Grand Sable, where further arrests were made.

Byrea presented their greatest challenge. Captain Da Santos described the situation there:

> There was a large, ugly and boisterous crowd armed with stones, sticks and cutlasses. The Patrol was held up here for quite a long time, and had to endure a great deal of provocation. But for the great restraint exercised the casualties would have been heavy. One man was shot on the leg.
>
> After the arrest of Lem Williams, identified as one of the leaders, the crowd dispersed, but the patrol was again attacked by a crowd throwing stones from the top of a hill in the area. The discharge of rifle shots prevented any further attacks and the patrol continued to Kingstown without further obstruction, arriving at the Police Headquarters at about 11:00 a.m.[62]

Disturbances at Camden Park–Chauncey

The other area of disturbance was the Camden Park–Chauncey region, about four miles from Kingstown on the western side of the island. Early signs of trouble manifested on the evening of Monday, 21 October, but took a more serious turn on Tuesday morning. It started on the Monday evening with the stoning of a business place belonging to John De Sousa, of Portuguese origin, who owned a shop and poultry farm in the Camden Park area. In fact, he informed the court at McIntosh's trial, "I study poultry." De Sousa had lent a box of bullets to a friend, Syl DeFreitas, who was a member of the volunteer force. When word about this got out, persons in the area accused him of lending bullets to shoot black people and began to vent their anger on his property. In the early hours of Tuesday morning, he was escorted through the cane fields at the back of his home, down the river and to the sea, where he used a boat belonging to Allen, manager of the Camden Park estate, to get to Kingstown. Not only were stones thrown at De Sousa's home but windowpanes were broken and his shop and home looted.[63]

The stoning of De Sousa's house was accompanied by the cutting of telephone lines and placing of trees across the street. A nineteen-member team of police, volunteers and special constables was despatched from Kingstown at 8:30 a.m. after news was received about the disturbances in that area. On their way to Camden Park, they encountered telephone poles and wires cut and lying on the ground. The stoning of De Sousa's shop had come to a halt by the time they got there, but they saw evidence of broken windowpanes and other forms of damage at his shop and home. The crowd had by then moved north to Chauncey village. The patrol lorry was stoned as it moved into that area, and the team were only able to calm the situation with threats of firing into the crowd. Further along, they were again met by a hail of stones, at which point they disembarked and fired shots at the crowd, killing one person and wounding four. Among the wounded was Osment Williams, who was later interviewed by this author. During their return to Kingstown, they had to stop at different points to clear obstacles thrown onto the road. In the process, a member of the patrol, J.H. Otway, the colonial treasurer, was struck by a stone. According to Williams, some of the persons who were involved in the trouble at Camden Park had actually gone to Kingstown on Monday, mainly out of curiosity. They seemed to have become motivated by what happened there. The patrol returned to police headquarters at 12:30 p.m.[64]

Table 5. Numbers of Injured in October 1935 Riots

	Detained in Hospital	Treated as Outpatients	Total
Police	5	2*	7
Warders	1		1
Volunteers		2	2
Special constables		1	1
Civilians	15#	12	27
Total	21	17	38

*Including the chief of police

#Among them were two women, one of whom died in hospital subsequently.

Source: Telegram from St Vincent sent to the Secretary of State, 24 October 1935, Confidential file 97/1935, SVA.

Since telephone communication was still disrupted, the authorities decided to send a team in a motor vessel to investigate the area north of Chauncey. Their report was to the effect that there were no disturbances further north. The disturbance in the Camden Park–Chauncey area was the last to have been experienced.

Six persons were killed during the riots, three of them being Adolphus Lovelace and Cornelius John in Kingstown and James Burnett of Camden Park (see table 5 for the numbers of the injured). The other three, consisting of two women, Nesta Grant and Marie Ollivierre, and Conrade Clarke, died from wounds inflicted during the riots.[65]

Reports of damages arising from the riots revealed that, in Kingstown, apart from the prison, four other public buildings were damaged, ten private ones, seven commercial buildings; four houses and five shops were looted and eight motor cars damaged. Outside of Kingstown, most damages involved the cutting of telephone wires and poles. At Camden Park, one store was broken into and a shop looted. Personal claims for damages were submitted by officials C. Ross, the attorney general; C.G. Williams, chief justice; A.K. Briant, agricultural superintendent; Administrator Grimble; and members of the legislative council A. DaSilva and F.A. Corea (see table 6 for details of the damages and losses incurred in the riots).[66]

In a notice published on 24 October, the authorities tried to answer the issue of increased taxation on basic necessities. The administrator, in an attempt

Table 6. Summary of Damages and Losses Incurred in the Riots

Damages	Amount £
KINGSTOWN DISTRICT	
Damage to public buildings	120.0
Damage to private buildings (including residences, offices and business premises)	132.0
Damage to motor cars:	
Public officers	310.0
Private owners	167.10
Loss by looting:	
Trade stock of Corea and Company	2,100.0
Trade stock of other persons	15.1
Household effects and personal property	306.12
Total: £3,150.32	
LEEWARD DISTRICT	
Public property:	
Telephone system	21.15
Bridges and culverts	12.18
Private property:	
Damaged	25.11
Looted	142.14
Total: £202.18	
WINDWARD DISTRICT	
Public property:	
Telephone system	77.15
Roads	8.0
Buildings	0.18
Private property:	
Damaged	16.15
Looted	21.9
Total: £105.18.09	
ABSTRACT	
Total Damages	**Amount £**
Damage to public property	241.06
Damage to private property (including motor cars)	651.16
Loss by looting – private persons	2,567.06.09
Total: £3,460.08.09	

Source: Conf. 97/1935 (45d), SVA.

to pacify the protestors, declared that the purpose of the new legislation was to raise funds for works and services by imposing higher duties on a number of luxuries. He had to come to grips with the issue of the tax on matches. He argued that the price on matches was not justified and had no bearing on the tax imposed. He indicated, too, that the price of raw sugar was protected by law. The notice explained that "if there had been general increases of the local prices of necessities, the increases are due to causes which cannot with any justification be attributed to the new duties".[67]

On Wednesday, 23 October, the governor indicated to the secretary of state that the situation in St Vincent remained satisfactory; that there was no further rioting since the previous day, Tuesday, 22 October, and that the roads to the windward and leeward sides of the island were free to accommodate traffic. He notified him, too, that the men of the HMS *Challenger* were advised that they could return to the ship by 8:00 a.m. on Thursday, 24 October. He wanted them, however, to remain in St Vincent until 28 October, a day that was celebrated as West Indian Day, to be on standby in the event that they might be needed to assist in stopping any meetings or addresses that could have resulted in further trouble.

The medical officer on the *Challenger* had assisted at the hospital on 22 and 23 October by attending to those who were injured. During the remainder of the ship's stay, the men were allowed free time between 4:00 p.m. and 6:15 p.m. each day and, on 25 and 26 October, entertained themselves with cricket and football matches between teams from different sections of the ship. A football match was played with the Boys Grammar School on Monday, 28 October. The *Challenger* eventually left for Grenada early on the morning of 29 October.[68]

The governor believed that something of the magnitude of what happened had to have been organized and, furthermore, that the poorer classes of people who were said to be implicated in the riots were not capable of that level of organization. There had to be, therefore, some mastermind behind the disturbances, and the person he identified as the brain behind the events was McIntosh. Grier was concerned about the possible negative effect of the riots on his administration. No effort was therefore to be spared in building a case against McIntosh. This took centre stage, even while arrests were being made and charges laid on others. The arrest of persons believed to have been implicated in the riots was accompanied by the institution of measures designed to restore law and order, to prevent any further violent outbreaks and to limit any bad publicity that could be sent out by the Canapress agent or other journalists who had come to St Vincent to cover the events.

CHAPTER 3

AFTERMATH OF THE RIOTS
Restoring Law and Order

FOLLOWING THE RESTORATION OF SOME SEMBLANCE OF CALM, the authorities set about attempting to recover stolen goods and to arrest persons suspected of being implicated in the riots. Investigations of persons alleged to be involved in the riots and searches for stolen goods were carried out, particularly at Sion Hill, Murray Village and Bottom Town.[1] On Wednesday, 23 October, there seemed to have been some trouble at Stubbs, although not of any great magnitude. By the following day, Thursday, 70 arrests were made, and 169 by the end of October. The prison was filled, forcing the use of Fort Charlotte and the government cotton factory to house prisoners. These were only temporary measures, so the governor was quite anxious to put permanent arrangements in place. Plans had been drawn up before the riots for a new mental asylum. He hoped that if such a building would be completed before June 1936, the existing mental hospital at Fort Charlotte could be transformed into a prison. There was some urgency, since it was expected that at least fifty of the persons arrested were likely to be convicted of felonies.[2]

Since the riots appeared to have been sparked by ordinances that prompted price increases on consumer goods, the authorities were quick to put their propaganda machinery at work, emphasizing their view that the tax measures did not justify price increases. Import duties on a limited number of luxury items were geared to secure funds necessary for the welfare of St Vincent. Careful precautions were taken to ensure that these did not touch articles used by the poor. He attempted to justify the additional tax on matches, stating that it was about one-fifth of one cent on a single box. He then concluded, "In the opinion of the Government the price of matches should nowhere exceed one cent per box as a result of the new taxation."

Emphasis then shifted to the issue of security. There was concern about the small size of the police force, making it necessary to retain a section of the volunteer force to maintain guard at the prison where some of the persons charged in connection with the riots were being held. Security was tightened, and twenty-four specially armed constables were made available for night patrol and as prison guards. By 12 November, following the termination of the services of some of the volunteers and special constables, a decision was made to add ten recruits to the police force, and shortly after, ten non-commissioned officers and men.[3]

The governor seconded his aide-de-camp, Lieutenant Commander C.D. Milbourne, to assist the chief of police, Major Grist. Milbourne left for St Vincent on 17 November.[4] There still remained a degree of uncertainty and unease among the authorities. The administration's concern was with what it regarded as the continuing tension in Kingstown. They felt that additional precautions would be necessary once the trials started.[5]

A few incidents would have added to the feeling of unease. There was, for instance, the death of estate owner Claude Hadley. Hadley, who was the proprietor of the Mount William estate, was regarded as a man of high moral standards and was well respected. He was, for many years, a lay preacher in the Anglican church in Georgetown and was described as being kind to everybody. He died on the morning of 18 December, having been killed by Lem Williams, one of his workers. Williams, who had worked as a chauffeur with him for fifteen years, had been arrested and charged in connection with the riots, after being identified as one of the leaders in the Byrea-Georgetown area. He was surprised that his employer "had not interested himself in procuring bail for him". He was to be greeted with even worse news when Hadley refused to allow him back to work until he was cleared of charges in connection with the riots. His response was to attack Hadley. He entered his former employer's premises on the morning of 16 December and hid in the pantry, after having bought arsenic. When Hadley entered his pantry, Williams attacked him with a hatchet, piercing his skull. Williams then took a drink of rum into which he had poured the arsenic. He died on the evening of the same day, and Hadley two days later.[6]

Although Grimble had expressed the view that the riots did not reflect the mood of the people, an incident such as this would have bothered him. There were other incidents, even two months after the riots. In December, one of the policemen on patrol at Sion Hill was hit by a stone thrown by an unknown person, who apparently hid in the dark. The Sion Hill assailant was not recognized, and it was not possible to pursue him because of the time of night when the incident occurred. The authorities then proceeded to investigate news of the presence of a large gathering on Middle Street. Milbourne sought the advice of Attorney General O'Reilly for legal steps to handle that matter. Some thirty to fifty persons described as disorderly had gathered at a rum shop in Middle Street owned by Cyril Williams, and it was feared that any news of the Sion Hill incident would inflame the crowd.

The authorities took the decision to close the shop, the neighbouring drug store of McIntosh and a club in the same vicinity from which gramophone music was being played, which had attracted some of the persons.[7] The street was subsequently cleared of the crowd. The attorney general indicated that, apart from the state of emergency which had previously been imposed, the liquor licence ordinance imposed a penalty for persons who refused to close licensed premises when asked to do so by order of a magistrate or justice of peace in the case of "apprehended or actual riot or tumult".[8]

Grier had suggested to the secretary of state that a warship be sent to cruise along the islands. He feared the continued intensification of racial feeling, an offshoot of the Italo-Abyssinian War.[9] The news he received from St Lucia indicated that similar feelings existed there and had been aggravated by the St Vincent riots. In fact, he claimed to have had reason to believe that a strike was to take place there on 4 November, when the next ship was due for coaling. Grier eventually proceeded to St Lucia on receipt of news that meetings focusing on the Italo-Abyssinian War had been arranged.

The legislative council resumed its aborted meeting on 28 October and passed the measures that were interrupted by the riots. On that same day, the governor summoned a meeting of the RGA, which he addressed at the Carnegie Public Library, on issues arising from the riots.[10] Apart from the possible negative effect on his administration, it bothered him that no member of the council, including himself, had "pre-knowledge of any unrest at all". He declared that the fact that the participants in the riots were not genuine workers, and that they had criminal records, gave the impression that there were no legitimate grievances. But then, he said, he had to assume that there was "a section of the community" not represented on the council, and he felt that it would be to the administration's advantage to have representatives, "preferably from among the workers themselves". He felt that they needed, above all, "men who are honest in their intention, who are prepared to think of the people first and of themselves not at all, who have no wish to distort facts and mislead the ignorant and who are prepared to cooperate with the administration of this Colony in improving conditions amongst the poorest classes". In his opinion, occasions such as those of 21 and 22 October demanded stern measures to deal with those implicated in the disturbances.[11]

Fear of disturbances in the period leading up to and during the trials was not the only matter of concern to the authorities. The picture presented to the outside world about the riots and their aftermath worried them. They were particularly uneasy about the role of the local Canapress agent, Clement DeBique. The other issue that they felt demanded their attention was the operation of two of the three local newspapers (most likely the *Investigator* and *Times*) that, in their view, catered to a low class of reading public and were not always free of subversive tendencies.[12]

CENSORSHIP, STATE OF EMERGENCY AND SEDITIOUS PUBLICATIONS ORDINANCES

Censorship

The efforts to keep matters under control and to prevent any further outbursts, particularly in the period leading up to the trials and at the trials, were buttressed by three ordinances relating to press censorship, a state of emergency and seditious publications. On Tuesday, 22 October, the day of the disturbances at Camden Park the executive council met to decide on granting powers to censor news reports. This was confirmed at a meeting of the executive council on 28 October 1935.[13] Grimble was appointed as press censor and P.W. Verral as assistant press officer.[14] The power of censorship, once granted, was quickly enforced and the censoring of news began. Censorship limited what newspapers were able to print about the riots. On 31 October, the *Times*, under a caption entitled "What Is Wrong with St Vincent", carried a statement indicating that the article planned for that space was censored and that it was too late to supply another. The *Investigator*'s editorial of 2 November 1935, entitled "The Governor's Address", noted that, because of the state of emergency and rigid press censorship, "press comment on the cause or possible causes is ruled out of order. Review of this address must be deferred for some future time."

The idea of censorship appeared very early, in a telegram of 22 October 1935 from the officer administering the government of Grenada. His communiqués to the press were thwarted by sensational news regularly received from St Vincent. He suggested then that they might wish to censor it "at the source".[15]

The *Times* of 24 November reacted to the issue of censorship: "We agree that it would be wise and politic to refrain from any comments on recent happenings which may tend to incite the populace to any acts of violence. But this does not mean that we are prepared to refrain from the publications of facts as such." It used the "mother country", Britain, as its point of reference, noting that it was one of the few countries "where there is no censorship, either open or covert". The paper felt that it had an obligation to every section of the community but was aware that its "outspoken manner" was "distasteful" to some. It regarded itself as a section of the British press, "the fourth estate of the Realm", and demanded the full rights and privileges given to the press "at the heart of Empire". It had no admiration for fascism or Hitlerism, where the press was a tool of dictators. It hoped that as "a small unit of this universal Empire", it could continue to enjoy the privileges and justice "which has made Great Britain truly great". It concluded by stating:

> We sincerely hope that in this question of censoring there will be no misunderstanding arising between the local Press and Government which may lead to a journalistic riot. There is no sane thinking person who does not regret the happenings of the past few days, and none but a madman would in any way assist in prolonging the disorder. We fully appreciate the difficulty of the moment and are prepared to render every assistance in restoring the "even tenour" [*sic*] that has been disrupted. But we must have no infringement whatsoever of our rights.[16]

There was some sensitivity to what the newspapers might have published in the wake of the riots and about the state of public anxiety in the face of the trials. Even later, when it was felt safe to end the state of emergency, there still existed fears of possible sensational releases from local Canapress agent DeBique.[17] Reference was made to the text of a release he had prepared. The distribution of the releases, the authorities felt, distorted the truth and could have had serious repercussions outside St Vincent, although there was no indication of what those repercussions were likely to be. It was under those circumstances that there was a suggestion that they consider working through Stollmeyer, the

West Indies trade commissioner in Montreal, since they did not want to be accused of muzzling the press.[18]

A release by DeBique dated 3 February 1936 noted that the state of emergency was raised and censorship lifted. It went on to state that twenty-nine persons were convicted by Judge G.C. Williams, "whose car was smashed by rioters", and that twelve prisoners were banished to Grenada. The administrator advised the headquarters of Canapress news agency in Halifax, Nova Scotia, that the reference to the chief justice amounted to contempt of court and drew their attention to other misleading statements.[19] Canapress regretted any misstatements but assumed that, in view of the recent censorship, the approval of the chief censor had been given. They were prepared to give the government the opportunity to make a statement setting the record straight. In response, the local authorities indicated that complaints had been sent to the divisional agent of Canapress in Barbados, even before the riots, about misleading statements by DeBique.

In their alternative news release, it was indicated that "no one has been charged with damages to the Judge's car" and the prisoners sent to Grenada were not banished but transferred temporarily to relieve congestion until the prison accommodation in St Vincent was sorted out. It was suggested, too, that if DeBique was to be retained, he be instructed to submit any telegram about which he had doubts to the representative of the administration before it was despatched. The local manager was warned that the repetition of any misleading news similar to that of 3 February could result in legal action being taken. Canapress, even while expressing regret about the disturbances, informed the Vincentian authorities that they preferred to do their own censoring. They had, furthermore, advised the local cable company not to circulate reports from St Vincent until approval was had from Halifax.[20]

Canapress appeared, however, to have gone somewhat overboard to satisfy the authorities. On 5 August 1936, following Workers Day activities in St Vincent at which Albert T. Marryshow addressed a rally, in Georgetown, he had cause to complain to the administrator, A.A. Alban Wright, that a text about the rally that was approved by him was "mutilated" by Canapress. He was clearly angry about it and suggested that the release sent entirely ignored the one approved by him and was thus unfair not only to the organizers of the rally but to the administrator's position too. He told the administrator, "You will remember at what pains I put myself when speaking on Monday to stress the need for publicity concerning happenings in St Vincent. Monday was a time to send a message showing that good order and loyalty prevailed and that a new chapter was opened. Instead of stating that, 'banners flying' and the 'band' were inserted which do not matter."[21]

There was obvious sensitivity about any news that was sent out. This was a matter taken up by the Jamaican *Daily Gleaner* and quoted approvingly in the *Times* of 28 May 1936. The *Gleaner* argued that the censorship issue made it difficult for the outer world to learn anything of what was going on in St Vincent. As the *Gleaner* expressed it, "in any case we do not for one moment imagine that a British West Indian newspaper would continue to stir up strife after a riot; hence the practical value of a censorship in a West Indian colony is not at all apparent". In an earlier issue, that of 6 February 1936, the point was made that the West Indian press almost unanimously looked disapprovingly on the censorship issue. In an issue on that same date, the *Times* had argued that, before appropriate steps could be taken to restore order in the colony, it was first necessary to ascertain the cause of the riots, but this was not possible during the period of press censorship.

The *Times* went further:

> Before we can ever hope to make the first step in the right direction of restoring St Vincent to normal we must first arrive at the cause of the disturbances of four months ago which have entirely thrown things out of gear. . . . Soon after the disturbances, we reviewed the whole situation in a leading article under the caption "Who is to blame?" Unfortunately, at the time Government thought that such an article could not help so our readers were not given the benefit of our views.

In the view of the newspaper, therefore, censorship limited what newspapers could say about the causes of the riots, and postponed any serious analysis.[22] The *Investigator* noted that, because of the "State of Emergency" and what it described as "rigid press censorship", "press comment on the cause or possible causes is ruled out of order and so any comment on that matter was to be deferred".[23] Other newspapers in the region, including the *Port of Spain Gazette* of Trinidad and the *Crusader* of Grenada, took a keen interest in the matter. In fact, the West Indian press followed developments in St Vincent closely. C. Wickham, editor of the *West Indian* from Grenada, and J. Broome, of the *Barbados Advocate*, arrived in St Vincent shortly after the riots. The *Port of Spain Gazette* had regular reports from a special correspondent in St Vincent and even printed articles on the riots from other West Indian papers.

Someone writing in the *Times* of 2 January 1936 under the name "Quiz" put a different spin on the matter. The concern was with lack of serious comment on the riots. He referred to the "choked and lifeless account of things which have taken the breath out of the community" and wondered why that was so. The author acknowledged the existence of censorship but could not imagine that censorship affected the statement of facts. He argued that the expression of facts did not infringe the censorship laws and asked if the editors were not independent thinkers and writers, obviously suggesting that, even under the existing circumstances, better reporting could have been done on the situation since the riots. He emphasized his point by stating that "if news are excluded from our newspapers by censorship, then it is time to leave St Vincent".

But the issue was broader than that. Grier was very much aware of the attacks on Grimble's administration, prior to the riots. In a letter to J.H. Thomas, secretary of state for the colonies, he referred to them, noting that all kinds of accusations were levelled against him, from inefficiency to injustice. He was of the opinion that the attacks on Grimble, "in a certain section of the St Vincent press, did have a very marked effect in the more ignorant section of the community in Kingstown and did, indeed, as was intended, produce an attitude of mind towards the administration which contributed towards the open disturbance of October 1935".[24] The governor identified DeBique with the attacks. It was this kind of view that led the authorities to search for evil minds behind the riots and to arrest McIntosh and H.E.A. Daisley as instigators. As was indicated before,[25] DeBique was indeed in the forefront of attacks on Grimble in the *Times*, of which he was a regular writer, and came also into contention later as the Canapress correspondent. The calls for Grimble to go continued up to the eve of the riots.

State of Emergency

The state of emergency that was declared on the morning of 22 October was another of the measures established to bring the situation under control. Although there appeared to have been little objection to it when it was enforced, the length of time during which it was in place did generate some opposition. A notice of 28 October 1935 reminded the public that a state of emergency still existed and noted that persons were still spreading false news and creating a state of sedition and unrest. It went on to appeal for information leading to the arrest and conviction of any person so involved.[26]

The *Times*, in an editorial captioned "A State of Emergency – Various

Aspects", in its issue of 7 November 1935, made note of the fact that two weeks had passed and the government had not considered it safe "to remove the interdict under which St Vincent has been placed on 21st ultimo". It went on to make the point that the existence of the state of emergency was uncomfortable for both a government and a people who lived under a constitution where liberty of the people was fundamental. The editorial noted, too, that their condemnation of the rioters and looters "was not entirely in keeping with the common touch", for while they had taken that position, a "racy ranconteur" in an unnamed American journal on 22 October 1935 provided a "grotesque distortion" of the situation and had given the impression that this country "still possesses pack or packs of savages". In a later issue, 15 August 1936, it actually reproduced the article under the caption "A Smile a Day Keeps the Doctor Away". The state of emergency continued into the following year, preventing, among other things, the organizing of large political meetings.[27]

Later, the administrator found it necessary to justify the continuation of the state of emergency. Fear was still being expressed about public gatherings, and so another notice in the *Gazette* of 9 November 1935 reminded about the existence of the state of emergency and warned against any gathering of persons after the annual Remembrance Day ceremony at the War Memorial on 11 November.[28] What seemed to have concerned the administration most of all were the trials and the expected public reaction to them. By 24 January, sixteen of the worst offenders were convicted. It was felt that the public would have reacted strongly against the heavy sentences that were likely to be given. It was therefore necessary to continue with the state of emergency, making it easier for the police to prevent any further trouble.

It served its purpose, too, in accommodating the retention of censorship. Grimble informed Grier that, as chief censor, he often had to delete passages apparently calculated to mislead persons of "low education". Under those circumstances, he was of the view that, if censorship was removed, the press would focus on the trials and was likely to present "the facts in a garbled, sensational or otherwise dangerous form".[29] The executive council had already supported that position and advised that the state of emergency and censorship remain until convicted prisoners were sent to either Grenada or St Lucia.[30] Grimble argued that, while the majority of citizens were calm and peaceful, it was difficult to calculate the attitude of certain elements within the "slum" population of Kingstown and the environs. He suggested that the dangerous elements numbered no more than two hundred persons, but that the lessons of

21 October demonstrated that a small number was capable of drawing "a much larger number of irresponsibles into simultaneous though unpremeditated acts of violence".[31] There was also added concern about the general reaction of the public to the trials. The administrator believed "that the condition of readiness ensured by the continuance of the State of Emergency will enable the avoidance of serious trouble in the days when the prisoners are sentenced and shipped out of the colony". Public safety on those days, he argued, could not be guaranteed without maintenance of the state of emergency.[32]

By the end of January, some of the more serious offenders had been convicted and transferred to Grenada, and the situation was considered safe enough to revoke the state of emergency. The minor cases, it was felt, did not constitute any major problem. In consultation with Administrator Grimble, a decision was therefore taken to end it.[33] An Order in Council dated 29 January 1936 declared that a state of emergency would not exist after 31 January 1936.[34]

The state of emergency did indeed generate a lot of opposition. Someone writing under the name John Citizen in the 19 March 1936 edition of the *Times* summed up the opposition in very colourful language: "But what a three months during which the State of Emergency existed. A law-abiding citizen could not even breathe loudly and the sword of Damocles did threateningly hang over the necks of all of us, the writer and all."

He referred to visits made by the governor to Georgetown and Chateaubelair and speeches made which he considered "unstatesmanlike and un-becoming the dignity of His Majesty's representative". He suggested that if Governor Grier was to see those speeches in print, he would have been very embarrassed. Reaction to the state of emergency was such that, after it was lifted, few persons in Georgetown turned out to listen to him.[35] All of this, despite the statement of the administrator that every means was taken "to ensure that it did not obtrude on the general life of the community".

Seditious Publications Ordinance

The other measure put in place to restore law and order and prevent any further disturbance was the Seditious Publications Ordinance, which had its first reading in the legislative council on 14 November 1935. It was "to provide for the punishment of seditious libel, to facilitate the suppression of Seditious publications and to provide for the temporary suspension of newspapers containing seditious matter".[36] In introducing the bill, the administrator informed members that similar legislation existed in other parts of the British West Indies and the British Empire. It was, he noted, an adaptation of the St Lucian Seditious Publications Ordinance, except that the St Vincent ordinance provided "for summary trial in all cases".[37] The administrator was at pains to suggest that it was not an attempt to "muzzle the Press" or interfere with free speech, but that it was modelled on principles accepted in Britain and elsewhere. He made reference to the governor's speech of 28 October, where he stated that "there is a distinct difference between constructive criticism and deliberate misrepresentation coupled as it often is with abuse of the Administration or of those responsible for it". The administrator argued that "malicious or seditious lying" was not to be regarded as "inalienable rights of human kind; nor can any sane person think that legislation to prevent such calculated distortions of the truth will even remotely affect a single one of those sacred prerogatives connoted by the terms 'freedom of speech' or 'liberty of the press'". He noted further that "the seduction of the people by statements that are false and by wilful misrepresentation either of facts or of the motives or intentions of the Government can no longer be tolerated in a community that claims to be civilized".[38]

The Seditious Publications Ordinance detailed in ten clauses what it considered seditious intent. These included:

> By means of any false statement or wilful misrepresentation of facts or of the motives or intentions of the Government, or any officer of the Government, to excite dislike of or discontent with the Government or constitution as by law established of the United Kingdom or of this Colony or of any British Possession or Protectorate or either House of Parliament or the Legislative or Executive Councils of this Colony or the administration of justice;
>
> To excite any person or class of persons to attempt to procure the alteration of any law or any matter in the State by law established otherwise than by lawful means;
>
> By means of any false statement or wilful misrepresentation of facts or of the motives or intentions of any person to create discontent amongst any of His Majesty's subjects;
>
> To advocate, teach or defend disbelief in or opposition to organised government.

It included under its provisions "power to prohibit importation of publications; suspension of newspapers containing seditious matter and power to prohibit circulation of seditious publications". The ordinance was quite broad in its provisions and content and was geared to limit opposition to the government and any discussion of matters related to the riots. The provisions that seemed to have generated most criticism, however, were those related to punishment for seditious acts and seditious libel. A fine not exceeding one thousand pounds, or imprisonment with or without hard labour for any term not exceeding two years, or both fine and imprisonment were to be meted out to anyone who "does or attempts to do or conspires with any person to do any act with a seditious intention and whoever utters any words having a seditious intention".

A similar punishment was to be meted out to anyone who "publishes, sells, offers for sale, distributes or, with a view to its being published, prints, writes, composes, makes, produces, imports or has in his possession, power or control any seditious publication". Anyone arrested or charged under the provisions would not be convicted if, in the case of a speech or publication that is considered seditious because it contains a false statement, it could be established that the person believed "in good faith that the statement was true and could not by reasonable inquiry have ascertained its falsity". In the case of the importation of or having seditious publication in "possession, power or control", once it could be established that the individual "did not know and had no reason to suspect that the publication was seditious", a conviction could similarly be avoided.[39]

Among the persons and organizations that were critical of the ordinance was Susan Lawrence, a member of the Labour Party in Britain. She had been on speaking engagements in Grenada and Trinidad on behalf of associations in those two countries that were affiliated with the British Labour Party. She indicated to the Vincentian authorities her strong opposition to the ordinance and suggested the establishment of a "large and efficient police force" as an alternative method of dealing with the problem. She argued that the model on which it was based had become obsolete in St Lucia and suggested that its provisions were "too drastic and in places ridiculous". Among the options suggested by her was an emphasis on propaganda. Based on discussions with Lawrence, Governor Grier was of the view that the ordinance was likely to be raised in the British Parliament and that the secretary of state for the colonies would be questioned and attacked for permitting the legislation.[40]

The matter was indeed raised in the House of Commons. Two questions were addressed to J.H. Thomas, secretary of state for the colonies, on 20 May 1936. One enquired about the grounds for the ordinance "and for the measures prescribed therein for suppressing all the different kinds of publications set out in it and for preventing the importation of publications". The other sought to find out if the secretary of state felt that, in the long run, repressive measures achieved what they were designed to do. In replying to the questions, Thomas indicated that it was modelled on one that had been in existence in St Lucia for many years. The object, he outlined, was to "check the dissemination through the press of propaganda calculated to inflame the population against established order".

He nevertheless expressed some dissatisfaction with the penalties, which, he admitted, in some cases appeared to be excessive. He was considering the possibility of reducing the penalties. The secretary of state admitted that he did not believe in repressive measures, but felt that, at times, they were necessary to establish law and order. The question that was left hanging was whether that was the best or only way of establishing law and order.[41] In the 19 March 1936 edition of the *Times*, "John Citizen" referred to the severe criticism of the ordinance from the West Indian press and noted that "the clauses in this Ordinance are so drastic that the Empire Press Association has taken up the matter with the authorities in England with the view to get this provocative ordinance removed from the Statute Books of St Vincent".[42]

The *Times*, in its edition of 7 May 1936, referred to the reaction of the West Indian press to the Seditious Publications Ordinance and suggested that, "if it was the harmless ordinance that it was outlined to be for protecting the St Vincent public all these editors would not have cried out against it as they did". It also made reference to a section of the Barbadian press which was of the view that the St Vincent press was incapable of any abuse of liberty.[43]

George McIntosh, once he had got beyond his immediate wavering reaction, as is described later in this chapter, hit out at the Seditious Publications Ordinance in two speeches, one at Kingstown and the other at Georgetown when his new organization, the St Vincent Workingmen's Cooperative Association (SWMA), celebrated Worker's Day. He referred to the ordinance as a stain that should be removed, since it prevented people from speaking freely. He felt as if there was a sword hanging over his head, since "the slightest word I say may be taken to be seditious". He asked that they be "treated as British subjects as any freeman in any part of the British Empire".[44] While admitting to the excessive nature of the penalties and being prepared to redraft the ordinance if so desired by the secretary of state, the governor was prepared to defend it. One of the things he touched on again was what he considered the vicious campaign against Grimble that obviously influenced the measures adopted. In response to Susan Lawrence's suggestion about the use of propaganda, Grier was of the view that in the Crown colonies which he administered, the government was unable to control the press, and there was always the possibility that any pronouncement by the government was likely to be distorted or misrepresented.[45]

The administrator had earlier pointed to the limitations of the Seditious Publications Ordinance. Although certain activities could, to an extent, be checked, it was not sufficient in the immediate situation. Its effect was limited to the prosecution for publication of seditious articles only after their appearance. He noted that articles could be inflammatory without being seditious. He admitted that the articles which he censored could not "justly be called seditious"; but he was able to delete many passages which might have misled "persons of low education" and increased tension.[46] It was for that reason that censorship of the press, the Seditious Publications Ordinance and the state of emergency were meant to work in tandem.

Given the objectives and concerns that prompted the government to introduce the Seditious Publications Ordinance, they were unlikely to revoke it until they believed those were met. Instead, they responded to criticism about the excessive fines by amending the sections dealing with punishments for its infringement. But some of the concerns still remained. The *Times*, while noting that the ordinance had not been challenged by any member of the legislative council, asked if it was necessary and intimated that the common law would have been sufficient to deal with sedition and libel. It suggested that the Colonial Office was not going to admit that the whole bill was unnecessary and felt that it was necessary to go further. As it stated, "now that the opportunity has been given to put the thin edge of the wedge on the question of fines, drive the wedge home and smash to atoms every clause of the bill".[47]

The 1937 Amendment Bill focused on sections four, five and nine of the principal ordinance. These sections dealt with punishment for seditious acts and seditious libel, the power to prohibit importation of publications, and summary procedure and punishment. The scope and reach of the ordinance remained quite broad. With the revocation of the state of emergency and censorship, the Seditious Publications Ordinance gave the authorities something to hold on to. By 1937, some of the concerns that motivated the state of emergency, censorship and the Seditious Publications Ordinance were no longer in existence, but the experiences of 21 and 22 October were not far removed from the political memory of the authorities.

REACTION TO THE RIOTS

A wide variety of individuals and organizations, both within the country and outside, reacted not only to the riots but to the response of the authorities. The Negro Welfare and Cultural Association of Trinidad called a meeting at Woodford Square in Port of Spain that was said to have attracted fifteen hundred persons. The association, as a result of that meeting, forwarded a telegram on 30 October 1935 to the governor demanding the arrest of those whom they described as murderers of the workers.[48]

The concern of London-based black civil rights organization the League of Coloured People went beyond the emergency measures. It was, indeed, critical of and concerned about the Seditious Publications Ordinance, which in its view "inflicts the penalty of imprisonment as an example, on anyone who receives innocently through the post, literature which His Excellency the Governor considered seditious". It pointed, however, to the firing on the crowd. A letter written to the secretary of state by its president, Harold Moody, said that it had no doubt that he had given instructions "for these circumstances to be thoroughly investigated and that you will issue a report therein in due course". He suggested that the measures taken and the general reaction of the administration in St Vincent savoured of dictatorship, which was "alien to the best traditions of British administration and directly violating the liberties of His Majesty's most loyal subjects in the colony".[49]

The league hoped that the secretary of state would seek an explanation for the actions of the governor and felt that an inquiry was needed "to allay the more than anxious fears of the two millions of His Majesty's loyal subjects now domiciled in the British West Indies".[50] In response to what might have been another letter by the league, it was told that the ordinance had the approval of the secretary of state and was then on the statute books. It informed that "the Secretary of State is not disposed to question the decision of the Governor to impose a censorship during a time of emergency". The league considered the reply unsatisfactory and made it known that they were disposed to question the actions of the governor, especially since, based on the information at their disposal, the situation did not warrant the dramatic steps taken.[51]

In the immediate aftermath of the riots, the Vincentian middle class, as reflected by the newspapers, appeared to be distancing itself from the events of 21 and 22 October. The *Vincentian* stated, "they were to all appearances without the advice of anyone who could impress on them the adoption of a constitutional process, but they vented their fury after the manner of a revolutionary party which unfortunately several from the island who have been forced to travel in search of work, doubtless have concluded is worthy of imitation".[52]

The *Times* later expressed the view that "no decent law-abiding middle class man had any hands in it". They were really trying to emphasize the spontaneity of the riots, and in attempting to defend representatives of the RGA from any involvement, they went on to say that "many of these men were as surprised at the outbreak as the officials themselves".[53]

The *Times* referred to the grievances of the people and argued that they had the right to voice their grievances, but the paper resented the use of force to make their grievances known. But even after saying that, it suggested that petitions might have been found to be of no avail. It was, however, difficult, in its view, to justify the "indiscriminate" destruction of property. It regretted the loss of lives among "the mob", even while they had taken no lives. The debate in the future, they considered, would be about whether the deaths could have been avoided.[54] The *Vincentian* of 26 October 1935 likewise, admitted that the people had hardships that needed to be remedied but concluded that "their cause is not helped by disgraceful scenes as marked last Monday's happenings". Nothing, it felt, could have justified "the riotous behaviour", particularly "of an uncontrollable collection of people who violently resorted to the ruthless destruction of motor cars, windows and doors of places of business".

There was, however, some ambivalence from two bodies that were organs of middle-class thought, the RGA and the Kingstown Board, on which many members of the RGA sat. The RGA, which had many members sympathetic to the plight of the working people, was divided on the issue. This led to the resignation of the vice-president, Byron Cox, whose request to send a letter to the governor expressing regret for the disturbances, did not get approval from the secretary, Ebenezer Duncan, and the president, Cyril McDowall. Other leading members of the association, when contacted, supported the position of the president and the secretary.[55] Later, the secretary and a few other members offered their personal services as special constables.[56] Some members of the RGA had long seen the working class as allies, albeit outside the formal political struggle in its fight for constitutional reform. The reaction of the crowds had surprised them and had moved beyond their control.

Duncan, secretary of the RGA and editor of the *Investigator*, was of the view that lawful means existed to work out the settlement of any problems and grievances. It was quite strange, too, that Duncan, in his *Brief History of*

St Vincent, published in 1941, had little to say about the riots except to quote from the governor.

McIntosh's reaction was also very instructive. In a meeting of the Kingstown Board on 29 October 1935, he asked for leave to move a resolution expressing "deep regret" at the incident, which he felt was going to retard the efforts at improvement in the colony. In his resolution, he even congratulated the government on the stand it had taken. The resolution was unanimously supported by members, who endorsed all that was said.[57] But McIntosh's reaction went even further. In his address to the RGA on 28 October 1935, Grier made reference to a letter he received from McIntosh on 22 October, where, according to the governor, "he dissociated himself entirely from the conduct of the people who had, as he said behaved, 'like a bunch of uncivilised savages'". In that letter, he also offered his services to the government, an offer that was not accepted by the governor because of his anger at what he felt was McIntosh's involvement as a central figure and his refusal to let the government know about the intentions of the mob. The governor stated further, in justifying his rejection of McIntosh's offer, that "it was the bounding duty of any law-abiding citizen, who knew that the mob had collected and was advancing on their Council Chamber to give that warning at once".[58]

McIntosh's response in the immediate aftermath of the riots might have been influenced by an awareness that he was being singled out by the authorities as one of the architects of the affair. He might also have been overcome by his inability to control the situation and to see those who had long sought counsel from him taking matters into their own hands. As will be seen later, with the dismissal of the case against him and the enthusiastic response of the people, who regarded him as something of a hero, he began to move in a different, more radical direction and became quite critical of the authorities.[59]

There were others who displayed no such ambivalence. The Methodist Church denounced the disturbances and pledged cooperation "within its own sphere by insisting on the utter wrong and folly of all forms of lawlessness and the duty of every citizen to render obedience and respect to the powers which are ordained of God". The church claimed that, as far as it was aware, none of its members was involved in the affair.[60]

Persons associated with the Supreme Court, at its sitting on 2 November 1935, were appalled by the damage to the courthouse, which counsel for the defence A. Amelius Richards regarded as abhorrent and disgusting. He was also concerned about the racial factor that had been introduced. He emphasized what he considered the sanctity of the court and the condemnation which he felt would always come from his colleagues on the bar when that sacredness was violated. Some of his sentiments were shared by N.S. Nanton, counsel for the plaintiff, and Chief Justice Williams, who noted that, unlike the recent disturbances in St Kitts, that of 21 and 22 October was directed at the government.

Williams pointed to the positives in the affair, since the government was in a position to recognize those on whom it could rely. Moreover, "they had proved that the great bulk of the population had no colour feeling, that it is loyal and law abiding and does not welcome mob violence".[61] The *Vincentian* also took up the theme and was critical of the fact that violence took place at the courthouse. It felt that few persons had paused to understand the true significance of that building "in which Justice is administered without fear, affection or ill-will, regardless of colour or creed".[62]

Other persons and bodies, in commenting on the disturbances, called for the holding of a commission of inquiry. The calls came from sources in the country and outside. One of the earliest calls came from a resident, Randolph Williams, who sought the help of the West India Committee in doing so. He was informed, however, that the committee could not act on an "ex-parte statement" coming from an individual and therefore suggested that he make representation to the secretary of state through the normal channels.[63]

The *Times* referred to what it considered the "comparatively large loss of life", the unusually large number of prisoners and consequent cost, factors which among others "make the sending of a Commission imperative". But it noted that, additionally, "it would prove, as nothing else can, that the Home Government is interested in our welfare. It would confirm our faith in the high ideals and principles of Great Britain." The paper proceeded to quote the precedent set with the commission that was set up following the riots in St Kitts. It stated, too, that the large body of persons apart from the government and rioters would be concerned if a commission was not appointed. It proposed a commission that was broad-based, including not only the action taken in suppressing the riots but also the "excessive expenditures" and the "economic condition of the people", which, obviously, it saw as causes. The RGA took advantage of the visit to St Vincent of Sir John Maffey, permanent undersecretary of state for the colonies, to request the establishment of a royal commission.[64]

In a letter signed by its president, A.T. Marryshow, the Grenada Labour Party echoed the sentiments of others in requesting "that in the interest of all concerned His Majesty's Secretary of State for the colonies be pleased to send a Commission to enquire into the recent disturbances in the neighbouring island of St Vincent".[65] Prior to this, in the 19 February 1936 issue of his paper, the *Crusader*, he wondered why the state of emergency was ever declared and press censorship imposed, a censorship that he regarded as "the most drastic that has ever been put in force in West Indian history, in so far as the press and even public telegrams are concerned". He then made his call for a royal commission to be set up.

There were those in the colonial administration who did not see the need for an inquiry. L. Toney of the Colonial Office saw no necessity for it. He argued that "the fact that a woman who is believed to be in no way taking part in the rioting was killed, and another injured, is most regrettable but an accident which could not have been avoided in the circumstances".[66] The official position of the Colonial Office came from secretary of state W. Ormsby in a letter to Governor Grier dated 16 June 1936, in which he responded to the petition from the Grenada Labour Party: "I request that the Grenada Labour Party may be informed that after careful consideration of their request I have come to the conclusion that there is no necessity for the appointment of a Commission of Enquiry."[67]

But the governor had earlier seen the necessity for a broad-based enquiry. Shortly after the disturbances, he had suggested the early appointment of a commission with West Indian experience "to enquire and report as early as possible regarding riots and steps taken to suppress them and later regarding causes". This was much influenced by what he reported to have been tense feelings in St Lucia over the Italo-Abyssinian War. The enquiry into causes, he felt, should follow the trials, which were likely to unearth important facts.[68]

It is of interest that five years later, in 1941, George McIntosh again raised the matter in the legislative council, when he asked if the government had as yet instituted an enquiry into the causes of the riots. By then, the political landscape had changed. McIntosh had formed an organization that had a political arm and was then a member of the legislative council.[69]

TRIALS

Preliminary Trial of George McIntosh

The country's administration had difficulty accepting the view that the riots were spontaneous. It therefore looked for evil hands, among them persons who, they claimed, had returned from Cuba and had, in their view, soaked up communist ideas. It was also looking for some mastermind who, they felt, was behind what they interpreted as a plot. But, more pointedly, they focused their attention on members of the RGA, which had been involved in political advocacy since its formation in 1919. Among them, McIntosh stood out. He was an obvious and easy target, too, in that he was at the centre of the activity on 21 October, although, as was revealed later, not in the role the administrator suggested.

Part of the administration's immediate reaction was to send a strong signal by dealing with those they considered to be behind the rioting. They felt that "success or failure of other proceedings will be much influenced by issue of this case", the case that was being constructed against McIntosh.[70] In a memorandum to Governor Grier, Grimble stated, "It became necessary after the riots of the 21–22 October 1935 to investigate the extent to which persons of better education and more responsible status than the rioters themselves had been implicated in precipitating the disturbances."[71] The governor and administrator, in their reaction to the events, displayed the mindset of colonial administrators to colonial people. They saw the black masses as mindless, ignorant and incapable of taking any serious action on their own. They were simply tools of middle-class activists, by whom they could be manipulated.

The Wood Commission of 1921–22 was on the same wavelength when it stated that, with "an ignorant and uneducated population, it is comparatively simple for good organisers to arrange effective mass meetings to advance a cause, with regard to which not one person in twenty if cross examined as to what it was all about, would be able to give an intelligent reply".[72]

As Ken Post said about the Jamaican colonial situation, "it must be borne in mind that it was necessary to the colonial myth that the masses be seen as simple, happy people, who might on occasion be misled by agitators".[73] The governor was clear on this. In his address to the RGA on 28 October, he warned them that when it was decided to end the state of emergency, he would have to take precautions "to prevent any further dissemination of misleading propaganda amongst the many people of this colony who are so ill-informed that they are unable to distinguish between what is true and what is false".[74]

Grier, in a confidential communication to Sir Cosmo Parkinson at the Colonial Office on 17 November 1935, pointed to the view that McIntosh had started "the whole thing" and informed him that McIntosh would be arrested once "connecting links" could be found.[75] Interestingly, Daisley of Stubbs, a

Methodist preacher and headmaster of the Stubbs Primary School, was the first person to be arrested. Grier stated that "it is known that at 12:30 p.m. on 21 October he received a telephone message at a place called Stubbs . . . which was admittedly to the effect that the men and women of Stubbs should come into Kingstown at once". Attention was, however, focused on McIntosh, and a search of the headquarters of the RGA, of which he was a leading member, was suggested and carried out.[76]

The services of three non-commissioned officers from Trinidad – Sergeant Belfon of the San Fernando Detective Office, Corporal Hunte of the Criminal Investigation Department, and Sub-Inspector Eric Morgan – were offered to St Vincent. Inspector Morgan, who arrived in the country on 11 November, was to report later that it was his view that a "prima facie" case existed for the arrest of McIntosh, and he sought a legal opinion from the attorney general, C.C. Ross. Ross felt that, providing the facts suggested it, McIntosh should be charged for inciting the lower elements of the community to violence, "an offence of so serious a nature that the very charge would not only make him realize fully the gravity of his conduct, but would deter him and others from a repetition of acts of the kind that brought about the events of 21 October 1935".[77]

Ross was at pains to justify the position he had taken and to inform the administrator accordingly. The charge was narrowed to that of treason-felony. In trial, a majority verdict could be had on a treason-felony charge, not on one of treason. He went on to suggest that "defending counsel would not have the opportunity . . . of indicating the nature of the penalty which the accused might have to suffer if convicted of treason".[78]

The charge was defined as having "compassed or intended to levy war against our Lord the King in the colony of St Vincent in order to put force or constraint upon His Excellency the Governor of the Windward Islands and the Legislative Council of St Vincent and that he expressed or uttered or declared such compassing or intention by diverse acts or deeds".[79] He was convinced that the charge was warranted since it appeared evident that McIntosh was the leader of a mob, "the object of which was to compel changes of legislation in policy either by violent means or by intimidation". He went further, pointing to the English Treason-Felony Act that had, he noted, been adopted in the colony by section 276 of the Indictable Offence Ordinance:

> If the facts or matters alleged in an indictment for any felony under this Act shall amount in law to Treason such indictment shall not by reason thereof be deemed void, erroneous or defective, and if the facts or matters provided on the trial of

any person indicted for any felony under this Act shall amount in law to treason, such person shall not by reason thereof be entitled to be acquitted of such felony.[80]

McIntosh was arrested on 23 November at 11:30 p.m. on a charge of treason-felony. Because of the nature of the charges, bail was denied; however, the authorities were prepared to speed up the preliminary hearings. It was initially felt that the preliminary hearings would be held in November with two weeks' notice of special assizes to allow the trial to be held towards the middle of December.[81] The preliminary hearing against McIntosh started on 5 December 1935. The magistrate in charge was Stanley DeFreitas. The case was prosecuted by H.J. Hughes, Police Magistrate District 2, since a decision was made to omit Ross, who had suffered personal damages during the riots. L.C. Hannays, legal counsel from Trinidad, was contracted to defend McIntosh and was assisted by local barrister O.W. Forde.

Nineteen witnesses were called, including eight policemen. On the fifth day, the trial took a surprising turn. It was clear that the prosecution's witnesses had failed to show that McIntosh was guilty of any crime; rather, their evidence seemed to have been suggesting that he was, in fact, attempting to calm the crowd. Hannays, the defence attorney, after some squabbles over points of law, decided to intervene. Addressing the magistrate, he stated, "I do not think that this farce should continue. I do not think that this could happen anywhere else. Witness after witness is asked to establish the innocence of the accused, but the case is still continued and bail refused."[82]

Magistrate DeFreitas, too, seemed to have had enough and decided to bring the proceedings to a close. He addressed the court:

> This is one of the cases where the Magistrate has a very simple task. I am not confronted with any doubt, conflicting evidence or any nice points of law. All the evidence and all the depositions with the exception of the last witness who heard certain words that might or might not have some reference to the charge against the accused is in his favour.[83] . . . In going through all the evidence I feel that if the defence had set themselves out to select all the witnesses for the prosecution and ask them to say what they had said, it would have been difficult for them to have done better. I have found no thread of any incriminating evidence against this man.[84]

The government's strategy fell flat with the dismissal of the case against McIntosh since, as the administrator had stated previously, "success or failure of other proceedings will be much influenced by issue of this case".[85] The administrator blamed the collapse of the prosecution's case on the discrepancy between statements given by Leonard Mayers, Donald Romeo and George Thomas to the police and the ones made in court.[86] The problem was that the authorities were so anxious to find a scapegoat for the disturbances that they read too much into the statements given by those gentlemen and might even have exerted some pressure on them to make the statements they did. Thomas, for instance, was summoned to make a statement on three different occasions, the first about a week and a half after the incident. Only on his third visit on 22 November did he make a sworn statement. He was even, at one stage, reminded by Reverend Hatch, the superintendent of the Anglican church and headmaster in charge of the Anglican school, that he was a civil servant. His views and those of the other gentlemen might even have been influenced by the climate of reaction then prevailing.

In the immediate aftermath of the riots, the middle class expressed shock at the behaviour of those implicated in the riots, but, after a few weeks, and especially because of the attempts to implicate McIntosh, attitudes began to change and a great deal of sympathy was expressed for him. Thomas's statement to the police could only have been considered detrimental to McIntosh if one had set out to find every tiny bit of evidence, hoping to have it add up to something significant. He indicated that, when the crowd entered McIntosh's drugstore, he heard someone say, "Morning Dada, we come for instructions." In court, he said, "It seemed more or less a joke." He stated that McIntosh seemed not to have been surprised to see the crowd and that he subsequently spoke to the crowd and was gesticulating.[87]

Mayers, a peddler, had been arrested because he was seen in the vicinity of the riots. He told the police then that he had been crying in the cell, remarking that McIntosh was the cause and that nothing would have happened if they had not followed him. Some of his fellow prisoners urged him not to call McIntosh's name since he was "a good man".[88] In court, Mayers made no mention of that incident and instead suggested that McIntosh was trying to calm the crowd. It was following his testimony that Hannays tried to have the proceedings brought to a halt. In correspondence with the governor, the administrator admitted that the witnesses testified for the defence rather than the prosecution. He was also critical of Thomas, whose "evasions" in court, he felt, deprived his evidence of any weight it otherwise would have had.[89]

The question of penalizing Thomas seemed to have been contemplated but then discarded since, as the administrator suggested, it was "widely known that his statement to the Police and Gonsalves[90] represented the truth, what was said in Court untrue but difficult to prove since he will admit that what was said in Court was true and what said earlier had been exaggerated".[91] He asked the new attorney general, O'Reilly, however, to consider Thomas's position as head teacher of a primary school "and to give this factor full weight in his conclusion of the facts".[92] In reference to the police witnesses, he was of the view that they did not attempt to suppress the facts but were affected by "the turn given to their evidence by the defence". He felt that none of them "stated less than he knew or less than he had already stated to Morgan".[93] O'Reilly, who had succeeded Ross as attorney general, was given the responsibility to hold investigations into the conflicting statements made by the police witnesses.[94] The dismissal of the charges against McIntosh completely upset the strategies and intentions of the colonial authorities. Nothing further was heard about the case against Daisley, and it was likely that, with the collapse of the charges against McIntosh, it was realized that it would have been difficult to convict Daisley. There was, in any event, no evidence to support Grier's earlier claim that he had induced people from Stubbs to go to Kingstown to join the rioters there.[95] With the charges against McIntosh having been squashed at the preliminary hearings, the case against Daisley could hardly stand and was seemingly not pursued.[96]

Grier later accepted that the magistrate was right in deciding that the evidence given by witnesses did not justify sending the matter to trial. He was further advised by O'Reilly that the statements by witnesses justified a charge of incitement to riot but not for the more serious offence McIntosh was charged with.[97] He was still of the opinion that McIntosh and other colleagues in the RGA were the instigators of the riots and that the disturbances were not more widespread only because they were not allowed to have it their way. He argued that the arrest of McIntosh stalled further activity "at a time of high political tensions".[98]

One of the outstanding matters that had been occupying the attention of the authorities was the attempt to arrest Don Morgan, one of the alleged leaders of the riots in the Camden Park–Questelles–Chauncey area, and his colleagues Clifford Sutherland and Peter McDowall. Although the warrant for Morgan's arrest was issued on 12 November, it was not until 24 December, fifteen days after McIntosh was freed, that he was eventually arrested. The authorities got little support from the community in their efforts to arrest these three. This was a result either of threats made by Morgan and his colleagues or distrust of the police in the area. The police encountered other problems. They had dif-

ficulty identifying Don Morgan, who was armed with a knife and cutlass and
had been monitoring their movements. The police authorities were forced to
change strategies in their efforts to arrest Morgan and party. They concluded
that the presence of European officers in the parties sent out to arrest the men
drew too much attention to them and made it easier for Morgan to follow their
movements. But the dilemma they faced had to do with the report that Morgan and the others with him were armed. Police regulations stated that armed
police parties were to operate only under an officer of commissioned rank,
which meant, at that time, English officers.

Through his efforts at eluding the police, Morgan became something of a
folk hero, reinforcing his image by exhibiting his skills at knife-throwing as he
practised on surrounding trees. With each unsuccessful attempt by the police,
his prestige grew. The search for Morgan even took the police to De Voilet in
the far north of the country. On one occasion, they had encountered him early
in the morning but were unable to identify him and only realized that fact after
he had escaped. Morgan had actually evaded different attempts to arrest him
and had, on two occasions, attacked the district constable Cleophus Jessop,
whom he accused of informing on him. On 22 December, two days before he
was actually apprehended, he escaped again after another physical contact.

Lance Corporal John led a police party to Chauncey, north of Camden
Park. He was warned that the use of firearms was reserved only for occasions
that could be considered emergencies. He was also told that he had to assume
responsibility for explaining the use of firearms to any court of enquiry. At
Chauncey, the police party approached a house allegedly occupied by the
wanted men. During a struggle, two shots were fired at Morgan, who, despite
being wounded, escaped but was later found sitting "in some cotton bushes".
Clifford Sutherland and Peter McDowall were, in the meantime, captured.[99]
Morgan was taken to the hospital, where he died later, on 26 December. A
coroner's enquiry on 7 January concluded that he had died from a gunshot
wound in a situation of "justifiable homicide", although McIntosh lamented
the lack of inquiry into the incident, implying that Morgan was shot while
under arrest.[100]

The collapse of the case against McIntosh changed the whole complexion of
the trials, which were to be based on a conspiracy masterminded by McIntosh
and Daisley, involving members of the RGA and the Ranch boys. Although
official correspondence did not list the nature of the charges, those charged
would have included persons who allegedly participated in the riots both as

leaders and followers, ones responsible for damages and others identified as participants in the looting of Corea's stores and in stealing goods.

Special criminal sessions began on 8 January and lasted until 3 March 1936, by which time 114 persons (91 men and 23 women) were tried. With the number of accused held for trials and some of them facing two or three charges, the trials were held mostly in batches of four.[101] Fear of public reaction still haunted the authorities, so they decided on a path of leniency since, according to Grimble, many of those who were guilty of misdemeanours were encouraged into "unpremeditated disorders" arising from the sudden development of the disturbances, or "misguided by clever persons into action of which they hardly realised the gravity".[102] The need for precautionary measures had been expressed quite early by Grimble.[103]

The authorities concluded that many of them were simply shouting and waving their sticks and cutlasses. Grimble suggested that it was in the best interest of the colony to let "rigour of the law" be "tempered by mercy". In providing an update on the proceedings up to 27 January, the administrator noted that twenty of the more serious offenders were already convicted. He stated that not many other cases involved serious action. The remainder he sought to divide into two groups: the first, "a relatively small group whose offences, prima facie, render trial on indictment unfavourable". Then, a larger group, whose cases, it was felt, could be dealt with in the courts of summary jurisdiction. In both cases, the Crown was prepared to submit pleas for leniency and "to bind them over to future good behaviour".[104]

The most serious cases had been tried first, and, by the end of January, thirty-three offenders had been tried, of whom four were acquitted and twenty-nine convicted and sentenced. Because of the shortage of space to accommodate the prisoners, twelve were sent to Grenada. It was even considered necessary to send some to St Lucia, given the fact that there were other serious offences to be tried.[105] By the end of the trials in March, ninety-one men and twenty-three women had been tried under riot-related charges. Of them, one woman and thirteen men were acquitted. Of the remaining one hundred, thirty-nine men and two women were convicted by the jury; thirty-nine men and twenty women pleaded guilty. Of those who were convicted or who had pleaded guilty, forty-five men and five women were sentenced to imprisonment, thirty-three men and seventeen women were placed on bonds "to come up for judgement if called upon to do so within two years". Forty-three persons had been discharged at preliminary hearings and three persons dealt, by magistrates, with

Table 7. List of Convicted Persons and Their Sentences

Men	Sentences (in years of hard labour)
Martin Durham	10
Wilfred Joyette	5
Donald Peters	9
Chester Bulze	10
Samuel "Sheriff" Lewis	9
Gordon Joseph	7
Julian Charles	7
Hubert Delpeche	2
Claude Phillips	7
Samuel McCaulay	5
Donald Romeo	7
Clifford Hinds	7
Claude Gumbs	7
Henry Mc Carter	9
Bassie Welcome	7
Theophilus Hackshaw	9
Ebenezer Jordan	9
Alfred French	9
Brisbane Samuel	9
Edmund Birchwood	9
Reuben Phillips	5
Victor Applewhite	5
Joseph Baynes	5
Sydney Scipio	3
Ormond Clarke	3

Women	Sentences (in years of hard labour)
Beryl Ollivierre	5
Lydia Laidlow	5
Hermina Oliver	4
Beatrice George	4

Note: Neither the charges nor the incidences of multiple convictions were identified.

fines or bonds (see table 7).[106] The chief justice had allowed many of the sentences to run concurrently, thus limiting the number of years, with the result that the maximum sentence was for ten years.[107]

One of the criticisms raised about the trials was that some of the prisoners were not provided with legal counsel, a charge the governor tried to defend by stating that the facts against the first thirty offenders were so clear that defence counsel would have made little difference. However, because of the adverse comments, it was decided to provide counsel for the remaining 120 persons.[108] Included among the persons charged was a fourteen-year-old boy named George Arthur, who was held in prison since October, with bail being refused "on his own recognizance" because he was declared to be homeless and the argument was being made that he was ill-nourished and better off in prison.[109]

The trials did not unearth any new facts to substantiate the conspiracy theories of the authorities. With McIntosh already exonerated, new bogeymen were found in Vincentians who had worked and lived in Cuba and the Dominican Republic. Grier had expressed to the secretary of state the view that those men who spent time in either Cuba or the Dominican Republic became sources of political trouble on their return. In fact, to his mind, it was more than a view, for he indicated that it was "generally recognised".[110] This cannot, however, be rejected as mere idle talk. The governor might have been on to something, although how extensive this was is difficult to tell. It was true that Vincentians, like other West Indians who had returned from those countries, tended to be more politically conscious. Samuel "Sheriff" Lewis, who was recognized as one of the men in the forefront of the disturbances on 21 October, had spent six months in Cuba and seven years in Santo Domingo and had, during that period, travelled to Puerto Rico and St Thomas. Lewis had taken a keen interest in the Italo-Abyssynian War and, as a member of the Ranch, played a leading role in political discussions that were regularly held.[111]

Governor Grier continued to believe in a conspiracy theory. He claimed that some of the convicts acknowledged that it had been decided on Saturday, 19 October, to have a disturbance but they were not prepared to identify those who were the organizers. It is difficult to substantiate this claim, for there is little else to allow anyone to come to that conclusion. At the end of the trials, according to the governor, there were a few men wanted in connection with the riots that were still at large and were believed to have escaped to neighbouring islands by sloops.[112]

The authorities were pleased with the way the trials had been conducted and were satisfied that justice was done. They were prepared to review the cases of those who had not been represented by counsel.[113] The chief justice and attorney general were satisfied with the work of the juries. They indicated that the accused were given the benefit, in situations where there was an element of doubt. They could point to only one case where, in their view, the evidence was at odds with the decision of the jury, although this was not identified.[114]

CHAPTER 4

CAUSES OF AND REACTIONS TO THE RIOTS

WITH THE FAILURE OF THE TRIALS TO UNEARTH any new evidence and the absence of a commission of inquiry, the views of the governor assumed major importance in official circles. It is, therefore, helpful to use his views as a point of reference. The Colonial Office seemed to have been satisfied with his report, a report that was reviewed by Colonial Office official, L. Toney, who agreed with most of it. His only real point of difference, which, in his view, did not seriously affect the governor's version of things, had to do with the period that elapsed "between the time when the Governor gave orders for the Police to be armed and the outbreak of the stone throwing and the return of the first armed detachment from the barrack". Toney expressed the view that it would be better to await the result of the trials, particularly as it related to George McIntosh, before deciding on the need for further investigation. He felt, however, that the governor's account of the disturbances "could hardly be improved upon". He argued, too, that it would be best not to publish anything about the contributory causes until the results of the trials, but went on to make the point that, if it was found necessary to do so before, then it should be limited to the summary of the governor's views as to the causes.[1] With the trials concluded and no new information emerging, a lot more importance was, naturally, attached to the governor's views about the causes of the riots.

There was general agreement by commentators on the main causes of the riots, although differences arose regarding emphasis and how they were played out. The riots generated interest in neighbouring Caribbean colonies and in Britain, where it was raised in the House of Commons. We have made mention before of the arrival in St Vincent of Clennell Wickham of the *West Indian* of

Grenada and J. Broome of the *Barbados Advocate*[2] on the day after the riots. The *Port of Spain Gazette* gave wide coverage to the event, possibly because of the involvement of one of Trinidad's lawyers in the defence of McIntosh and the use of three members of their Criminal Investigation Department to assist the Vincentian police. The *Port of Spain Gazette* not only carried excerpts from other West Indian newspapers but secured the rights to the publication of the preliminary trial of McIntosh. The paper depended initially on reports from Clement DeBique, who represented Canapress, but, with the imposition of press censorship, secured their own contact.

The emergency measures imposed after the riots limited any thorough discussion of their causes. Because of press censorship, the newspapers in St Vincent tended to be cautious and moderate in their comments on the causes. By the latter part of February 1936, with censorship lifted, the *Times* ventured more widely into related matters. It called for an open discussion of the disturbances and identified some aspects that needed to be taken into account. There was, at that time, some emphasis on the economic situation.[3] The *Investigator*, in its issue of 26 February 1936, after highlighting the economic situation, called for a committee to enquire into the economic conditions of the people and to make recommendations for effecting improvements, showing, no doubt, where it thought the emphasis should be.

By 1936, despite the willingness and greater freedom to discuss the issues surrounding the riots, the immediacy had been removed. With general elections due shortly, the focus had shifted to the political sphere. Early in the new year, the RGA published notices urging members to register to vote. Later, with changes to the constitution and the formation of the SWMA, the emphasis in the country shifted to the elections. The *Investigator* of 1 February 1936 appealed for people who would represent the interest of the masses.

The dismissal of the charges against McIntosh had complicated matters for the authorities and destroyed the main tenet of their thinking on the causes of the riots. Grier, taken completely by surprise by the disturbances of October 21 and 22, attempted from very early to influence thinking on the causes. In a telegram to the secretary of state for the colonies on 22 October, he admitted that the origin of the riots was obscure. He declared, however, that those who participated in it were "primed with rum". He identified what he considered contributory causes and attempted to downplay any possible blame that could have been levelled at his administration. He highlighted them: a feeling of discontent arising from lack of employment and low wages on some of the estates;

the development of strong racial feeling that resulted from the Italo-Abyssinian War; and "misleading propaganda" that created the impression that it was
government's policy to raise the price of essential commodities. Grier informed
the secretary of state that when he was confronted by the crowd on 21 October, the cry was primarily about lack of employment and low wages, but he
suggested that the other two matters that he mentioned were also causes.[4]
The governor, however, sought to discredit the rioters and, by implication, to
suggest that there were no genuine grievances. The "original gang of rioters",
he argued, were not genuinely unemployed but persons known to the police
because of their "well-known criminal records".[5]

He was also concerned about the possibility of what he called "garbled
accounts" appearing in papers such as the British *Daily Mail* and *Daily Express*.
He expressed the fear that "local correspondents, one of whom is under grave
suspicion as being in part responsible for what occurred, are bound to write up
the events here and send them to England in a very exaggerated form".[6] At the
continuation, on 28 October, of the interrupted legislative council meeting of
21 October, Grier continued his examination of the events and tried to make
sense of what had happened, although this was affected by his efforts to remove
any blame from his administration and to find scapegoats.

He stated that he was informed about the rise in prices in some shops, in
Georgetown and other outlying districts, which he considered unjustified. He
tried to disconnect the riots from the ordinances that were introduced on 18
October. He felt, too, that the kind of shopkeepers to whom he was referring
would not have seen or understood the schedules attached to the ordinances
and were unlikely to be involved in such activities unless led on by others with
agendas designed to create strife. In his view, there were few genuine workers
and peasants involved. It shocked him that no one in authority had "preknow-
ledge of the event". Legislative council member F.A. Corea, whose business
place bore the brunt of the damages in Kingstown, supported his views and
emphasized his belief that "the people of the labouring class particularly have
been stirred up to a point of agitation by people who ought to know better".[7]

While, in his early responses, Grier had been reacting to the cry of the
crowds against lack of employment and low wages, in his official report of 12
November he pointed out that he had since revised his opinion and highlighted
the tense racial feeling from the Italo-Abyssinian War as the main underlying
cause. He argued that the general attitude of the rioters was one of bitter
hostility to whites rather than to the government.[8] This contradicted the view

of the chief justice, who, as indicated before, argued that, "unlike estate riots, directed against private individuals such as had recently taken place in St Kitts, the riots in St Vincent was an attack on government itself and was fomented by agitators for political reasons".[9]

Grier, in developing his argument about the central role of race, stated that, with a single exception, shops and houses looted were those of people of European descent. The single exception, he declared, was that of "a wealthy African whose house was entered and some valuables taken". He never explained why, if race was the motivating factor, the home of a wealthy African was attacked. Clearly, the governor was embarrassed by the riots and attempted to shift the blame from any deficiencies in his administration. The other major argument used by him centred on his view that the riots were organized. He stated, "I am definitely of the opinion that the Kingstown riot was organised . . . in my whole experience of work in the Colonial Service I have never known a similar case where a sudden outbreak has taken not merely the Government and the Police but also the great majority of the people in the community so completely by surprise."[10]

The fact that no member of government or police knew about the possibility of disturbances beforehand he interpreted to mean that it was secretly organized with the intention of causing discontent. His thinking on those matters appeared to be downplaying any major issues that might have played a significant part in the riots. But it must be argued that, with disturbances occurring in ten Caribbean colonies between 1935 and 1939, it is only natural that one would want to look for the regional connections and similarities and not see the events as originating primarily within the country and outside that regional context. The regional causes were certainly not unique to a particular country. The Moyne Commission, which was set up to investigate conditions in the Caribbean following the disturbances of the 1930s, pointed to a regional connection. While taking note of nineteenth-century disturbances, the commission, in referring to the 1930s, stated:

> The discontent that underlies the disturbances of recent years is a phenomenon of a different character, representing no longer a mere blind protest against a worsening of conditions, but a positive demand for the creation of new conditions that will render possible a better and less restricted life. It is the coexistence of this new demand for better conditions with the unfavourable economic trend that is the crux of the West Indian problem of the present day.[11]

The introduction of the Licences (Amendment) Ordinance 1935 and the Customs Duties (Amendment no. 4) Ordinance 1935 on 18 October was clearly not the reason for the riots. It merely acted as a spark to ignite a situation that had obviously reached boiling point. In fact, in events such as these, one has to draw a distinction between the spark that sets off an explosion and the underlying causes. It is not surprising that disturbances occurred in different Caribbean colonies. These colonial societies were similar in nature. They mostly emerged from plantation economies and were subjected to colonial rules and regulations. With common external factors interacting with local ones, the resulting regional nature of the disturbances can be understood. But, as the case with St Vincent shows, differences in the political economies would have influenced the nature of these disturbances.

One of the external factors that impacted on and seriously affected the colonies was the Great Depression. This added to and complicated the challenges facing the regional export economies and created severe hardships for the working people. Secretary of state MacDonald's remark that "these feelings of unrest are a protest against the economic distress of the colonies themselves, a protest against some of the consequences of that economic distress: uncertainty of employment, low rates of wages, bad housing conditions in many cases", was quoted favourably by the Moyne Commission.[12]

The harsh economic times created the context within which other issues and factors played themselves out. Contemporary analyses that highlighted economic conditions as playing a significant role in the outbreaks in the Caribbean region were applied to St Vincent. Within the country, economic conditions, as a cause, were highlighted. One writer in the *Times* even felt that Grier's failure to diagnose them could have been attributed to "a loss of nerves and a set of panic stricken and spiteful advisers".[13]

I accept the *Vincentian*'s position that unemployment and low wages were among the main causes of the riots, but do not see them as "twin evils" that "provide a mental background which coupled with his nervous tension leaves the victim an easy prey to insidious propaganda". In other words, the paper was suggesting that the economic situation created the mental state that made the rioters vulnerable to the designs of others.[14] This is really another version of Grier's conspiracy theory. Harsh economic times had been evident for some time, but some newspapers, as suggested before, argued that better times were ahead, since the country had reached the darkest point before the dawn.[15]

By the 1930s, there were definitely great concerns and anxiety about the financial situation. There was nothing to suggest, as Grier did, that the unemployment problem was less acute in St Vincent than elsewhere. Based on that view, he no longer regarded unemployment as a "serious contributing cause though it is probable that some unemployed joined the rioters". It was true, as Grier suggested, that the country's two major products, arrowroot and Sea Island cotton, had been receiving more attractive prices and that the planting of Sea Island cotton had provided greater employment for those who needed it.[16]

But the issue of the availability of land was important. Work was needed to provide the means of renting or purchasing land. The areas of greatest unemployment were on the Leeward side of the island, with the towns of Layou and Barrouallie being among those most seriously affected. Those areas, Grier noted, were not involved in the riots. This, of course, stoked his downplaying of the role of unemployment and low wages. He felt that a solution to the country's economic problems rested with the development of a peasant class.[17] While numerous commissions and commentators had already stressed the importance of the development of a peasant class, it was also the case that "the truly independent peasant holder entirely occupied on his own land [was] relatively uncommon".[18] Moreover, it is necessary to keep in mind the view expressed by the Moyne Commission, that "the normal peasant holding is too small to provide the means of an independent existence and most peasants are accustomed to supplement their income by wage work on the estates. Thus, the great majority of the negro population depend at any rate in a large degree on wages for their livelihood, however much they may supplement them by work on land that they own or rent."[19]

Admittedly, the country's two major crops were more conducive to production by peasants and agricultural labourers/proto-peasants. The land owned or rented by peasants and agricultural labourers were minute plots, but wages were low, and arrowroot and Sea Island cotton grown on plantations did not attract the number of labourers that sugar did. But the issue was much more complex, for even while the agricultural working people demanded wage work, which was important to them in providing down payment or paying leases on any plots of land available, they did not see the provision of agricultural labour on the estates as the real solution to their economic problems.

Prior to the riots, the purchase of the Three Rivers estate, in 1932, appeared to be the beginning of an effort to satisfy the land hunger, but the government was not prepared to continue in this direction since they were committed to the preservation of estate production.[20] There was, however, still the hope that another phase of land settlement was beginning. With those expectations prevalent, Administrator Grimble had pointed to the fact that, in the Leeward area, an area of acutest need, the estate owners were unwilling to sell.[21] Moreover, the Three Rivers scheme needed to be monitored. Governor Grier's belief that the only solution to the economic difficulties lay in the development of a peasant class was obviously shared by a significant portion of the working people. Forty-nine residents of Barrouallie, in petitioning for land in 1936, reminded the administrator of the loyalty of Barrouallie during the riots. In fact, they went further and expressed their belief that land settlement would assist "in restoring former prosperity".[22]

This connection between the purchase of land and loyalty during the riots cannot be dismissed. The people's hopes were on the acquisition of land. They did not see the answer to their economic problems tied in with increased employment on the estates. The availability of land to the working people was considered to be the solution to their economic problems, especially with the significant involvement of working people in the cultivation of Sea Island cotton and arrowroot. The fact that people in the depressed area of Barrouallie did not participate in the riots and reminded the administrator about it is therefore no mystery.

There was general agreement on the effects of land settlement, and this was recognized even before the riots. The *Vincentian*, in its issue of 6 July 1935, while drawing attention to what it considered the prospects offered by Sea Island cotton, argued that a land settlement scheme "would greatly assist in averting the perilous approach to the rocks". The importance of land settlement continued to be stressed after the riots. The *Times* of 10 September 1938 commented on the reality of a "surplus of land lying idle from year to year . . . while poor labourers continue to endure untold hardships". It stated, too, that "underdevelopment, poverty and discontent will always manifest themselves where the uneven distribution of land is very much pronounced".

The riots had stimulated the call for granting wider political representation. Following changes to the franchise requirements in 1936, the SWMA became the dominant political force in the legislative council after the 1937 elections.[23] Land settlement became one of the dominant issues on their agenda, and motions for the extension of land settlement schemes became numerous.[24] No longer was the plantation the focal point of struggle. With peasant involvement in the production of the two main crops, Sea Island cotton and arrowroot, and, consequently, in the export and regional trade, a different channel for struggle emerged. Even in Georgetown, where the only sugar factory was located, the rioters attacked symbols in the town rather than the estates. In the case of the Grand Sable estate, the attack was on the person of the manager, Child, rather than on the estate. Contrary to what the governor said, there was no strike on that estate prior to the riots.[25] The work stoppage that took place there came after Child halted work following the incident in which he was injured by a blow to his head and the medical officer was prevented for some time from getting to him.

On Monday, 21 October, and on the following Tuesday morning, workers had turned up at the Mount Bentinck estate to assemble for work but did so wearing "an ugly face".[26] No disturbance occurred, and the crowd dispersed after being reminded that the Riot Act had been read. When the police patrol from Kingstown arrived, they were informed that there was no serious disorder. At Orange Hill, the manager also reported that the situation was calm. The telephone lines to the Sans Souci estate house were cut, but this was likely to have arisen because it was the only telephone service in that area and hence the only instant contact with Kingstown.

The economic situation and economic issues, generally, not only represented a mental framework within which the dynamics of other issues were played out but were themselves a major factor. The new duties imposed, even that on matches, which the governor tried to downplay, represented a burden to the people, given their economic state. It was more so when, justified or not, merchants increased prices on their goods. A bad economic situation would also have manifested itself particularly in the areas of housing and health, which the Moyne Commission reported as being very primitive for most of the Caribbean.

While the Italian invasion of Ethiopia was a major factor, it has to be seen within the context of other forces with which it intermingled. A small and powerful elite, mainly white, dominated the politics and economy of the country. In this situation, ideas of race and class prevailed. Even though these ideas might have lain dormant for a long time, they began to emerge forcefully in the early decades of the twentieth century with the growth of the Marcus Garvey movement, the Universal Negro Improvement Association. Through its local branches situated at Stubbs and Lowmans (Leeward), it tried to put the plight of blacks into an international context and also to provide an ideological path for the struggle of workers. While the local chapters could not be described as mass bodies, their ideas spread far beyond their membership.

The *Negro World*, organ of the Universal Negro Improvement Association, was circulated in St Vincent and was considered a threat, to the extent that the authorities found it necessary to ban it.[27] The movement, in St Vincent, gained a foothold mainly among the peasants and working people. The middle class, made up of black and coloured professionals and small cultivators, held larger-than-average holdings, sought to demonstrate its mastery of British culture and civilization and, by that virtue, demanded rights to privileges held by the whites. In this kind of atmosphere, racial consciousness became a key factor, as the press tried to publicize the achievements of blacks from any-where.[28] An example of this can be seen with the wide publicity given in 1921 to a Martiniquan, Rane Maran, when he won a top French literary prize, the Prix Goncourt.

The *Times* was critical of anyone casting aspersions on the black race. In an article entitled "Wickedly Libelling a Race" (17 July 1930), the paper launched a strong attack on a work by Wentworth Hill entitled *The British Empire through the Ages*, which, in referring to West Indians, suggested that those descendants of freed slaves "have shown little energy or desire to advance". In its rebuttal and defence of West Indian blacks, the paper stated, "If it is intended that the objectionable work is for use in our schools, we say at once to the Education Authority – do no such thing as placing it within the view of our children, for the reason that we regard it as a wanton and wicked libel on a Race which is certainly undeserving of it and to which we feel proud to belong."

On the other hand, those who were regarded as advocates of blacks were celebrated. Among them, French general Charles Mangin, who claimed that "there really is an intellectual elite among the blacks, whom liberty has intro-duced to our culture. And experience has demonstrated that this elite possesses the ability to excel in every domain of human activity".[29] Despite its patronizing tone, this kind of thinking was swallowed up by the black middle class.

With the growth of race and class consciousness, the Italian invasion of Ethiopia served to fan certain emotions. In July 1935, when, according to the *Times*, war clouds hung over the nations of Ethiopia and Italy, dissatisfaction stimulated by racial oppression began to gain ground. While colonies such as Trinidad were in the forefront of protest, the *Times* of 11 July 1935 claimed that in St Vincent, despite the dissatisfaction, the situation was still relatively calm. By August of that same year, there was a marked change, and the issue was becoming heated, with persons congregating around the cable board to follow the latest developments. Meetings, organized by the RGA, were held to protest

Italy's aggression against Ethiopia. Persons who attended those meetings were even prepared to pledge their physical support.[30]

The *Times*, in its editorial on 11 July 1935, under the caption "The Italo-Ethiopian Situation and the West Indian Negro", tried to put the situation in a broader context. It argued that the situation in Ethiopia was causing "Negroes", wherever they were, to think in terms of "Negroid". Using Trinidad as an example, it noted that the West Indian "Negro" was beginning to express dissatisfaction and that one of the methods used to do so was the holding of mass meetings. It stated that in St Vincent, at that time, there was no "such public protest", but that "private talks with different Negros has [*sic*] revealed much dissatisfaction". "Sunday Night Stroller", in the *Times* of 17 October, decried the "murderous campaign" against "thousands of souls", all of them as precious as his, and perhaps even more so. He was deeply concerned that the "last independent African Kingdom [was] threatened with Italian overlordship".

These feelings spilled over into other issues in the society and created certain tensions. It was reported that, after a meeting at the Carnegie Public Library, an individual nicknamed "One and a Half" told a crowd, "Give me five more negroes as strong as I am, and we will drive every white man out of the island."[31] Other remarks showing heightened racial feelings were noted. John Sardine, a shopkeeper of European descent living at Chauncey, reported on heated discussions about the war, with threats being made "against people of European descent and against English rule". Sardine reported on remarks he claimed to have heard: "King George won't rule the world when we start our war"; "There will be no more white men in St Vincent when we begin to fight"; "We are the Abyssinians, the white men are the Italians; we will kill them all when we begin." Hayward, whose house at Cane Garden was attacked by rioters, described certain remarks made by Martin Durham, alleged to have been the leader of the gang rioting at Cane Garden; "We are the Abyssinians, the white men are the Italians. We chop off the white man's head tonight."[32]

Shortly before the introduction into the legislative council of the two ordinances that sparked the outbreak of disturbances, Marryshow of Grenada, who was vice-president of the International Friends of Ethiopia, spoke to an enthusiastic and cheering crowd at the Carnegie Public Library, and this was despite short notice. The newspapers carried regular reports on developments relating to the war, but, as suggested earlier, a significant number of people would gather at the cable office to follow what was going on.[33]

The depth and intensity of racial fears and feelings at that time can be detected from an incident that happened a month after the riots, on 25 November. Rumours had apparently been circulating about a proposed visit to schools by an Italian doctor whose mission was to distribute sweets and inject the children with a poisonous substance. Children might have been warned by parents and guardians to run out of school any time a strange face appeared. At the Kingstown Anglican School, a gentleman of "fair" complexion, Mr Branch, who was a relative of the headmaster, appeared at the school at about 1:15 p.m. The school was thrown into confusion, and there was an uproar as children dashed away from school with parents immediately on the scene. This was obviously a reaction to the fears and talk about the Italo-Abyssinian War. It appears that similar incidents occurred in Trinidad and British Guiana.[34]

The local authorities interpreted the seemingly strong racial feelings not as a reaction to the structure and functioning of Vincentian society, with its racial imbalances, but as a means of driving their conspiracy theory, and to absolve the administration of any blame. What emerged from their comments was a view that some elements used the Italo-Abyssinian War as part of a campaign "of subversive propaganda".[35] In a communiqué to Cosmo Parkinson on 26 October 1935, Grier states that, as long as "this Abyssinia business" continues, tense feelings were likely to exist, fuelled by local agitation.[36]

Even the *Vincentian*, which voiced the views of the ruling elite, angled in on this issue. It argued that, in such times, persons of low intellect get "carried away by emotion and lose their sense of proportion". "Consequently", it declared, "a great responsibility rests upon those who affect to interpret to their benighted brethren the news appearing on the Cable Board".[37] Grier's conspiracy theory, as it related to the racial situation, can best be seen in his report to the secretary of state on 12 November 1935:

> In every West Indian Community can be found men either of pure African descent or of mixed descent who devote their activities to fomenting trouble. In the majority of cases these men are imbued with a bitter hatred of any and every class of European. In normal circumstances their activities have little effect beyond creating resentment and distrust of the administration amongst a limited section of the population but for some months now they have had an opportunity of obtaining a wider hearing than they have ever had in the past. There are men amongst them who have been comparatively well-educated and have powers of organisation.[38]

The American weekly magazine, the *Literary Digest*, carried, on 2 November 1935, an article captioned "An Island's Reign of Terror", which had as its subtitle

"British Marines Land to End Two Days Civil Strife between White Masters and Blacks on West Indies Plantations". A few months later, on 26 March 1936, with the benefit of hindsight, the *Times* suggested that the idea of a race riot was started among "a panic-stricken section of the Whites" (and not native whites at that). It argued, too, that the government "lost its head", fuelling the idea of a race riot. John Knight, secretary to the government in the governor's office in Grenada, found it necessary to respond to the account of the events produced by the *Literary Digest* but carefully avoided the issue of racial strife.[39]

Earlier, on 27 February 1936, the *Times* had recognized the complexity of the factors that gave rise to the riots. It suggested that racial antagonism and the Abyssinian war, if they did contribute to the outburst, were minor causes. It asked, "Did not some 'Euro-West Indians move unmolested'? Were not the properties of coloured Vincentians damaged?"[40] It decried the fact that the country's good name was soiled by the falsehood. The governor had, in his comments, obviously missed the complexities regarding race and class.

It was no accident that the riots did not emerge from strikes or play themselves out on the plantations. The fact that they occurred during a meeting of the legislative council was significant and emphasized the political divide in the country. Here again, the words of the chief justice at the meeting of the Supreme Court on 29 October, where he drew a distinction between the riots in St Kitts and those in St Vincent, labelling the former as estate riots and the latter as an attack on government, are quite relevant.

Political consciousness in St Vincent had been developing through efforts to demand the reintroduction of representative government and the dismantling of pure Crown colony government. The main drive of middle-class activists was not only for the reintroduction of representative government but to have the franchise extended to accommodate more members of the middle class who did not then meet the existing regulations. The issue of mass involvement in the formal political system was then not on the cards. It was, however, necessary for the RGA to build links with the working people and have them as an extra-parliamentary force.

Editorial comments by an undisclosed Grenada newspaper that were published in the *Port of Spain Gazette* of 7 November 1935 would have found resonance with the thinking of Vincentians, since the views stated there were shared by many Vincentians and manifested themselves in the struggle against Crown colony government. The article noted, "If any of these Crown Colonies are on the rocks or near them it is not the fault of the people. They have had no responsibility for government and it is unfair to throw it in their teeth."[41] The economic hardships of the people had long been attributed to the reality of Crown colony government which did not allow them a say in their own affairs. Furthermore, when the governor stressed the need for measures to keep the country off the rocks, the feeling was that it was not the people who had driven it near to the rocks.

The reintroduction of representative government came with the 1925 elections, but little had changed, for the persons who gained places in the legislative council were, with one exception, those who had sat before under the "Pure Crown Colony" system. The one exception, Joseph Milton Gray, son of a "poor labouring woman . . . and transient Scotsman" was, in any event, of the same social ilk, a merchant and landed proprietor. The other elected members, W.M. Grant and A.M. Fraser, were of the merchant and planter class, respectively. Grant was the son of a "large family, poor but respectable", who became a successful and "public spirited" merchant. Fraser, the son of Scottish natives, born when his father was manager of the Rabacca estate,[42] controlled two estates of 1,017 acres. Following the findings of the Closer Union Commission, some efforts were made to adjust the electoral system, although the changes were minor in nature and did not aim to overturn the essential thrust of Crown colony government. In 1935, the nominated "un-official" and three elected members of the legislative council continued to be wealthy persons. Alex Fraser still sat, but as an elected member. A. DaSilva was a wealthy merchant, and Fred Corea was the largest merchant as well as an estate owner of 298 acres, with controlling interest in other estates.[43] The racial and class composition of the legislative council made it remote from the concerns of the working people, who did not feature in its political calculations.

After the removal of press censorship, this was a point taken up by the *Times* on 12 March 1936. In its editorial "Why Administrations Fail", it commented as follows: "Is there any wonder then that most of our Administrations fail? The masses have no representatives. In the 'higher' circles and in 'official' quarters they receive little consideration." It quoted from Grimble, who had left his position in St Vincent on promotion elsewhere: "The influential men and women of standing in the community did not interest themselves sufficiently in things pertaining to the welfare of the masses." He became critical of the members of council being drafted from a particular social class.

Clennell Wickham, editor of the *West Indian*, in a piece reproduced in the

Port of Spain Gazette of 8 November 1935, tackled that same issue from a different angle and in a broader framework. He wrote:

> The West Indian labouring Man lives under a perpetual sense of grievance or injustice. He believes that he is indeed forsaken of men; he believes that none of the good things of life are for him. I speak of the poorest and more ignorant class and especially in the smaller colonies. . . . His dumb acquiescence is very often mistaken for something else and there seems for him no half way house between servility and the pushful, impudent assertiveness which will infallibly get him into trouble.

Members of this same unrepresented class were the ones who stole the limelight on 21 and 22 October and revolted. It only dawned on the governor then that something essential to smooth and proper government was missing. The fact that the governor had only then arrived at that conclusion really sums up the nature of the problem.

When the governor responded to McIntosh's request for an interview with the news that he would meet with a delegation at 5:00 p.m. following the meeting of the council, the people who had gathered at the courthouse were not prepared to accept it. There was a great deal of mistrust. When Donald Romeo was asked, on cross-examination during McIntosh's preliminary trial, if people who had grievances desired to see the governor on his visits, Romeo replied, "People of my type have obstacles put in the way. My class is too poor. We can't see him. I hear the people say so many times. Many people have tried to see the governor. Many people do ask and they are not allowed to see the governor."[44]

Grier appeared to have accepted the failure to communicate with the working people but suggested that the task of responding to the underprivileged in the community rested with the administrator. He noted that it was evident that there was no contact between the administration and that sector of the community, but he was unsure how it could be remedied. He stated that "an Administrator in one of these islands however accessible he may wish to be can find little time for establishing close personal contact with all sections of the people, and he has no one to represent him. Grenada where he resided was an exception since part of the task of the Colonial Secretary was to carry out visits of inspection and establish contacts with the community."[45]

The people's reaction at the courthouse was not only about the ordinances in question that prompted price increases. It was also about the perceived insensitivity of those controlling the reins of power. Those persons who stormed the courthouse might not have carefully followed the legislation but recognized the insensitivity that was being reflected. The governor's argument that it was more logical to encourage the importation of motor cars and reduce the duties, while at the same time increasing licence fees on items that included matches, spoke to the insensitivity of the administration.[46]

The governor's reaction certainly carried with it a race and class bias. We must not forget, too, in examining the people's reaction that their initial effort through the assistance of McIntosh and other members of the RGA was to send a petition and seek an audience with the governor. Despite the governor's new-found realization that a section of the community was not represented on council, he failed to follow that to its logical conclusion in his analysis of the causes of the riots. Instead, his efforts were centred on removing the administration from any blame and trying to find scapegoats. He insisted that the riots were planned in a bid to cause discontent and ill feeling among the labourers on the estates, with the hope that they would follow the example set by the Kingstown rioters. He therefore drew a distinction between the origin of the Kingstown riots and those in Georgetown and Camden Park.[47] Moreover, Grier claimed to have evidence to that effect, which he never attempted to show.

McIntosh was considered the mastermind behind the disturbances, one who was guilty of manipulating the people. But he was not the only one. The governor's imagination seemed to have run wild, and he was finding conspirators everywhere, some directly involved and others indirectly by causing tension in the society. This last category included persons who created the kind of propaganda that forced the ignorant and unlettered people into actions they would not normally have taken. Even the Anglican bishop of the Windward Islands made it onto the governor's list. He was accused of making unwise speeches and often allowed "his somewhat impetuous verbosity to run away with him". Grier stated that he "was most imprudent in his farewell speech" on leaving St Vincent. After quoting or referring to statements the bishop was alleged to have made, the governor argued that such speeches might have been harmless to an English audience but were unsuitable to St Vincent, with its heightened racial feeling. Added to that, his speech was made just prior to that of Marryshow. Grier hoped, after all this, that the next bishop would be "less talkative and more discreet".[48]

A Russian Jew also fitted into the scenario that Grier was painting. He was identified by the governor as a linguist "who professed a philanthropic interest in the slums of Kingstown and Castries where he spent much of his time". Not surprisingly, he was said to have visited St Kitts, where disturbances had broken out prior to those in St Vincent.[49] The name of another group that surfaced was that of the "Ranch Boys", a name that Grier claimed had come from an American gangster film. He had indicated that he was investigating a possible link between that group and that of "another directing organisation which remained in the background". This was obviously a reference to the RGA.[50]

The dismissal of the case against McIntosh blew holes in the efforts to implicate H.E.A. Daisley of Stubbs. The evidence revealed in court showed that McIntosh, rather than masterminding any plot, had actually made every effort to direct the people's frustrations through formal political channels. He assisted in the preparation of the request for a meeting with the governor. Statements by witnesses, including police constables Joseph Banfield and Frederick John, pictured McIntosh as one who tried to control the crowd at both the yard of the courthouse and at his own drugstore. He also assisted Grier in his efforts to speak to the crowd, ringing a bell at one time to silence the crowd and then even escorting the governor out of the room of the courthouse when things appeared to be getting out of hand.

Efforts to link McIntosh with a so-called conspiracy would have had to do with his activities prior to the riots, but there was no evidence to show any suspicious activity, except that of speaking at meetings protesting the Italian invasion of Abyssinia. McIntosh, as a member of the RGA, had been involved in the struggle to secure elected representation and put an end to "pure Crown colony" government. His work as a pharmacist would also have been instrumental in building a bond with the working people who often visited his store,[51] so that when they felt that contact needed to be made with the administration, calling for a redress of their grievances, he was one of the men they were most likely to turn to. It is of significance that, in early Caribbean working people's struggles, a number of pharmacists played leading roles for that same reason. Among them were Walter Mills, first president of the Trinidad Working Men's Association, and his successor, Alfred Richards.[52]

If any case can be made about leadership of the riots, the person who stands out is "Sheriff" Lewis, alias "Haile Selassie". Oral history and general talk on the ground have always attributed that role to him, a role which he acknowledged and spoke about. Sheriff fitted the profile of those who had worked abroad; he had been in Cuba and Santo Domingo, where he had developed some level of political consciousness. He was a member of the "Ranch", a group of men who met in Paul's Avenue near the courthouse, where they played cards and dominoes and discussed different issues in the society. Sheriff indicated that he and his friends would often sit under an almond tree at the market square, listening to an old man named McKenzie discuss the state of the country.

The nine-year sentence handed down to him at the trials does, perhaps, indicate that he played a leading role in the proceedings.[53] That role, however, was assumed after the riots started. Members of the group, such as Donald Romeo, were attracted by the noise in the yard of the courthouse and went over to see what was happening. Sheriff, who seemed to have wielded some influence on other members of the group and, possibly, on others outside of the group, described his role to Oswald Peters and Kenneth John, "I instructed two men to tell the teachers not to allow the children to return to evening school, and I ordered a group to command Mr Isaacs to close down the arrowroot pool at once". His aim, as he described it, was "to see all business places closed until we could hear something".[54]

Clem Cato, who was one of the policemen involved in the attempt to control the trouble at the courthouse, indicated to this author that, during the rioters' invasion of the prisons, Sheriff had taken a leading role. He identified himself to the prison authorities as "Haile Selassie" and demanded that the chief warder open the gates.

The *Times*, in an article on 27 February 1936, gave as good an explanation as any to explain the outbreak of the disturbances on 21 October. It dismissed looting and robbery as prime causes, since the rioters would not have hesitated to approach the business places directly. Instead, "the people sought redress of their grievances. Misunderstanding arose, someone alleges that he was kicked and so the matters grew from bad to worse".[55] The paper was correct when it claimed that the Kingstown riots broke out because of certain misunderstandings at the courthouse and yard. But it was a much more complex matter, because these misunderstandings arose in a situation of mistrust, where the working people were facing severe social and economic problems and concluded that no one cared, particularly those who controlled political power and appeared to be insensitive to their plight. Even the governor's decision to set the meeting with the people's representatives for 5:00 p.m. that day – obviously set at a time when the meeting of the council would be at an end – was seen in that light. All of this operated in an atmosphere of heightened tension from the Italo-Abyssinian War, with a grown political consciousness among the working people.

Why riots broke out in some areas and not others cannot be easily answered, but there were enough issues and problems, shaping the mental framework, to ensure that any spark could have generated violence. Such was obviously the case in Camden Park, where the people vented their anger on the property of John De Sousa for lending bullets to a member of the volunteer force "to shoot black people".[56] The administration had been taking the people too much for granted and, at first, paid slight attention to the noise coming from the yard of the courthouse. Perhaps Clennell Wickham has a valid point that the people's "dumb acquiescence" was often misinterpreted. When the news of the riots reached Georgetown in the late afternoon on 21 October, some persons there were prepared to follow the example of Kingstown, since they were suffering from the same conditions that prompted the uproar in the court yard.

The St Vincent riots were not planned, but a number of issues and matters came together in an atmosphere where the people's efforts to have the administration listen to their grievances appeared, in their view, not to have been taken seriously. The environment in which all of this happened was of some significance. The control of the commanding heights of the economy, of both land and business, were in the hands of a small white elite, mainly the landed class, while the working people were mostly black and poor. Additionally, too, that same small elite monopolized whatever political power existed at the local level.[57] When McIntosh indicated to the people that the governor would meet with their representatives at 5:00 p.m., they cried "No! No!" Those in authority misread the situation, for they had little understanding of the problems, hopes and aspirations of those people who were locked out of the formal political structure and whose concerns were hardly taken into consideration.

The spark that created the explosion came out of the political process, but a number of different factors came together, and a misunderstanding and mishandling of the situation led to violence. People's consciousness and frame of mind would have been shaped by a multiplicity of things. Their one hope for a redress of their grievances faltered. A few minor incidents at the courthouse aggravated that situation, and violence was the result. What happened in the Georgetown area was prompted by the news from Kingstown.[58] There were, seemingly, particular issues that were heightened and individuals in place who were prepared to demonstrate their anger. In such situations, issues, events and people need to be in a position to exploit them. The people in Barrouallie and some other areas hoped that land settlement would solve their problems and waited for a new phase of land settlement to start, since they saw this as critical to their economic well-being. The 1932 Three Rivers Land Settlement offered them hope that land settlement would have been extended since Barroaullie was identified as an area where there was a great demand for land.

CHAPTER 5

POLITICS AFTER THE RIOTS

THE DISTURBANCES OF THE 1930S IN THE CARIBBEAN marked a significant turning point in the development of the British colonies. For St Vincent, as with other British colonies, it signalled a new phase that ended with the introduction of adult suffrage in 1951. The governor's belated acknowledgement, at the time of the riots, that there was a section of the population not represented in the legislative council was critical to what followed. The constitutional and political developments leading to adult suffrage in 1951 provided the context for and shaped other important developments, particularly in religion, education, labour and land settlement.[1] Adult suffrage brought a new momentum and different dynamics to the life of the country, and, to this extent, the period between 1935 and 1951, when a number of critical things were put in place, can be considered a watershed.[2]

Adult suffrage, in reality, signalled mass involvement in politics in a way that was never seen before and so ushered in a new era in the life of the people of the country. It is for this reason that some historians and political scientists have referred to this period as one that signalled the birth of the democratic revolution.[3] In St Vincent, the period was marked by the growth of political consciousness and the birth of trade unions. George McIntosh was on the right track when he argued that Britain had noticed St Vincent because "we had a riot",[4] but only up to a point. I had suggested earlier that one needed to look also at the interrelationships throughout the region and to the colonial interconnections. Bolland puts this in perspective. He writes, "Important as the individual rebellions are in the social and political history of each country in which they took place, the impact of the rebellions as a whole was greater than merely the sum of the parts."⁵ The imperial context was always the point of reference and defined what was possible. But, at the same time, colonial policies as they were presented in the colonies had to make adjustments to the milieu in the region.

Until the riots, the working people expressed little interest in the formal political structure. Their grievances and dissatisfaction were expressed through the medium of petitions and protests as concerns were raised about matters affecting them. Something significant seemed to have happened as they stood on the grounds of the courthouse and legislative assembly on that Monday morning of 21 October. They must have realized more than ever that their interests were not addressed in the "hallowed" chambers of the Legislative Hall, though the proceedings there had a profound effect on their lives. The response of the governor to the outburst on 21 October, expressed particularly through promises that were given, must have made them recognize the latent power they had. The colony's legislative agenda was being reset, and the colonial authorities realized that they could no longer take the people for granted. The governor was forced to admit that part of the problem was that the persons behind the disturbances were ones not represented in parliament. This was quite clear to him, late though it might have been, and he expressed the need to have persons of their own ilk represent them there.

After the submission of reports by the governor, the officials in the Colonial Office might have believed that they understood the source of the problems. Later, riots in other colonies occurring up to 1939⁶ would have deeply impressed on those officials the seriousness of the problems and made them realize that the problems were not necessarily localized ones. There were initial efforts to cater *in situ* to some of the issues and shortcomings as they interpreted them, but, in the final analysis, it was the regional scope of the disturbances that demonstrated that there were fundamental problems throughout the region. The developments that followed the disturbances were largely regional ones, although individual peculiarities and circumstances influenced the nature and pace of those developments.

The public's reaction to the dismissal of the charges against McIntosh at the preliminary trial, perhaps more than anything else, signalled the dawn of a new day. Vincentians were certainly no strangers to protests and demonstrations, but the riots and the reaction by the authorities seemed to have given rise to a new spirit that McIntosh ultimately captured and transformed into organizational form. The *Times* describes the moment: "Breathless the crowd awaited the decision. . . . On leaving the Court Yard, he was met by crowds of people some of whom lifted him on their shoulders and bore him many yards. Throughout the balance of the evening there was conspicuously in evidence among many people . . . a spirit of joy on Mr. McIntosh's acquittal."[7] Prior to this, a large crowd had gathered at the wharf to welcome Hannays from Trinidad, when he arrived to represent McIntosh at his preliminary hearing.

As I have suggested elsewhere, the riots were cathartic, purging the people of their political innocence.[8] An awareness that their actions could matter emerged. The statement that was made through their actions commanded the attention of the authorities and forced them to take note. The political agenda was being reset, and the formation of the SWMA by McIntosh became the vehicle "to carry forward this new feeling of political being".[9]

A writer in the *Times* recognized what he considered a new spirit in the country. When Grier visited Georgetown after the riots, he "did not receive as warm a reception as was accorded colonial governors in the past in this small island".[10] The *Times* of 13 February 1936 had earlier made the point that they had been taught "to copy and practise English courtesy" and that "a polished English gentleman" was a fine product. Taking note of what it considered the discourtesy meted out to the governor, with tongue in cheek, it hoped that it was not by example, for "the ass is a partial and docile brute. Lead him gently and he will furnish a great deal of labour, even he is sensitive to kindness. But he will kick sometimes."

The paper also pointed to the great gap between the governor and the common people. This gap existed before, as was suggested by the governor when he responded in the legislature to the riots of that day and as Donald Romeo pointed out in the evidence he gave during the preliminary trial of the case against McIntosh. The response in 1936 was quite different. There was a different level of consciousness and a realization that the mystique surrounding the governor was broken.[11] While touching on the impact of the depression, columnist "Quiz" had described the period as a time "when the underman caught his first imperfect glimpse of the futility of a labourer trying to better his position; when the labourer having nothing and seeing little or nothing to look for in the future, cared for nothing". What was needed under those circumstances was not a "strong man with mere iron will" but a "sympathetic tactician", a clear reference to the response of the authorities to the riots.[12]

The middle class, on the other hand, had been agitating, through the RGA, to have what was then a limited franchise extended to accommodate them. Kenneth John aptly sums up the purpose and intent of the RGA by describing it as "the dissentient voice of a disgruntled middle class which believed it had mastered all the cultural shibboleths and political idioms of the mother country to qualify for some measure of constitutional advance. Little thought was directed to the man in the street."[13]

In 1932, what was dubbed the "West Indian Unofficial Conference" was held in Dominica. The aim of the conference "was to bring together the exponents and guides of public opinion in the West Indian Islands to discuss common problems and if possible to formulate a common comprehensive policy in regard to the cognate questions of Federation and Representation, as well as other matters of common concern".[14]

One of the central concerns of the delegates was the desire to end Crown colony rule. In a foreword to the conference report, the chairman, Cecil E.A. Rawle of Dominica, stated clearly, "Crown Colony Rule unquestionably stands to-day at the bar of public opinion throughout the Caribbean archipelago indicted on three major counts." He then proceeded to elaborate. The underlying argument at the conference and among other organizations represented, including the RGA, was that the middle class was educated and mature enough to take control of the government of the Caribbean countries.

In his address at a public meeting that marked the opening of the conference, Ebenezer Duncan was quick to point out that the association he represented was made up of people from all classes. Even though Captain A.A. Cipriani of Trinidad staked out a claim for adult franchise as an essential part of the federation being proposed by the regional labour movement, he had to admit at a public meeting which signalled the end of the conference that he was unable to carry his friends "of the Conference the full length of Adult Franchise". However, he maintained that it was "the only weapon that can be put in the hands of the working man to save him from the grip and strangulation of the Capitalist and employer class". He continued, "I put it to you this way that when those who now lead you shall have gone, you must have something in your hands with which to fight and the only weapon you can use with success and efficiency is Adult Franchise."[15] Adult franchise was seen as the ultimate goal but not something they were likely to get in the short run. In the conference's draft proposals for "the Federation and General Government of the British West Indies" that they were advocating, the section under "Qualification of Voters" stated that "adult franchise is the ultimate aim of the Federation: The qualifications of voters to be reviewed triennially in each unit with a view to bringing adult suffrage gradually into the general operation."

In explaining this at their final public meeting, Chairman Rawle stated, "That means, we hope that the day will soon come when every man and woman who is a British citizen of the age of 21 years who is born or domiciled in this country or has otherwise acquired a permanent stake in it, and who pays taxes directly or indirectly will have the right to cast his or her vote at the election of a representative to the Legislature."[16]

The attitude to adult franchise displayed at the conference reflected the thinking among members of the RGA in St Vincent. Although the immediate intent was to get members of the middle class who qualified under the existing franchise elected to the legislative council and to seek further extension of the franchise to accommodate more persons in that body, some of the leaders recognized the importance of the working people as an extra-parliamentary force. To this extent, Kenneth John might have been guilty of exaggeration when he said that little thought was given to the man in the street. In fact, as was suggested before, a sympathetic wing of that organization, led by McIntosh, had gone further and was building bridges with the working people. It was because of this that they consulted him on the occasion of the passage of the two bills that precipitated the riots.

The riots of 21 and 22 October 1935 led to a split in the ranks of the association over its reaction to them. This was ironic since, in the immediate aftermath of the riots, as we have seen, leading members of the association, including McIntosh, were united in their condemnation of the rioters.[17] Despite this, however, the die was cast, and McIntosh, following the tumultuous reception he got after the dismissal of the charges against him, decided to place his fortunes with the working people.

Even before the riots, plans were in place to have an extension of the franchise that would have accommodated more members of the middle class. The RGA was expected to participate in the electoral process by contesting the next general election. Although working people would not have qualified under the new franchise yet, the connection with the working people would have been of great importance to the RGA.

What was, in fact, happening was the continuing evolution of a process that started with the introduction of the new constitution in 1924. The franchise was still extremely limited and catered largely to the same class that occupied political positions before 1924. The battle for further extension of the franchise continued. In 1931, the 1924 Order in Council that gave birth to the new system was amended, providing for three *ex officio* members, one nominated official, one nominated "unofficial" and three elected members. The call throughout the West Indian colonies, even at the beginning of the 1930s, was for self-government, but the belief that the British government would have been unwilling to grant it to each colony led those in the forefront of the movement to locate it in a federation of the West Indies.[18]

There were other developments in the early 1930s that helped to fan the flames of constitutional advance. The Closer Union Commission was preoccupied with the constitutional issue, although it drew strong criticism at a very early stage from the persons behind the setting up of the 1932 Unofficial Conference, who considered its terms of reference too narrowly defined.[19] The commission was critical of the governor's casting vote in a legislative council that had an equal number of official and unofficial members.[20]

As was noted earlier, when the Closer Union Commission visited St Vincent in January 1933, it was of the view that the people were more interested in the financial prospects of the colony than the issue of closer union. The two issues, however, were interconnected. For some time, particularly since the 1880s, critics related the economic difficulties faced by the colony to the existence of Crown colony government. At the 1932 West Indian conference, in highlighting the suffering of the people, Chairman Rawle argued that "the want of any serious effort to ameliorate such conditions is the measure of the interest shown in the welfare of the West Indian peoples by Crown Colony Government".[21]

The Unofficial Conference and the Closer Union Commission provided opportunities for pushing demands for an extension of the franchise.[22] At the 9 November 1934 meeting of the legislative council, the administrator introduced a motion, notice of which was given before, that catered to some measure of constitutional advance. It stated

> that the official majority should be abolished; that only those officials whose presence is necessary for the conduct of business should sit as members of the Legislative Council; that an unofficial majority should be created with elected as well as nominated members, on the definite understanding that (in addition to his existing power of veto) the Governor would be empowered at any stage to carry any measure which he considered necessary in the interest of public order, public faith or other essentials of good government.[23]

There was only slight movement here and certainly not what those in the forefront of the movement for advanced constitutional change wanted. What this did was to reinforce the power of the governor, which was one of the central planks of Crown colony rule. That motion was, in fact, really to cater to some of the recommendations of the Closer Union Commission.²⁴

An earlier resolution had stated, "Be it resolved that this Council having considered the report of the Closer Union Commissioners together with the Secretary of State's announcement in this connection and estimates of expenditure, is of the opinion that effect should be given to the report subject to such modification as may seem necessary and desirable to the Secretary of State."²⁵ No additional changes were implemented before 1936, when the riots helped to change the political landscape and to demonstrate to the authorities the urgency of the situation.

Issues relating to race came to the forefront during the riots of October 1935, and the reception given to Marcus Garvey when he visited St Vincent in 1937 was testimony to feelings similar to those expressed in 1935. With blacks beginning to occupy prominent positions in the new political environment, the focus was really on advancing their role, and the battle was between the colonial government and the political-constitutional advocates led by McIntosh. Garvey seemed to have mellowed somewhat when he delivered two addresses in St Vincent where he appealed to blacks to uplift themselves and to be proud of who they were. The white administrator, who was present, heard little to which to object. What Garvey and the Garvey movement had actually done in St Vincent was to provide a broader context for the struggles of the working people.²⁶

THE BIRTH OF THE WORKINGMEN'S ASSOCIATION

The second of March, 1936, was an eventful day in the annals of the colony's political history, for it was on that day that the colony's first mass-based organization, the SWMA was launched. It happened on Middle Street, on the upper floor of the business place of James Davy and Son, in close proximity to McIntosh's drugstore. The meeting room was crowded from early in the evening, with the crowd spilling over into the street, creating traffic problems.²⁷ Approximately four hundred persons attended, and 276 of them joined the organization and paid the necessary fees. McIntosh was the main architect behind the venture, and the newspapers of the day paid tribute to him.

The *Investigator* of 4 March 1936 described him as one who was "fired with zeal to help lift them [the masses] to higher levels in their economic and general well being". The *Times,* concerned perhaps about the possibility of political divisions, was, at first, quite lukewarm, as was indicated in its editorial of 15 March. Under the caption "A State Divided", it declared, "There is some talk of a Workingman's Association. This Association should join hands with the RGA and a powerful body formed." In its next issue, however, it was much more positive and hopeful. It noted that an appreciable number of middle-class men had joined its ranks, something that augured well for the future. It appealed to Vincentians to join the association and expressed the view that if it had been in existence before, the riots might not have occurred.[28]

The need for an organization to cater to the needs of the masses was not debatable, and the *Times* continued to welcome its birth. In its 4 June issue, it spelled out its value in some detail:

> Every thinking individual who considers the economic conditions of the colony cannot fail to realise that the masses, the wage earners, stand in desperate need of help and upliftment. The lot of the poor labourers is appalling; and any move made to alleviate their suffering, to place these fellow human beings in a better position to feed, clothe and educate them, should be considered a laudable effort deserving the support of every member of the community and not a move to be viewed with suspicion as a possible source of trouble.

At the 2 March inaugural meeting of the SWMA, one of its members, A.C. DeBique, gave details of its objectives:

> to encourage thrift by establishing penny banking facilities, to promote industrial, educational, social, economical and political improvements, to protect its members against exploitation of any dominant class or institution or person, to assist any deserving member in the defence and maintenance of his personal and property rights, to oppose by all constitutional means all or any measure introduced or intended to be introduced into the Legislative Council of the colony which may tend to the detriment of members generally; to relieve members in sickness, indigence and unforeseen circumstances over which they have no control; to provide for the burial of its members; and to do all other things and acts conducive to the financial, social, economical, educational, political and industrial benefit of members.[29]

At a time when trade union laws were ineffective and political parties non-existent, the association could not help but be a diverse body. It embraced aspects of friendly societies, labour and political organizations. The new body had been experiencing great difficulty deciding "whether it should be registered as a Cooperative body or Trade Union". Its guiding principle was "From which will the greatest good accrue to the majority of working men".[30] Its political role was anticipated, for, after all, it had incorporated many of the members of the RGA. There were suggestions that it should join hands with what remained of the RGA, forge a formidable body and follow the pattern set by similar organizations in Grenada and Trinidad to form a political party.[31]

At some of its early meetings, attention was focused on its different and diversified objectives. At a 30 April meeting, J.L. Cato, secretary of the association, stated that the organization must express its opinion on the Minimum Wage Ordinance that had been passed before the riots but had not yet been implemented. One other speaker advised that members settle differences among themselves and avoid the law courts.[32] The Colonial Office's *Annual Report* for 1936 stated that the SWMA[33] "provides sick and funeral benefits for their members". Later, when McIntosh and a delegation from that body appeared before the Moyne Commission, he informed the commissioners that their function was to represent the working people. He indicated that "prior to the formation of this Association there was no representative in St Vincent for the working classes".[34]

Although started in the capital town, Kingstown, the SWMA began to spread itself throughout the villages and small towns. By 13 May, it had begun to organize in Georgetown. The large crowd that attended its recruiting meeting and signed up as members included persons from the surrounding areas of Byrea, Grand Sable and from the Carib country north of Georgetown. On 13 June, organizers of the association went to Barrouallie on the western side of the island. One newspaper correspondent described the scene there: "They reached us about 7:30 pm. Crowds greeted them from every side as they drove through the streets." He noted that, despite the rain, a big crowd was in attendance.[35] By 21 June, the Mesopotamia branch was functioning, with C. Jack as chairman. The growth of the association was phenomenal. It had passed the thousand-member mark by March and, in April, reached approximately fifteen hundred, with membership estimated at six thousand by July.[36]

RALLY OF 3 AUGUST 1936

The organization had the distinction of being the first body to represent the mass of working people. Its first mass rally on 3 August, which was greeted with enthusiasm, was the first public demonstration of its strength.[37] The period of mass involvement in formal politics had begun. The newspapers celebrated the occasion:

> Within the annals of St Vincent history there never was witnessed a giant demon-
> stration as the rally of the St Vincent Workingmen's Association held on Monday
> 3rd instant. From midnight of the day before until the morning of 3rd inst. the
> buses roared into Kingstown and the tramping of workers feet brought thousands
> of workers either to take part in or witness what turned out to be an unparalleled
> demonstration of workers. Ninety seven towns, villages and other places of abode
> stretching through the length and breadth of St Vincent were represented.[38]

The addresses for the occasion echoed the position of the colonial middle class, which wanted Dominion status within the British Empire. They attacked Crown colony government but sang praises of the British connection. They were proud of that allegiance because they regarded the British as the greatest colonizers. When their grievances were expressed in a proper manner, they were accorded full justice and fair play by the British. The problem, there-fore, was not with the British connection but with poor administrators who thwarted and distorted British justice and fair play. At least, that was how the SWMA leader, George McIntosh, saw it. It has to be remembered that the leadership of the association grew out of the RGA, whose immediate goals were quite limited, seeking largely to extend the franchise to accom-modate themselves. If, however, the leaders of the association had any doubt about the direction to take, the massive response to the rally must have pointed the way.[39]

McIntosh began to lay out issues that were to form the plank of the associa-tion's agenda in and out of the legislative council. These centred around the lopsided distribution of land; conditions of the working people, particularly as related to housing; scholarships to secondary schools; and, in the early period of the existence of the association, the Minimum Wage Bill. Marryshow, who was in St Vincent shortly before the riots, was a special guest. He had paid pre-vious visits, mobilizing support for the condemnation of the Italian invasion of Ethiopia. The administrator was indeed concerned, the riots still being fresh in the minds of the people, especially with the trials having been completed only a few months before. Marryshow appeared, in Administrator Wright's view, to have lived up to the commitment given to him prior to the rally, and, in fact, he did comment on the moderate tone of his speech, attributing it to the presence in St Vincent, as the administrator's guest, of Sheila MacDonald, daughter of the late prime minister of England, who had hosted Marryshow on one of his trips to England.[40]

Marryshow expressed pride in the way the people responded to the SWMA and suggested that it was the making of history. He sang McIntosh's praises, one whose name, he felt, would be "carved imperishably on the annals of the West Indies and will be remembered even after other great names were forgotten . . . [one] who was prepared to give his heart and soul and serve his day and generation".[41] Marryshow paid attention to labour matters, particularly the Minimum Wage Bill and the Workmen's Compensation Ordinance. He was confident that the Minimum Wage Bill would become a reality. He spelled out, however, what he regarded as the political orientation of the association, a view that would obviously have been formed from his deep association with and influence on McIntosh: "You are Socialists", he said, "and the British Labour Party will do more for you than any other party", a line taken by Cipriani's Trinidad Workingmen's Association and Trinidad Labour Party.[42] McIntosh regularly wore a red tie and kept a picture of Stalin in his drugstore. Byron Cox, who had refused to associate himself with the leaders of the SWMA, referred to them as the "Reds", which, he said, was based on the nature of their anthems and songs, the colour of their ties and the colour of their flag, "popularly known as the Red Flag of the Revolution".[43] Gordon Lewis, however, saw McIntosh as no "Leninist insurrectionist", basing his view on the evidence of McIntosh's role during the riots, as revealed at the preliminary hearing.[44] Whatever was his personal ideological orientation, his group followed what can be called a moderate socialist line as they pledged their commitment to the working people.

The association next shifted its attention to Georgetown. Apart from highlighting some of the issues he touched on in Kingstown, McIntosh explored a theme that must have struck a chord with the people of the area, an area that had experienced riots on 21 October. He justified the work and aim of the association as having arisen out of a situation where "nobody in the higher walks of life seemed to interest themselves in you to get you together to interest yourselves in your own selves . . . have no fear in saying this because the last Administrator said it openly the better classes of St Vincent takes [sic] no interest in the poorer people and it does not appear as if they are willing to do it".[45]

The association's decision to register as a limited liability company had very much to do with the limitations of the Trade Union Act of 1933 that did not give adequate protection to workers, not providing them "with the right to peaceful picketing or protection against action in torts".[46] It became poised to correct one of the major problems that became blatantly obvious during the riots – that is, the absence in the legislative council of representatives of the working people. The *Investigator* of 1 April 1936 argued that it was now possible through the association "to have direct touch between the people lowest down and the Government through those people's representatives, selected by themselves in their own labour assembly". This was especially so, the paper felt, since it was a foregone conclusion that McIntosh would be put forward as a candidate on a labour ticket.

The *Times* had expressed the desperate need for assistance to the masses. Along with the *Investigator* it had been helping to map out a role for the association. It has to be remembered that the editors were members of the SWMA and close associates of McIntosh. Not surprisingly, their views corresponded with the direction in which McIntosh seemed to be moving, based on his speeches during the workers' rally and in campaigning for election to the legislative council.

Administrator Wright, in his address at the rally on 3 August, was clearly aware of the strong possibility that the association might move into the area of electoral politics. He informed them that he was aware of their political expectations but indicated that he was not going to talk party politics. Even before the association had established itself as a formal entity, there had been keen interest in the colony in the forthcoming general elections. The RGA had, early in 1936, put a notice in the newspapers urging their members to register to vote.[47] The middle class welcomed the intention to extend the franchise and became keenly interested in the chance to become more strongly involved in the formal political process.

There was some discussion about the kinds of persons who should seek membership in the legislative council. The newspapers led the way, with the *Times* of 5 September 1936 asking,

> Whom do we wish on that Council? Is it the popular man, the man who can entertain the electorate by raising their spirits? Is it the big landowner who wants to secure his own interests and is very little interested in the colony as a whole? Are we to be satisfied with Mr. This or Mr. That because it would not be just the correct thing not to have the other man? Or are we to have Mr. So and So who is only desirous of obtaining a seat on the Council to be termed honourable when in reality he is very dishonest?

Like the *Times*, the *Investigator* began to pay some attention to the forthcoming general elections. What, in its view, was needed were people who would represent the masses, but it accepted the fact that the choice was limited, since the franchise was still relatively high. It emphasized the point that they could not have elected persons earning incomes of less than two hundred pounds per annum or who own property of a value of less than five hundred pounds above all encumbrances, and noted that peasants, artisans and labourers were not in that category. One possible way of dealing with this was to have the administrator nominate such persons.[48]

In looking at future legislators, one name clearly stood out even before the formation of the SWMA, McIntosh. He was someone from whom "the smallest, the poorest, the most depressed can always get a sympathetic hearing".[49] The riots had changed the political landscape, and McIntosh became the man of the moment. The association's link with politics came naturally, since it had become obvious to the masses, after October 1935, that the major decisions affecting their lives were made in the legislative chambers. In highlighting the role of McIntosh, the 1 April 1936 issue of the *Investigator* made the point that "work among the masses is difficult, but it is necessary for the advancement of a civilised community". There was little doubt that McIntosh would be put forward as a candidate at the next election but on a "labour ticket" – that is, as an SWMA candidate. Since his December 1935 trial, McIntosh was the victim of a great deal of harassment.[50] This had possibly to do with his perceived or expected political role or with a genuine belief that he had actually been one of the ringleaders and still had to be monitored.

Constitutional changes were already in motion before the October riots and so were expected. This was a response to the continuing agitation for greater constitutional reform. The changes, grudgingly given, did not affect the basic thrust of Crown colony government, for the governor retained the power to enforce any measure that he considered necessary for carrying out the work of his imperial masters.[51]

Even though agitation for constitutional advancement predated the 1935 riots, the riots gave some degree of urgency to the matter and ensured that it would involve much more than accommodating a wider representation among the middle classes, since the working people had placed their concerns on the national agenda.

THE 1937 ELECTIONS

On 16 December 1936, the legislative council was dissolved in preparation for elections and for a new council. Changes in the qualification of electors applied to women over twenty-one years instead of thirty, as it had previously been. They had, of course, to meet the other qualifications.[52] It must be noted that the elected members would have been outnumbered by the nominated and official members. The council was dissolved by proclamation on 17 December.[53] New boundaries were carved out, with the Grenadines being separated from Kingstown, and the Windward constituency divided into North and South Windward.

Preparations for the elections began with the putting in place of the required structures and regulations. Arrangements were made for the expansion of electoral districts to five instead of the prevailing three. The closing date for registration of electors was 31 January. The middle class had begun to take the whole election exercise very seriously, and the newspapers had been highlighting the need to be registered as it urged persons eligible to vote to not leave things to chance. As one of them expressed it:

> It is now well known that many of the evils that persist here cannot rear their heads in more fortunate islands that have councils to keep them low. . . . Lives have been lost, poverty persists and conditions generally are too one-sided owing to the lack of good councillors. If these do not force upon every man who is qualified to vote the urgent need of registering his name to elect the men who will largely contribute to making his home what it will be, what else will?

Apart from that news item, the editor found it necessary to address a special letter to the readers. He stated, "There is to be the general election for the new constitution, the passing of the Minimum Wage Bill, serious efforts at Land Settlement that could really benefit the man lowest down etc. etc. I feel it my duty to remind your own vast amount of readers that these are every body's business and to entreat you to have a live and deep interest in them during the coming year."[54]

The old landed class that had for so long dominated politics was not leaving anything to chance and began to put a great deal of emphasis on having their people registered. This was reflected in the Kingstown Board elections held earlier. The SWMA was being urged to follow in line and become serious in an effort to defeat what one columnist described as the "Capitalists". He was concerned about rumours of division in their ranks.[55]

The atmosphere became enlivened as both parties put a great deal of effort into the registration process. There were complaints, however, that even up to the closing date for registration the candidates for "Labour" were not declared. The designation *Labour* seemed to have been given to the association by the newspapers, which wanted to highlight their commitment to the working people. It was known, however, that McIntosh was to be one of them. Confidence continued to be expressed in him, as he was seen as a man with very practical rather than theoretical knowledge. "He never minces matters but speaks straight from the shoulder."[56]

The absence of public meetings up to that time and the failure of the SWMA to declare its candidates caused some concern. But, not long after that, the public meetings began. Eight hundred people listened in Georgetown to N.S. Nanton, a barrister who was one of the candidates of the Labour Party. Nanton was an island scholar who had returned after a period of study abroad. At that meeting, held in an area where the plantations dominated, McIntosh revealed that the planters had sent a petition to the secretary of state asking for the abolition of the elective element in the legislative council.[57] He described them as "enemies of the people" and urged that they be frustrated in their attempts to get representatives into the legislative council.[58]

Among the issues raised at the meeting by Nanton were land settlement and the Workmen's Compensation Ordinance, two issues that continued to be highlighted in later meetings. Nanton pledged to work with McIntosh to ensure that some of their concerns were addressed, and he was greeted with shouts of "Mr Nanton is our man" and "We will vote for you." The meeting was thrown open for comments from the listening public, and many persons took the opportunity to express support for him since he was on the side of their hero, McIntosh.[59]

Of the colony's three newspapers, the *Times* and the *Investigator* followed the events leading up to the elections quite closely and kept reminding their readers of the significance and importance of the elections. The third paper, the *Vincentian*, became a voice of, or, at least, was sympathetic to the political fortunes of, the planters but was quite lukewarm about the forthcoming elections. Indeed, apart from the contribution by one of its columnists, M. Byron Cox, and an occasional comment from the editor, it appeared quite uninterested. Cox had an axe to grind after parting company with the leadership of the RGA over its reaction to the riots. He used the *Vincentian* to voice his opposition to the "Labour Party"[60] which included members with whom he had had the disagreement. In the issue of 6 February 1937, in his column "Notes and Comments on Current Events", he expressed, apparently tongue in cheek, his dissatisfaction that little was heard from his erstwhile friends who were now vociferous politicians.

The *Vincentian*, in its editorial of 13 March, two weeks before the elections, decried the political inactivity, but its comments then seemed geared to the planter class. The paper stated that "it is indeed deplorable to observe how little enthusiasm is shown by the majority of that section of the community which is really intelligent and influential". It warned the voters that the destiny of the country was tied up with "the gentlemen you select to advise the administration". On 20 March 1937, it did little more than publish a list of candidates and times for polling.

The Labour Party's slate of candidates was soon known. Apart from McIntosh, who was contesting the Kingstown seat, and Nanton, the others were H.A. Davis for the Leeward constituency, O.D. Brisbane for the Grenadines and O.W. Forde, who had been on the defence team for the preliminary trial of McIntosh. Forde, who was a planter, eventually threw in his lot on the side of the planters and was replaced by A.C. Allen. The withdrawal of Forde appeared not to have caught many people by surprise since he was a big landowner "and represents the interests of his class".[61] Before his withdrawal, Forde had actually addressed one of McIntosh's meetings and expressed his full support for him.

The meetings of the association's candidates were well received. McIntosh described himself at one of his meetings as "an out and out labour man". He continued on the issue of the expansion of the franchise, being critical of those who opposed it and asked for a reduction in the franchise because, he felt, they were afraid to face the electorate. As candidate for the Leeward District, Davis hammered home issues that were important to the electorate in that district. One of them was land settlement. He called for a better distribution of land, which he considered a "crying need", and pledged that the members of the association's team were prepared to expend their energies on realizing a practical land settlement scheme. The Leeward area had long been recognized as one of the more deprived areas in the country, and Davis re-echoed a sentiment that had long been expressed, that land monopoly was one of the culprits for the existence of that situation. He described it as "the dire poverty and nakedness of the people". The other matter that got a great deal of attention from him was that of the minimum wage, which had also been of great concern in that part of the colony.[62] In some quarters, the electoral fight was seen as one between capital and labour. Candidates like Alban Da Santos were singled out as being among those who had drafted a petition against an extension of the franchise. Forde was seen as reverting to his "class interests". This was his second time at the polls, not having managed, in his first attempt, to save his twenty-five-pound deposit.[63]

The week of the elections was a lively and busy one. Vehicles were transporting persons to meetings, reflecting the heightened interest. The two contesting "parties" were leaving little to chance.[64] The atmosphere on the day before the elections was captured by one of the newspapers. That day "was the climax of the political campaigning when shortly after midday a procession of some twenty cars circled the town [Kingstown] decorated with small Union Jacks and bearing posters; Vote for MacDonald, Forde, Da Santos, Providence and D.C. McIntosh". They were described as persons who lived in their districts, who stood for orderly and progressive government and whose slogan was "the greatest good for the greatest number". Then came the time for the candidates of the Labour Party, "cars and buses dressed with red flags and led by West Indian music gave out the propaganda from the SWMA. 'Vote for George McIntosh, the People's friend'. 'We need better conditions for our Working People'."[65]

Election day, 25 March, was a busy one, with polling booths opening at 7:00 a.m. and closing at 8:30 p.m. There was some concern in Kingstown from supporters of the Labour Party when it appeared to them that the planters' party had been mobilizing a large number of vehicles to take voters for their candidate McDonald to the polls. There was, however, no real cause for concern, for the SWMA, running under the unofficial name Labour Party and led by McIntosh, achieved an almost clean sweep. McIntosh easily defeated McDonald, having received 364 votes to his opponent's 178. His victory, as was to be expected, was greeted with great enthusiasm. He "was lifted and put into his car, the crowd cheering as he drove to his home". "No one who heard that midnight shout of the populace on the announcement of McIntosh's victory can ignore it", the *Times* proclaimed.[66]

In the South Windward constituency, Allen won a decisive victory, humbling Forde in the process and demonstrating the strength of the Labour Party. That constituency had the highest turnout of registered voters, with 95.8 per cent of the voters exercising their right to vote.[67] The North Windward area, the heart of the plantation system, was where the fight seemed to have been most intense. That constituency had the "most independent and largest number of voters". Thirty-seven votes separated the candidates, and Nanton's victory was due largely to his support in Georgetown, the only town in the North Windward constituency, where he led Da Santos by one hundred to fifty-two votes.[68] In the Leeward area, there was not much of a fight except in the village of Troumaca, which was the home of Providence, the planters' candidate. Davis won relatively easily. The area where the Labour Party faltered was in the Grenadines, where the candidate backed by the planters, D.C. McIntosh, was victorious.[69]

The victory of the Labour Party led to a great deal of rejoicing among the working people, who celebrated until the early hours of the morning. The man who obviously stood out in this victory was McIntosh, about whom the establishment was wary but in whom the working people had overwhelming confidence. The victory was even more remarkable because of what appeared to have been a determined fight put up by the planter class in the last week before the elections. The *Investigator* of 27 March 1937 made mention of the planters' group working valiantly "in their seven or eight days of electioneering".[70] Enormous responsibility was now placed in the hands of the Labour Party, a responsibility that was in the consciousness of many people, even though they might have articulated it differently. The *Times* was quick to point this out. In its view, the thrust that it had undertaken by its victory at the polls amounted to the idea of liberating labour from wage slavery, "a power which must be used with care". It warned the victorious party not to become "intoxicated with its victory"; it was just about to assume the task that was put in its hands. The paper appealed for support from the public even in attending meetings of the legislative council, a presence that, it felt, would give encouragement to those elected to the council.[71]

The planters seemed determined to fight those whom they considered political upstarts depriving them of their accustomed places in the legislative council. The *Vincentian* was again at their service, and Cox led the fight. He acknowledged that the new party had earned its rewards from "foresight, energy, organisation and hard work". He resented their tactics, "packing the Electors Roll with their own followers, going about getting them to enrol . . . while those of the opposite views sat quietly by and did nothing". This was a strange argument. The extension of the franchise for the elections, including making it available to women over twenty-one years, would have meant the inclusion of more persons not necessarily sympathetic to the cause of the planters. Since they were new electors, it was absolutely essential that the Labour Party facilitate their registration.

Cox claimed further that it was only at the last moment that the other party recognized what was happening and tried to organize, but it was then too late. He was high in praise of the conduct on election day, "except for a few irresponsibles in the red camp". The battle between capital and labour, as one writer described it, was well and truly on, even in the minds of representatives of both groups.

Cox felt, too, that the new representatives were unlearned in matters of the council. He was, nevertheless, happy for he was heartened by the numbers who voted for the "party of the right". It was, to his mind, an indication "that there is substantial percentage of the electorate who can be relied upon to watch the colony's welfare with care and attention". For him, "they are the real backbone of the island who can give the bread of reality and not the stones of spurious promises". Cox also raised an issue that is of significance and spoke to the impact of the riots. He recognized the "unprecedented interest in public affairs" from all quarters. But, for him, the interests of those on the "right" were the important element. As he put it, "The men of wealth and influence have been roused to come forward with the expressed view of saving the poor and ignorant from exploitation and great goodwill will result to all."[72]

His diatribe did not go unchallenged. One writer, who described himself as "Red", using the language of Cox, acknowledged that he was a working man and a member of the SWMA. He was convinced that the emergence and victory of the party "will sound the death knell of many evils that exist today". He argued that the "common labourer" was wiser and more enlightened than he had been two years before. He took exception to Cox's claim that McIntosh's opponent, MacDonald, had the support of the majority of the intelligent classes, for he was "convinced that a strong middle class intelligence was at the back of George A. McIntosh at the polls".[73]

In another article, captioned "Humour or Ridicule: A Criticism", Junias, obviously a nom de plume, failed to see any humour in Cox's reference to the Labour Party as "red". The insinuation was obvious to him, "Bolshevik, Communist, Reactionary". He noted that the red flag of labour was universally adopted and appropriate. He took exception to the general tone of Cox's article, arguing that "base indeed is he who would cast aspersions and degrading insinuation at the honest efforts of labour in its honest struggle for liberty against overwhelming odds". He mocked Cox's suggestion that "capital would come forward to protect labour from exploitation of itself. Behold a New Teaching!" He adds, "Who, be he never so ignorant of sociology, does not know that labour has been in all ages the defenceless prey of capital." He let it be known that labour's salvation was in its own hand and "that's why labour is uniting much to the uneasiness of its earstwhile [sic] masters, 'the men of wealth and influence'".[74] The battle lines were drawn. The riots had changed the political momentum, and a number of things were put in motion that led eventually to the historic elections of 1951 conducted under adult suffrage.

The new legislative council comprised Henry Bradshaw Popham, governor of the Windward Islands; Arthur Alban Wright, administrator (colonial secretary); Harry Allan Oswald O'Reilly, attorney general; and John Felix Hamilton Otway, treasurer, all being *ex officio* members. The nominated bench contained A.M. Punnett, A.M. Fraser and William Alexander Hadley, all planters. Fraser was a former elected member of council who was selected for the nominated bench. The elected members were G.A. McIntosh, A.C. Allen, N.S. Nanton and H.A. Davis, all of whom represented the Labour Party. D.C. McIntosh of the Grenadines ran as an independent. The death of D.C. McIntosh shortly after led to a by-election that was won by default by Bonadie of the Labour Party. S.G. DeFreitas, who was supposed to have opposed him, was found to not be a registered voter.

There were two other general elections, in 1940 and 1946, before the historic 1951 elections. In 1938, a by-election was held following the resignation of N.S. Nanton, for the post of magistrate. That election was quite heated, reflecting the growth of political consciousness and the changing times. Frank Child, manager of the Grand Sable estate, ran as an independent candidate but was backed by the planters. His opponent was Scott Stephens, a small merchant of Georgetown who represented the Labour Party and won by twenty-two votes. "There is no denying the fact that, the St Vincent Workingmen's Association today wield[s] an influence over the electorate that cannot be ignored", commented the *Times* of 8 October 1938. That paper went on to emphasize what, it felt, was a "growing distrust of the large landowners" throughout St Vincent and the West Indies. It argued that "these feelings are based upon deep rooted facts which have impressed themselves upon the middle and labouring classes during years of struggle for existence against hard economic pressure".[75] It sought, however, to soothe the fears that some persons had about the preponderance of labour members by noting that three large landowners were nominated by government and there were also three *ex officio* members.

THE WAR YEARS: MOVING TO THE 1940 AND 1946 ELECTIONS

The Child-Stephens struggle was perhaps a forerunner to the heated elections of 1940. Political activity was at a height; "even the children in the streets are thinking and talking politically".[76] The planters' challenge of the credentials of about eleven hundred voters in the North Windward, Kingstown and Leeward districts was strongly resented by the working people and made them determined to rally around the SWMA. This was especially so in the plantation-dominated North Windward area. "Quiz", writing in the *Times* of 2 March 1940, was of the view that 95 per cent of the electorate "rallied against the unprecedented mass of objections". The objections were, however, overruled, and the Labour Party once again won an overwhelming victory. The winners for the Labour Party were the leader (McIntosh), Cato, Bonadie and Davis. Labour's candidate was once again defeated in the Grenadines, A.G. Hazell defeating P.C. Lewis.

The victory of the Labour Party's team was attributed to its advocacy of issues of concern to the working people. The leader, McIntosh, was described as "a strong Socialist . . . advocates a more even distribution of the colony's wealth. He is a member of several local committees and is possessed of wide experience. He was confined in prison for 3 weeks in connection with the October disturbances." Davis was "sincere and fearless, with a strong Christian background". Bonadie was "one of the colony's youthful politicians with an intelligent socialist and labour bias. He is editor of the *Times* newspaper and Vice President of the Association." Cato was the youngest legislator and secretary of the association. "He has wide and varied knowledge of the many local labour problems, perhaps more so than most of his colleagues. His representation made on behalf of so many people have made him extremely popular in the middle and labouring classes."[77]

The 1940 elections, perhaps more so than those of 1937, demonstrated the extent to which the 1935 riots had changed the political landscape. What stood out was the fact that the working people, most of whom were not enfranchised, gave full support to the Labour candidates, whom they recognized as representing their interests. It was also considered good for the overall political development of the colony, because the political consciousness that was developing "will act as a watchdog over the deeds or misdeeds of the new legislators".[78]

A 1943 by-election to replace Cato, who had vacated his seat on the legislative council, was won by R. Brisbane of the Labour Party. The party was, however, becoming a victim of its own success. It was credited with the responsibility for the rising political consciousness but was beginning to suffer from internal divisions.[79] The split within the Labour Party, which will be discussed later, affected its preparation for the 1946 elections.[80] It led to a reorganization of the party's team for those elections. Two of the party's representatives in the legislative council were dropped from the 1946 team. They were Davis from the Leeward District and Bonadie from South Windward. Bonadie pledged "to use a chastening rod to clear out the dirty muck that is running the Association" and to do so from within the association. The 1946 elections, like the two previous ones, generated a great deal of interest. Edmund Joachim got the nod as candidate for the Leeward District. A columnist writing for the *Times* felt that Joachim was favoured despite the excellent work that Davis had done. Joachim's youth seemed to have worked in his favour.[81]

As indicated by a political commentator in the *Times*, there was concern about the possible negative impact of the split within the ranks of the party, since it had "conjured up dreams of a return to power by St Vincent's plantocracy. And they are spending and are prepared heavily to take advantage of this opportunity before the advent of Adult Suffrage and a reunion of labour takes place. Or better let me say, before the colony's labour reverts into the hands of wiser, more stable, more intelligent and more educated leadership."[82] Other members of the public also feared a return to dominance of the legislature by the planter class.[83]

Bonadie, who was dropped as a candidate, maintained his position as vice-president and managing director of the SWMA. At one of their early meetings, he felt it necessary to pray for the party, "which he said was running backwards downhill and without breaks".[84] Because of the high regard in which Davis, Bonadie and Brisbane were held, the character of the leader of the association and party was being put "under the microscope", since he was seen as the person behind the decisions. There was even more cause for concern when the public had begun to become critical.[85] McIntosh's support for Sydney McIntosh, a former proprietor of the Bequia Hotel, was puzzling; columnist Evoe, describing it as an unlikely alliance, felt that "strange things happen sometimes".[86]

The planters made every effort to stem the tide that was moving against them, spending a lot of money, "parading the country side laughing with and pinching up the cheeks of black babies".[87] They acted fully aware that adult suffrage was on the cards for the immediate future. In some areas, especially in the Windward district, there was talk of big feasts of goat and vegetables meted out to the electorate. This did not achieve its objective, since the area remained loyal to the Labour Party.[88] There was even a saying by supporters of Labour that if they dressed up a lifeless object and put it on the Labour slate, it was certain to win.

The planters' dominance of the nominated side was being threatened, and this was another cause of concern for them. O.D. Brisbane, a black merchant, was nominated to the council in May 1942. The *Times* reported that "the middle and labouring classes are jubilant over the selection while a 'big interest' minority has expressed shock and disappointment". The reference was naturally to the planters, who failed to capitalize on the divisions within the Labour Party. Times had certainly changed, but an even bigger battle lay ahead with the onset of adult suffrage. Despite the criticisms of McIntosh centred on his age (he being then sixty) and questions about the political direction he appeared to be taking, he still retained public support. Evoe commented, "Great thing this weapon of workers' votes."[89]

The planters had been seeking McIntosh's head. They held meetings with big and small businessmen to find a candidate to oppose him. The increase in the number of registered voters from the lower middle class was making a difference and creating further problems for the planters. McIntosh was, however, put to the test before the 1946 elections. He had lost his seat on the legislative council in 1944 because of a decision in 1943 by the Kingstown Board, of which he was chairman, "to compensate its Chairman 'momentarily' for the duties which took up so much of his time". The attorney general gave his legal opinion, and it was decided that his seats on both the Kingstown Board and the legislative council were void under article 9 of the Letters Patent, St Vincent (Legislative Council) Order in Council, 1936. The attorney general informed that the Kingstown Board Ordinance did not allow "holding an office of emolument within the gift of the Board".[90]

At the by-election to fill the seat, McIntosh was elected unopposed but questioned the decision that led to his removal from the legislative council. He argued that the government's interpretation of the Letters Patent was wrong and indicated that he had strong legal opinion to support his position.[91]

Despite the earlier concerns about the slow build-up to the 1946 elections, once the registration process was completed, the pace picked up. The Kingstown electoral district remained relatively calm because of the difficulty of finding someone to contest against McIntosh. The Leeward constituency was one of the areas where political activity was at a height. Davis, having been rejected by his party initially, announced his unwillingness to contest but, having been pressured by supporters, reversed that decision. He was up against the much younger Joachim, a man who was only forty, a resident of Barrouallie, one of the larger population centres, and was prepared to put a lot of hard work into his campaign.

In the South Windward area, there was, at first, some uncertainty about the candidates, although it was felt that Bonadie, though discarded by his party, was going to contest the election. The candidate Julian Baynes had created something of a stir, first for introducing a novelty when he spoke from his car with a loud speaker. There were reports of heated discussions between Bonadie and Baynes, something that helped to bring further excitement to the campaign. It seemed to have been the practice, at that time, to open the meetings to persons who wanted to make a contribution. At one meeting held at Mesopotamia in the South Windward constituency, two supporters of Baynes took advantage of that opportunity to mount the platform and have their say, speaking at great length. Bonadie, as editor of the *Times*, certainly got good coverage from that paper, particularly from its political correspondent Evoe.[92]

In the North Windward area, the new candidate for the Labour Party was Ebenezer Duncan, editor of the *Investigator*. The Labour Party even resorted to some of the tactics of the planters' group by having, following one of their meetings, a big feast of goat and vegetables. The area had always held firmly to the Labour Party and selected Duncan as its candidate. Like Kingstown, the political climate in the Grenadines was quite lukewarm. It was one of the smallest constituencies, having only 250 registered electors, and, again, there appeared to be difficulty finding someone to contest against S.G. DeFreitas. Eventually, Sydney McIntosh, the son of the former representative, emerged as candidate and, despite not being a member of the Labour Party, had the support of George McIntosh.

Again, two of the country's newspapers, the *Times* and *Investigator*, played leading roles in the electoral campaign, their editors being candidates for the 1946 elections, Bonadie of the *Times* running as an independent. The *Vincentian* was quite uninterested and mostly avoided any mention of the campaign. On 5 October, the eve of the election, its editorial was on a school-building programme. On 12 October, it was about the governor's visit, which was primarily for the opening of parliament but with a little mention of the elections. It was not until 19 October that it carried a release with the results of the elections, a release that was signed on 8 October. A large part of this had to do with the personality of the editor, Robert Mowbray Anderson. He was described by one who knew him as an Anglophile.[93] He had a particular admiration for Administrator Grimble, who held office during the 1935 riots. On the eve of the administrator's departure in February 1936, he wrote, "ignorance of some of the masses and misunderstanding, wilful or otherwise, caused some regrettable disturbances toward the close of this administration. The contributing factors were manifold and only time will reveal them all. It has not served, however, to undo the brilliant achievements of the period of administration now under review."[94]

The *Times* kept its readers updated on the political situation at that time. Evoe provided weekly highlights of the political campaign. The paper, through its editorial, indicated that it was its intention to start preparing the populace to take the opportunity of contributing to the destiny of the colony.[95] It was of the view that they were into a critical period in the development of the country and region. This demanded representatives that were "well balanced, sober, sound, intelligent, educated and far-seeing". The destiny of the colony, it felt, hung on the results of the elections. It pointed to the upcoming conference in St Kitts that was to deal with the amalgamation of the Windward and Leeward Islands and suggested that the country needed to have the right delegates with "great powers of mind and statesmanship if they are to pull their proper weight in shaping the future of these colonies for weal or woe".[96] As elections drew near, it stepped up its call to the electorate. It cautioned them and urged voters to be judicious in casting their votes, "lest history judge them by their actions on that day". It hoped that posterity "would endorse their verdict".[97]

The Labour Party won three of five seats. McIntosh was returned unopposed. In the North Windward area, Duncan won over Eric Hadley of the Planters' Party, and Joachim was victorious over Davis, who had contested as an independent. In South Windward, Bonadie was given the nod over Baynes in the tied contest, through a decision of the legislative council.[98] In the Grenadines, S.G. DeFreitas defeated Sydney McIntosh, even with McIntosh's support for the latter.

What was significant for the working people was that issues of importance to them were being placed high on the agenda by the representatives of the Labour Party. There were still severe limitations, since power remained where it had always been, with the executive. What they were able to do, however, was to present themselves as strong advocates on behalf of the working people. In the next chapter, I highlight a few of the issues that were pushed vigorously by

McIntosh and his colleagues as they ensured that the concerns of the working people took centre stage and became part of a new agenda. Their advocacy was carried out not only in the legislative council but in all other forums that were available, including the newspapers. The need for further constitutional changes to allow the political enfranchisement of all adults remained an issue, which was only settled in 1951.

CHAPTER 6

RESETTING THE COLONY'S LEGISLATIVE AGENDA

THE COLONY'S LEGISLATIVE AGENDA WAS BEING RESET AND the battle lines drawn, though blurred. Despite the governor's bravado and attempt to find a hidden hand behind the riots, he must have recognized the changed circumstances and realized that it could no longer be business as usual. The elected members of the Labour Party in the legislative council had begun to highlight the issues which they considered central to the lives of the working people, with whom they had thrown in their lot. In the election campaign, they had pledged, if elected, to have the issues they were highlighting addressed. They saw the working people as strong allies in their struggle with the planters, who were still the dominant force in the society. The political climate was ideal for this, for the rioting on 21 and 22 October 1935 had forced the working people into the picture as never before. The Colonial Office had also recognized the changed circumstances, not necessarily or only because of the St Vincent riots but also because of the many disturbances that rocked the British colonies during the period of the 1930s. Workers' unrest was not new. There were riots and other kinds of disturbances before.[1] What was new, as the Moyne Commission noted, was "a positive demand for the creation of new conditions to 'render possible a better and less restricted life'".[2]

John La Guerre puts this in perspective: "What distinguished the Moyne Commission from its predecessors was the recognition by the Colonial Office, for the first time that the unrest in the West Indies was neither the work of agitators nor blind protest, but the expression of a more fundamental malaise in the region as a whole and, by way of corollary, that a regional programme rather than mere island palliatives was required for its solution."[3]

There was some urgency in understanding and addressing the conditions that might have created the disturbances of 21 and 22 October but Grier continued to spend much of his time on his conspiracy theory in an effort to remove any blame from his administration. McIntosh and his colleagues, however, began to force the attention of the colonial authorities to what they considered pressing issues affecting the working people.

We identify here some of these issues.

LAND SETTLEMENT

Grier, as he responded to the shouts of the people at the court yard on 21 October, informed the crowd that a land settlement scheme was at that moment being considered by the Colonial Office, something that seemed to have grabbed their attention.[4] Yet he did not seem to give it urgent attention.

In his first campaign meeting in Kingstown for the 1937 elections, McIntosh had been pushing the view that little interest was taken in the poor man. This was part of the effort to strike a bond with the common people, whom he urged to awake from their slumber.[5] The recommendations of the Moyne Commission were presented to the British Parliament on 20 February 1940, but some of the areas highlighted were already being discussed in the St Vincent legislative council, matters related to land settlement, labour conditions and education, among others. On the issue of land settlement, the commission pointed out that several estates were financially embarrassed and recommended that the government take powers for the compulsory acquisition of agricultural land for land settlement and similar purposes.[6] Land settlement was clearly the most dominant issue that surfaced in the period between the riots and the advent of adult suffrage, certainly up to 1946.

The Three Rivers scheme, as was noted before, raised expectations of further expansion of land settlement in other areas. Grier was of the view that "except where sugar is being cultivated, the day of the large estate is passing".[7] In light of the uneven distribution of land, the view that land settlement was a solution to the economic problems continued to be a persistent one. In his address to the legislative council on 15 December 1936, in pointing to the uneven distribution of land, Grimble noted that the thirty estates or groups of estates that exceeded one hundred acres each comprised approximately thirty-three thousand acres, representing almost half the privately owned land, including "most of the best cultivable areas".[8]

The newspapers continued to highlight the need to keep land settlement high on the agenda and singled out "the middle leeward district with the town of Barrouallie as its centre". They carried the administrator's speech in the legislative council on 15 December 1936, where the issue of the uneven distribution of land was raised. The *Times* and *Investigator* reported on debates in the legislative council on the matter of land settlement, ran editorials on the issue and carried letters from the public and articles from McIntosh.[9] They sometimes resorted to strong language, as can be seen in the issue of the *Times* on 10 September 1938 when it warned that "the Haves will not readily give up any of their possessions to the Have-Nots". The implication here was that it was necessary for the government to intervene. Grier, on the other hand, as suggested before, seemed then to not have ruled out the possibility of compulsory acquisition if necessary, despite the long-held policy that they needed to maintain a judicious balance between estates and small holdings.[10]

In 1936, C.C. Skeete, assistant commissioner of agriculture at the Imperial College of Tropical Agriculture in Trinidad, was invited to St Vincent to examine the suitability of the Leeward District for peasant settlement. He was opposed to the purchase of land in the southern portion of McDonald's estate because of what he described as uncontrolled land exploitation and devastation and the existence of numerous narrow valleys with steep, rocky slopes. He recommended a scheme of agricultural development in the northern estates based on sugar production, to facilitate the peasants. The governor did not agree, possibly because of the long history of difficulty with sugar production, sugar having long ceased to be a major industry in the country.[11] He could also possibly have been concerned that they would then have been treading on an area that was virtually reserved for the planters.

Fraser, nominated member of the legislative council who owned an estate in Rutland Vale, adjoining the town of Layou, was willing to rent out some of that land, information that the administrator brought to the attention of the executive council.[12] The finance committee, with one dissenting voice, agreed to rent fifty acres of land at Rutland Vale.[13] Similar arrangements were sought for Barrouallie, to the north of Layou, and in Bequia in the northern Grenadines. The committee was in full agreement once the advice of the Board of Agriculture was obtained for each proposal.[14] A notice by superintendent of works S.B. Isaacs, dated 20 March 1939, invited applications for lands at Rutland Vale.[15]

The land settlement question, the acting administrator informed secretary of state Malcolm MacDonald, was fully ventilated during the visit of the Royal Commission, but action was unlikely to be taken without the commission's report. He stated, "I am, however, anxious that wherever possible land should be made available for the use of the working classes especially in districts where the supply of labour is permanently in excess of the requirements of the estates and where there is an appreciable number of labourers who are not in possession of any land, either as peasant owners or as tenants of an estate."[16]

Lands had also been purchased at Mount Alexander to meet the needs of residents of Chateaubelair, although there were criticisms that the land was poor.[17] There were major difficulties with the situation in Barrouallie. T.M. McDonald, the sole proprietor, after appearing initially to be willing to rent lands, decided later to fall back on his previous policy of giving the labourers on his estates land free of charge to use as small plots for growing food crops. There were obvious problems with that arrangement. The lands were limited to workers on his estates. The size of the plots, three-fifths of an acre each, was quite small. Moreover, they were restricted to the production of food crops, and there was, above all, no security of tenure. The situation in Barrouallie worried the authorities, and they were willing to spend five hundred pounds on renovating the leeward highway, in an effort to provide employment in the area. They were quite aware, however, that it was not going to be sufficient to meet the need for employment.[18]

While the Barrouallie situation remained worrisome, the authorities received offers from other estates in Layou for land to rent. At a finance committee meeting on 27 November 1942, approval was given for the purchase of the Camden Park estate, some 399 acres. The purpose was to establish an agricultural station, with 60 to 70 acres to be used for land settlement, the cost to be met partly by a Colonial Development and Welfare grant and partly from a loan.

The developments that were taking place had, however, been prompted by continuing pressure from McIntosh and members of his Labour Party. McIntosh, in a letter to the *Times* of 11 February 1939, depicted the uneven distribution of land as a heritage of the days of slavery. He wrote:

> In a sense it is the root of all West Indian problems. To it can be attributed directly the poverty of the masses of the people reflected as we have already seen in inadequate wages, insanitary housing, illiteracy etc. What is now most urgently needed

in the West Indies is that the abolition of slavery be taken a step further by destroying the economic foundations of slavery and redistributing the land more equitably – the power of the West Indian Capitalist is also strengthened by the absence of trade unions and the inadequacy of industrial law.

In the legislative council, four motions by representatives of the North Windward, South Windward, Kingstown and Leeward Districts, respectively, urging provision of lands for the further establishment of a peasantry were presented. The petitions were rolled into one and accepted by the council. Statistics for landownership in 1940 revealed that fifteen persons owned more than a half of the privately owned land but there were only four thousand peasants in a population of sixty thousand. Faced with this information, even the nominated members who were large landowners were obliged to give way.[19]

The newspapers continued their strong advocacy for land settlement. The editorial in the 11 February 1939 edition of the *Times*, entitled "Tinkering with Land Settlement", quoted from W.M. McMillan's book *Warning from the West Indies*, where he argued that large landowners were unwilling to part with good land "and it may often become necessary to acquire good lands, if the government is honestly interested in the success of land settlement schemes".[20]

A land settlement policy was ultimately adopted in 1943. By then, the recommendations of the Moyne Commission had already been known. It placed emphasis on leasehold rather than freehold ownership, which had been central to the earlier land settlement schemes. The Royal Commission had suggested that governments not commit themselves to freehold ownership but experiment with both freehold and leasehold tenures.[21] The argument advanced in the land settlement policy was that the leasehold system would prevent allottees from having to spend large sums of money buying land rather than investing in working it. Efforts were made to address the issue of security of tenure by having leases of twenty-five years, with the right to renew for another twenty-five years after every ten years.[22]

The next step in the process, following continued pressure from the legislative council and through public opinion, as expressed through the newspapers, was the passage of an ordinance to create a body to regulate and control land settlement and development, and the establishment of a land settlement board.[23] There was enthusiasm among elected members. McIntosh pledged to ensure that persons appointed to the board "have the sympathy and consideration of the people at heart". Davis, from an area where land hunger was most evident, was determined to ensure that, with the board in place, the horrible conditions in Layou and Barrouallie would no longer exist. McIntosh and Bonadie of the Labour Party were elected to the board along with two other members, one a planter, the other an *ex officio* member and officials of related government departments.²⁴ In 1948, when a new board was appointed, an additional member of the Labour Party, the newly elected Joachim, was added.

The *Times* was enthusiastic about the developments. Its editorial of 30 June 1945, shortly after the meeting which created the board, was captioned "A Great Piece of Legislation". It stated, "When the members of the Legislative Council left the Council Chamber on Thursday evening amidst gathering darkness after an all day session, they did so with the feeling that unborn generations of Vincentians would look upon that day as perhaps the most historic in the life of the Legislature for the present century."

Later, in December 1945, legislation was passed for the acquisition of estates in the Leeward area.²⁵ Approval was subsequently given by the secretary of state for the purchase of estates in the north and central Leeward areas.²⁶ F.A. Casson, who then owned estates that had formerly been in the hands of T.M. McDonald, offered a number of those estates for sale in two blocks, a northern and southern block (see table 8).²⁷ Financing for their purchase was to be met by a grant from Colonial Development and Welfare funds, a government loan from the colony's surplus funds, and part "in debentures at three and a half percent repayable in twenty five years (held by previous owner)".²⁸

The land settlement policy, the creation of a land settlement board and the purchase of estates in 1945 had moved beyond what the *Times* had described as "tinkering with land settlement". The earlier reluctance to seriously push the effort to make land available to the landless was quite clearly dictated by the government's unwillingness to antagonize the planters, their political allies. This was restated in 1944 when administrator Ronald Garvey expressed, in his budget address, that "it is the intention of government to pursue a policy of land settlement but not at the expense of the continued existence of estates". He was of the view that estate production was most economical for exports, and so it was not their intention to run the plantations out of business.²⁹

The planters saw the drift towards land settlement and even tried to capitalize on it. It is also of interest that two of the planters who made land available for peasant production, Fraser and Casson (formerly Corea), had been members of the legislative council. Other planters, too, offered their estates for sale, often land unsuitable for peasant cultivation, as shown in the report of the 1931 com-

Table 8. Land Settlement Scheme of 1946

Estate	Name of Settlement	Acreage	Location
Richmond Vale	Richmond Vale	625	North Leeward
Petit Bordel/Sharpes		295	
Cragaburn		16	
Richmond		830	
Evergreen		60	
Wallibou		654	
Petit Wallibou		173	
Wallilabou	Wallilabou	460	Central Leeward
Resource		5	
Reversion		183	
Belle Isle		261	
Mount Stewart		110	
Keartons		332	
Total (Acres)		4,004	

Source: Minutes of the Land Settlement and Development Board, Lands and Surveys Department, St Vincent, 1946; Karl John, *Land Reform in Small Island Developing States: A Case Study on St Vincent, West Indies, 1890–2000* (College Station, TX: Virtualbookworm Publishing, 2006), 77.

mittee that had been appointed to look into land settlement. Where the government did not accept their offers, they privately organized sales in small lots. The *Times* of 13 May 1944 supported a bill to control the sale of land since planters were cutting up their estates and selling lots at "ridiculously exorbitant prices" and poor people were spending their last penny to get the small pieces of land.

Land settlement had, undoubtedly, begun to find its way into the thinking of the authorities with the governor's response to the rioters who confronted him at the court yard. The increased activity had very much to do with the pressure exerted by the leadership of the SWMA and its legislative arm, the Labour Party, and their allies the *Times* and *Investigator*. This was validated by the Royal Commission that helped to inform the colonial government's policy.

LABOUR

Matters relating to labour also took pride of place on the agenda of the SWMA. After all, it was the working people who had taken centre stage. Their demands for work and land had echoed throughout the disturbances and in the following period. Issues related to land settlement and to labour can hardly be divorced from each other, given the nature of the Vincentian economy. Even when estate workers were able to get access to land, given the small size of their lots, they still depended on part-time work on the estates, where and when it was available, to help pay for the purchase or lease of the land.

Labour issues were important even before the riots. What the riots did was to give them central place and to attach some degree of urgency to them. The Minimum Wage Ordinance passed before the riots was quickly implemented. The somewhat archaic Trade Union Law of 1933 was quite limited in its scope and offered little protection to trade unions. Orde Brown, in his report on labour conditions in the West Indies, had recommended for St Vincent the draft legislation that was pending in Jamaica.[30]

The colonial authorities, taken by surprise at the suddenness and spread of the disturbances in the region, sought ways to control and bring some order to the situation. The formation of trade unions and structures to accommodate labour demands and to channel them into more organized forms was put on the colonial agenda by the British government. The British Trade Union Congress was encouraged to facilitate the development of what were considered responsible trade unions. Subsequently, training courses were organized, and, even before that, members of the Moyne Commission included trade union personnel, who dialogued with labour representatives and working people during their visit to the colonies.

Since 1929, the governing Labour Party in England had recommended that governors give legal recognition to trade unions. The secretary of state was of the view that they were "'a natural and legitimate consequence of progress', but a source of disturbance if they were not officially recognised".[31] The unprecedented disturbances throughout the region in the 1930s gave some urgency to the matter and intensified the policy of the British government to push "responsible trade unionism". The British Trade Union Congress was to assist with this, and its general secretary, Walter Citrine, used his position as a member of the Moyne Commission to hold meetings and render advice to workers and their organizations. He discussed with officers of the SWMA the possibilities of establishing trade unions. Crowds of workers had gathered outside the courthouse building, eager to hear from him. He agreed to address them for a few minutes and did so to a packed house. His address, he informed them, was in his capacity as general secretary of the British Trade Union Congress and not as a member of the commission.[32]

The issue of responsible trade unionism was underscored by Bolland, who highlighted the anxiety of the British Fabian Socialists that Caribbean trade unions be led by people who could be considered to be responsible.[33] This concern of the government influenced the provision of training for trade union leaders. On 22 December 1939, a letter from the secretary of state addressed to Governor Popham advised him about proposals of the British Trade Union Congress to assist trade unionists and the trade union movement generally in the West Indian colonies.[34]

Susan Craig emphasized a different aspect of this when she argued that the establishment of trade unions and collective bargaining "was the express design of the Colonial Office and the major capitalist interests in the Caribbean, to stifle the militancy of the workers", a position which, she noted, coincided with the workers' optimism about the value of trade unions.[35] The official position on trade unions was spelled out by former administrator Arthur Francis Grimble, who was then governor of the Windward Islands, during an address in 1946 to the legislative councils of the Windwards on matters affecting the islands. They were, in his view, meant to promote peace in industry and trade through the development of responsible organizations of employers and employees. He spoke of the desire to establish collective bargaining machinery for the regulations of wages and working conditions and resolving problems by joint negotiations.[36]

It was not until the formation of the SWMA that an organization had attempted to embrace and voice fully and openly the concerns of the working people. This was in the post-riots period, when the working people had forced themselves into the consciousness of the colony. McIntosh, recognizing the significance of the working people, used the association as an organ to struggle on their behalf. Inadequate laws prevented the association from being registered as a trade union. The organization, nonetheless, focused on the legislative council and used those chambers to raise the concerns of workers. Although it made interventions on behalf of the working people with employers and government, it was not until the 1940s that it seriously began efforts at forming unions.

It might then have been stimulated by the formation of the Caribbean Labour

Congress (CLC). In fact, McIntosh and Bonadie represented the organization at the official launching of the CLC in Barbados in 1945. At that conference, McIntosh described the situation in St Vincent as one where there was a strong labour movement but without a registered trade union. He enquired of the conference whether they should concentrate on building one. An employers and employees association, meant to be a counter to the SWMA, had actually been registered as a friendly society. These bodies, although not legally trade unions, were attempting to do that work as well. The St Vincent Employers and Employees Association was formed in 1937, seemingly motivated by concerns arising from the disturbances of 1935 and the disarray in society that followed. It was supported strongly by the planters, most of whom were members. Its president was O.W. Forde, barrister and owner of the Argyle estate. It was registered under the Friendly Societies Ordinance 1843, its objective being "to create and maintain a better feeling among all classes in the colony of St Vincent and to provide funds by means of weekly contributions and donations for sick allowance of members subject to certain rules, for the payment of $30 on the death of any member to his or her executors, administrators or assigns".[37]

With McIntosh and his group in council, labour issues were brought to the legislative council. At a meeting on 5 February 1938, McIntosh spoke on the issue of the workmen's compensation ordinance, asking that it be brought forward "so as to give immediate effect to it as has been done in sister colonies". He questioned whether the government was "aware of the fact that on several estates throughout the country labourers who lived and worked for a number of years are given seven days notice to quit and remove their houses or huts and leave their food crops planted on the small plots allotted to them".[38] Later, in 1940, among four motions which the Labour Party presented to the legislative council was one that asked for the strengthening of the Labour Department to enable it to deal more effectively with labour matters.[39]

The 1939 Trade Unions (Amendment) Ordinance removed some of the inadequacies of the earlier ordinance. Included in the new ordinance were sections dealing with peaceful picketing and the prevention of intimidation without liability or tort, the removal of liability for interfering with another person's business and the prohibition of actions of tort against trade unions.[40] Advocacy on behalf of workers also took place outside of the legislature. In 1940, the SWMA held a labour conference that attracted fifty-eight delegates from throughout the island. It is important to note that, at that labour conference, the question of land settlement featured strongly.[41]

The 1939 ordinance facilitated the establishment of trade unions. At the beginning of 1945, there was still no registered trade union in the colony. In fact, in the Windward Islands, only two registered trade unions existed, in Grenada and St Lucia. During 1945, however, the Stubbs Peasants Growers Association was established by the SWMA. It was the first step in the formation of a peasant cultivators union.[42] At the beginning of 1946, two unions were registered and, by July, a third came into existence. The total recorded membership by the end of 1946 was 802. In 1947, three unions were in existence: the Peasant Cultivators Union with 284 members, the General Workers Union with 472 members and the Growers Union with 50 members.[43] By 1948, only the St Vincent General Workers Union was functioning. It had a total membership of 1,207 by the end of the year.[44]

Labour issues naturally went beyond the formation of unions, and activity took place both at the executive level and through the SWMA, both within and outside the legislature. The association brought the grievances of workers before the appropriate bodies. At a meeting of the executive council on 19 February 1937, the representatives of the Labour Party took the grievances of workers from Chateaubelair before the administrator. He was informed that representatives of the workers came to Kingstown on 17 February "in a rather excitable state to complain of treatment dealt out to them by MacDonald the owner of several of the estates on the Leeward District". The statement of the labourers was presented.

> We are in a terrible state of distress. We are more oppressed than ever by Mr. MacDonald since the introduction of the Minimum Wage Bill. Before this bill was introduced pasturage for our cattle was 1 shilling per month, now we are charged one shilling and six pence per month; pigs formerly free now six pence per month; goats formerly free now six pence per month; sheep formerly free now six pence per month. Formerly we paid no rent for the estate land where we have our houses, now we are made to pay one shilling per month. Formerly we got 10 days work in a month at 11 pence per day, now we get only 5 days work in a month . . . We have no land to work so as to help ourselves, though there are acres of land lying uncultivated. We scarcely have food to eat. . . . There is no other estate to go to look for work. We have to hire breadfruit trees to get something to eat. Mr. MacDonald charges us in proportion as the trees bear. Not long ago, he was about to ship bananas and a half hand of ripe grains, 8 to 9 dropped – a labourer in the banana gang picked them up and he was charged 60 cents.

The administrator agreed that the government should take definite action to deal with the situation and felt that they should try to "ascertain whether Mr. MacDonald would sell some of his estates, especially Petit Bordel and Sharpes".[45]

The Labour Party also presented to the administrator, in 1940, complaints from workers at the fifteen-hundred-acre Grand Sable estate, one of the largest estates in the colony. It had been the custom for permanent workers to get provision grounds rent free. According to the *Times* of 17 February 1940, "It is this practice which has saved many of our people from dying of starvation or openly committing crimes. And when it is remembered that in some months of the year, many if not most, of the labourers get only from 3 to 6 days work averaging 30 cents a day on which to feed and clothe himself, wife and children, one wonders how they manage to exist."

The labourers at the Grand Sable estate refused to continue working following allegations that Child had given notice to them to give up the mountain lots which they had been using rent free. It was also stated that he refused to increase their pay for digging arrowroot.[46] Workers at the Camden Park estate had gone on strike because the task allotted to them was considered too great. Their case was taken to the SWMA, which met with one of the owners of the estate at the office of the attorney general and had the matter settled.[47]

The newspapers regularly took up the plight of workers, and McIntosh also used the papers to continue to voice the workers' concerns, as he did in an article in the *Times* on 22 July 1939. He referred to the terrible conditions in the Leeward area, where persons were unable to get sufficient work and also lacked land:

> If they go on these idle lands and pick wild yams to eat they are prosecuted; if they get something and they try to get a few sticks to cook it they are prosecuted; and so these charges continue. It is often heart rending to see the victims of such charges as larceny of a coconut, larceny of mangoes, larceny of breadfruit, larceny of firewood, larceny of wild yams; and what must I consider the Labour Commissioner to be doing; I have not seen him bring any charge for larceny of labour.

And so the SWMA fought the struggle on behalf of workers both in and out of the legislative council. The colonial authorities remained conscious of what had happened in 1935, and so the Labour Party's relationship with the working people outside of the legislative council served to exert pressure on the government. It is not clear why the SWMA was so slow to get trade unions started, for, certainly, the 1939 ordinance had given some measure of protection.[48]

As early as 25 August 1937, the executive council dealt with the appointment of a labour commissioner. It noted that similar appointments were made in other colonies. It recognized that certain questions related to labour required investigation and noted the lack of adequate machinery for addressing workers' grievances. Ordinance No. 27 of 1937 provided for the appointment of a labour commissioner and, by 1938, an appointment was made. The *Colonial Office Annual Report* of 1938 commented positively on the work of the labour commissioner, saying that it ensured "full ventilation of the grievances of labourers" and provided government with detailed information about labour conditions and possible remedies. Provision was made for staffing the Labour Department with other assistants, with the duties and obligations of the commissioner to be decided by the governor, who was also responsible for the appointment of a labour advisory board that was to advise on all questions related to labour.

The duties of labour officers were pointed out – the promotion of good industrial relations; mediation in trade disputes; collection of information relating to wage rates, hours of labour and working conditions; the compilation of statistics relevant to working-class expenditure; and the construction of living index figures. Also singled out was the need to examine conditions under which manual labourers were recruited for work overseas and to assist trade unions in promoting and maintaining good industrial relations. Officers saw 718 persons in 1947; 268 enquiries were made regarding local employment, 193 about termination of services without notice or payment of wages, and 65 about employment in Aruba.[49]

The establishment of these structures and machinery, and the general climate that was being created, were clearly having a great impact. In November 1947, the St Vincent Planters Association made a voluntary decision to increase the wage rates of agricultural workers. On 23 March 1947, the Labour Advisory Board agreed to increase prevailing rates for unskilled workers employed by the government. In a notice informing of this agreement to increase rates, the labour commissioner, R. Nicholas Jack, urged other employers to comply with the set rates.[50]

The workmen's compensation ordinance had become a reality, after having been in committee stage since 1934. The Workmen's Compensation (Amendment) Ordinance No. 5 of 1949 amended Ordinance No. 21 of 1939 and provided for increased compensation for injuries sustained by workmen during the course of their employment.[51] The Minimum Wage Ordinance was also being implemented. In 1940, five planters were convicted and fined one pound each for breach of the ordinance.[52] The Trade Disputes (Arbitration and Inquiry) Ordinance 1940 allowed for settlement of trade disputes by arbitration tribunals and for the appointment of boards of inquiry to investigate the causes and circumstances of existing or apprehended disputes. These, of course, were similar to legislation enacted throughout the British West Indies in the period 1938–45.

Industrial disputes continued, nevertheless, with a strike by male employees at the St Vincent Cooperative Arrowroot Association on 22 February 1949. The Labour Department, however, assisted in bringing about a settlement. In that same year, the department reported that 612 persons had sought their assistance. The situation was, in any event, certainly an improvement on what it was in 1938, when Orde Brown made the following observation:

> Local legislation again, was frequently lacking in provisions for the establishment of trade unions on modern lines and such bodies as came into existence were in consequence generally unregistered and uncontrolled; they were subject to no requirements as to election of officers, management or auditing of accounts, so that in certain instances members speedily grew dissatisfied with the way in which affairs were controlled and left the organisation in disgust, the whole movement being perfectly discredited.[53]

Much had undoubtedly changed since 1935, and trade unions were becoming a part of the social and economic landscape. The *Vincentian*, however, seemed not to have been impressed with developments within the trade union movement. On 25 December 1950, it commented, "It is nevertheless disappointing that the Trade Union movement in St Vincent appears to make no reasonable progress, as organised labour assists everyone but disorganised labour is a help to no one." Contrary to what the *Vincentian* said, the labour movement, as opposed to the trade union movement, was becoming a formidable political force. The SWMA sought first the political kingdom and then addressed itself to the formation of a viable labour movement. Their focus on the legislature might have taken away from the organization and strong development of the unions. This left gaps in the struggle outside the legislative chamber.

Labour matters became part of the programme of the colonial government, but the work of the SWMA, in the legislative council and outside, helped to keep the pressure on the executive to give urgent attention to addressing some of the raised issues. A giant leap was made in 1951 when a newly formed trade union, the United Workers Peasants and Ratepayers Union, capitalized on the opportunities presented by the pending introduction of adult suffrage to enter formal politics and to further lift the profile of workers. This, however, will be addressed in the next chapter.

THE STRUGGLE OF THE SHAKERS FOR THE RIGHT TO PRACTISE THEIR RELIGION

The issue that proved most difficult to get the colonial authorities to accept was that of the recognition of the Shaker religion, which had been prohibited since 1912. The concern here was with the struggle led by the SWMA and its political arm for repeal of the 1912 Shakerism Prohibition Ordinance. McIntosh gave special attention to it, not only struggling in the legislature but also using newspapers and other public forums to pursue that struggle. While Albert Gomes began overtures to the Shouters in 1949 in return for their votes, in St Vincent, when McIntosh began to struggle on their behalf, the Shakers were among that sector of the population that was not politically enfranchised.[54] Gomes, of course, had long championed local culture.

The reality of ninety-four prosecutions in 1934 was earth-shattering. The Shakers felt that they were, in fact, being persecuted. A member of the religion later reflected on this in an interview with Jeannette Henney:

> The police used to persecute us like in the days of Saul. At meetings you couldn't shout. They would imprison you, take you under arrest and make a case, One Sunday there was a baptism and from it they were in a meeting. Some Police arrest and beat them. They had little carts. They had handcuffed them and thrown them in the carts like beasts. Some got away and ran and hide. Some got six months, nine months, 4 years.[55]

This was the environment in which the new legislators took up the cause of the religion of the working people. The Shakers had been doing whatever they were able to, in an effort to protest what they considered religious persecution and the violation of their right to worship. In one case, this involved sending a petition to the king. The petition was signed by Hilton Fiffe of Barrouallie, who had suffered prosecution in 1913 and 1933 and was still practising the religion in 1934.[56]

A new phase started with the control of the elected side of the legislative council by McIntosh and his Labour Party. McIntosh took revocation of the

1912 Shaker Prohibition Ordinance very personally and vigorously led his organization's efforts to have it removed from the statute books. Members of the Shaker religion were mostly poor and not among those qualified to vote in elections. The struggle by McIntosh and his colleagues to revoke the ordinance banning the Shaker religion was among the list of issues they were prepared to champion. That issue was brought before the legislative council but was also taken to the general public through a series of articles in newspapers and advocacy at other public forums. McIntosh, who led the struggle, went as far as allowing a Shaker prayer meeting to take place in his yard at Paul's Lot, at a time when its practice was forbidden in Kingstown.[57] He gave notice of his intention to bring the issue of repeal of the ordinance before the legislative council. The executive council meeting of 3 April 1939 discussed the motion for repeal of the ordinance that was to be moved by McIntosh at the next meeting of the legislative council. The following decision was taken:

> In view of the fact that it was generally known that the practice of Shakerism fre-
> quently caused ill effects to a number of its followers; and that under the operation
> of the present law the practice has been greatly diminished . . . the general feeling of
> Honourable members was that it would be unwise to amend any of the provisions
> of the existing law with a view to allowing the practice of Shakerism.

There was therefore to be no change to the existing law.[58]

The bill that was introduced on 13 April 1939, under McIntosh's name, read as follows: "That Government be requested to repeal the Shakerism Prohibition Ordinance, chapter 172 of October 1, 1912, pg. 1091 of the Revised Edition (1926) of the laws of St Vincent." Speaking on the motion, McIntosh felt that the ordinance created a blot on the statute book. It amounted, in his view, to placing hardships on a set of people because they were poor. He argued that, under the British constitution, people had a right to serve God as they thought fit. In response to the charge about the mental effects of the religion, he noted that there were "few if any Shakers among the people at the Mental Asylum". But then, he added, "fanatics of any religion would go out of their mind". Many were the times, he argued, when they were holding ordinary prayer meetings and had been arrested by the police. He noted that the ordinance did not define exactly what was meant by the practice of Shakerism and that it was left in the hands of the magistrates to make that decision. The ordinance, he felt, was an ancient relic designed to prevent persons considered ignorant from worship-ping as they pleased.

The motion was seconded by the member for the Grenadines, who argued that if the members were committing crimes, they could be dealt with under the common law. Other elected members stood with McIntosh in support of the motion. The member for South Windward cited the case of a woman whom the authorities suspected of indulging in Shakerism in an effort to cure her ill husband. The police went into her house, found her praying at her husband's side and were disappointed but proceeded to arrest her, resulting in her being fined by the magistrate.

Nominated member A.M. Punnett supported freedom of worship but not, he argued, the case of the Shakers, who, in his opinion, went to extremes. The acting attorney general also spoke against the motion, and, in reference to the South Windward case, he said that there was a certain amount of jumping up and noise which, under the ordinance, was enough to have the person charged. McIntosh, in winding up the debate, said that "he believed that those who practised Shakerism had a very high conception of God and how to serve him and should not be prevented from worshipping in the manner which was peculiar to their religion".

The vote went in favour of the motion, six votes to four, with one of the nominated members, Fraser, voting for the motion, something that was unexpected from the nominated bench.[59] The political atmosphere had certainly changed.

In an article in the *Times* of 28 October 1939, McIntosh defended his motion and was critical of the "un-British law in a British colony", as he described it. The law, he stated, did not define a "Shaker meeting" and left it to the police to take before the magistrate persons they felt inclined to charge. It affected innocent persons who, through curiosity, might have been drawn to the meetings and could possibly be charged. He objected strongly to the denial of the right of appeal and emphasized the hardships imposed on "the oppressed working class people of the colony for trying to serve God as their only consolation for the half starved, naked, miserable and deplorable condition in which they have been kept". He noted that his motion was carried by a majority and declared that all that was left was for the government to introduce and pass a bill giving effect to the motion.

A new feature, he argued, was the role of the established churches, whose clergy realized that the so-called Shakers comprised "a very large section of the community". Since the Shakers were prevented from serving God as they pleased, and they assisted in the upkeep of those churches, the ministers were more motivated to "save their collections" than in saving souls. He referred to

a petition organized by the churches that defended the existing ordinance, and
was meant to coerce innocent persons into signing. McIntosh drew attention
to the Second World War that was in progress and felt that the people's loyalty
was unquestioned. If these persons were denied their right to serve God, "how
are they to be expected to fight outside aggression"?[60]

While the newspapers had strongly supported the passage of the Shakerism
Prohibition Ordinance in 1912, following the riots, by 1939, public opinion had
changed radically, and two of the colony's three newspapers strongly supported
the efforts to have the ordinance repealed.[61] The *Investigator* of 25 November
and 2 December 1939 supported repeal. The *Times* provided space for McIntosh
to argue his case before the public.

The *Vincentian*, known for reflecting the planters' position, dealt with the
issue of repeal in its editorials of 2 and 9 September 1939. It made much of the
fact that the ordinance had the royal assent and that the secretary of state was
satisfied with it but that the member for Kingstown desired to have it repealed,
anyhow. It was as if the satisfaction of the Colonial Office and royal assent
precluded any objection from persons in the colonies. The paper went further
and referred to what was happening as representing a "misguided idea of the
meaning and limits of liberty and freedom". It was of the view that advances
in science provided abundant evidence of the morally degrading and mentally
unbalancing effect. The paper warned that if McIntosh succeeded in his efforts
to have the ordinance repealed, he could possibly go on to introduce bills for
ordinances "to remove the censoring of films, the banning of undesirable literature, [and] prosecutions under the law for the use of indecent language",
which, in reality, meant recommendation for a period of unchecked licence in
every department of life. It urged the government to stand firm "and allow no
specious arguments adduced by any unreasoning and unreasonable politicians"
who aimed mostly "to pander to the whims of the masses".[62] The *Vincentian*
had certainly lost touch with the sentiments of the times.

The churches, which strongly supported the ordinance, were quick to react
to the changing circumstances. In a letter dated 19 June 1939, the Clergymen's
Fellowship expressed surprise and regret that the legislative council had, by
majority vote, recommended repeal. They considered it a "retrograde" step,
since the ordinance had been passed to prevent practices that had a "pernicious
and demoralising effect upon the colony". That was, in their view, a fact that
had not changed.[63]

On 23 June 1939, McIntosh wrote to the clerk of the legislative council indicating that, in an effort to give effect to the resolution, he was going to present a motion "for the introduction and first reading of a Bill for an Ordinance to repeal the Shakerism Prohibition Ordinance".[64] On the following day, 24 June, the executive council discussed the bill presented by McIntosh and the letter from the Clergymen's Fellowship. It was agreed that the government would adhere to its previous position – against any change to the ordinance – taken at a meeting of the council on 3 April.[65] The council also agreed to reply to the letter from the Clergymen's Fellowship, informing them that their views were noted and that, following the next meeting of the legislative council, when the motion was to be brought before them, they would communicate further with the fellowship.[66]

At a later meeting, on 29 September 1939, the executive council confirmed its decision to not support an appeal. It felt it necessary to take into account what was likely to be the view of the imperial government. If the bill was passed by a majority vote, the governor's assent was to be withheld. It was prepared, however, to have an amendment to allow the right of appeal.[67]

In a letter of 16 October 1939, Administrator Bain Gray explained to Governor Popham what was likely to happen with McIntosh's motion when it was introduced in the legislative council:

> It is probable that the Members of Council will be equally divided in regard to this subject – all the elected members voting for the Bill and the ex-officio and the nominated members voting against it. The nominated member who voted previously for the motion to repeal is absent on leave, and the member now filling his place has intimated that he will vote against it. Should this occur, I propose subject to any instructions from Your Excellency, to give a casting vote against the Bill, in view of the advice of the Executive Council which is strongly against the repeal of this Ordinance, and which, so far as I can ascertain, represents the majority of responsible opinion in this Colony.[68]

Secretary of state Malcolm MacDonald disagreed with any attempt to repeal or amend the ordinance and wanted that position secured by the casting vote of the administrator or by the governor's power of veto.[69]

The Shakers appeared to have become emboldened by the new environment and provided support to the SWMA. In October 1939, two worship meetings were actually held in Kingstown on two consecutive Sundays. One, which the chief of police described as "disgusting and savage", was held in an open yard in Paul's Lot. The second was more problematic for the chief of police because it was held in McIntosh's yard. He consulted the attorney general and took no action, based on the advice given to him.[70]

The *Times* reported on an interesting case involving some Shakers who were taken to court in June 1940 at Barrouallie "for practising Shakerism". The report stated that the Shakers got the "spirit" and started shaking in court. An embarrassed Magistrate Cox warned them to give up the practice "as he felt it was definitely injurious to themselves". After cautioning them, he dismissed the case.[71] McIntosh appears to have been the person who instigated that action of "shaking". At a meeting of the legislative council on 5 October 1950, he stated

> There have been several attempts to take these so-called Shakers before the Magistrate, and hitherto there have been many prosecutions. I remember once about 40 of these people were hounded down and brought to Barrouallie for prosecution. I went down to Barrouallie and asked the people; "Are you conscientious that this is the way you should serve God?" And when they said "yes", I told them "If you are arrested it will be nothing more than being a martyr to your cause, and if you are put in prison there is nothing to prevent you from shaking there." And those 40 people shook in the Court House at Barrouallie and were prepared to shake in prison. . . . The case was dismissed.[72]

The position of the executive council, supported by the secretary of state, to use either the casting vote of the administrator or the power of veto of the governor to frustrate the possibility of a majority vote demonstrated to elected members of council the obstacles colonial rule and the existing constitution presented to them. This may have delayed McIntosh's introduction of the motion that he had pledged to present. After the success of his resolution on 3 April 1939, he was of the view that it was then up to the government to pass a motion in conformity with the wishes of council.

McIntosh continued to use the newspapers to build public support. The Anglican bishop of the Windward Islands appeared to have broken ranks with the clergy of the other churches. In a letter dated 14 January 1945, he expressed his views on "Shakerism" to the administrator, based, he said, on a request by someone to do so. He was of the view that no magistrate should have the power "to decide what is or is not 'Shakerism'". He should only deal with offences that came within the orbit of the common law. Furthermore, he felt that repressive measures were counterproductive and he never did "believe that it does good to drive any practice underground if it can be avoided".[73]

Administrator W.F. Coutts, who assumed office in 1949, had some doubts and concerns about "Shakerism" but was unsure about the best method of dealing with it. Based on discussion with Archdeacon R.S. Maxwell, recommendations from the clergy were to be solicited, with the administrator initially being kept out of the discussion.[74] The clergy, following a meeting on 27 September 1949, presented to Coutts a memorandum prepared by E.A. Pitt of the Methodist Church. Pitt described the religion as a "subtle attempt to revive an original primitive African religion" and saw it as a "symbol of daring excursions into the esoteric and occult". He referred to free sexual intercourse at the "Mourning Ground" and of polygamy and insanitary conditions.[75]

The clergy recommended that "Cult" houses be examined with respect to the "Sanitary conditions and Disorderly Houses" regulations.[76] It was felt that, with regard to meetings and noises at night, the law prohibiting disturbances and nuisances should be more strictly enforced. It maintained its position that a high percentage of inmates of the mental asylum were Shakers and asked that the government request statistical information to confirm that.[77]

The debates reflected the changed political climate in a situation where the number of persons enfranchised remained extremely small. This is precisely why McIntosh and his association took their struggle outside the legislative council. The governor had the power to veto bills, and the administrator still had a casting vote, but the colonial authorities were quite aware of the new atmosphere and tried to discredit the movement in the public sphere. The churches were useful in allowing the authorities to create the impression that they were largely responding to the clergy's outrage and to what they considered "responsible public opinion".

The administrator, reacting to the clergy, sought medical data from the medical superintendent and senior medical officer. The effort to revive the old issue of associating Shakerism with mental derangement was not helped by the responses from the medical personnel. There was a relative increase in the number of inmates known to be Shakers, but there was nothing to show that they constituted a high percentage of the total. Nor could they confirm that Shaker leaders professed to possess healing powers.[78]

The opinion of the magistrates was also solicited. Coutts, convinced that Shakerism was on the increase, sought recommendations to keep it "in bounds without actually suppressing it". This was an interesting development which reflected not only Administrator Coutts's uncertainty but also the changed circumstances confronting him. Magistrate Dasent urged that they "establish and encourage group work as the leading factor of rural reconstruction" and wanted the existing churches to simplify their forms of worship. He did not think that there was any "appreciable" increase in "Shakerism" and was of the view that powers given to the police under the ordinance were sufficient to deal with the problem.[79]

The response from the magistrates was pointing in the direction of social reconstruction through social welfare. Complementing this was a letter from J. Griffiths of the Colonial Office to Governor Arundell stating that Pitt's submission was "couched in exaggerated terms". What was needed was an objective study. He urged caution, to avoid any charge of religious persecution, and wanted the local authorities to ensure public support. The emphasis on the religion's association with mental derangement was one way of trying to avoid the charge of religious repression. Griffith pointed also to the social welfare perspective. He argued for the need to provide alternative outlets by "the organisation of community life, recreation (especially community singing and music making) and education and the provision of village halls".[80] Some of its detractors still believed that the religion was a result of ignorance and that, with a more "enlightened" atmosphere, Shakerism would disappear.

McIntosh, his colleagues, the Shakers and others who were involved in the struggle decided on a new strategy. Since the ordinance was directed at "Shakerism", with no clear definition of what it was, they decided to stake their luck on a change of name. At a meeting of members of the religion, a decision was taken to form what they called the Spiritual Baptist Church. As part of the new strategy, one of its aims was to put an end to Shakerism. In 1949, the Spiritual Baptists were allowed to hold a "patronal festival" in Georgetown in honour of their patron saint, John the Baptist. They held a successful ceremony at which about two thousand persons attended, as was acknowledged by the police. In the following year, 1950, another application was made to hold a march in Kingstown. This was denied and drew the anger of McIntosh, who decided to take the matter once more before the legislative council. On 17 July 1950, McIntosh gave notice of a motion in the legislative council.[81]

He submitted twenty-four questions, twelve of them dealing with Shakerism. In advising the administrator on answers to the questions, the superintendent of police seems to have hit on the strategy supposedly being employed by McIntosh. He warned the administrator that "most of the questions are framed in an ambiguous manner, the simple answer to which will tend to accept the correctness of the premise".[82]

One of the questions sought reasons why the Spiritual Baptists were given permission in 1949 to hold a patronal festival in Georgetown but were denied permission for a similar festival in Kingstown the following year. He wanted to know under what law they were refused permission.[83] The administrator acknowledged the peaceful procession in Georgetown but argued that bystanders openly declared that the participants were "Shakers". The police presence was as "guardians of law and order", to prevent any breaches of peace. There was also, in his view, no certainty that the majority of persons attending were members. Permission was denied for the procession in 1950 because nothing was known of the Spiritual Baptists except that they were commonly regarded as Shakers. They could not grant permission to an unknown, unorganized group "to take charge of Kingstown for two hours for unspecified purposes". If, as was commonly believed, they were Shakers operating under a different name, "there was reason to apprehend a breach of the peace, namely that a 'Shakers Meeting' as forbidden by law, might arise".

McIntosh's request to have an amendment to a new motion that he had submitted was accepted. The original motion had called on the legislative council to "put forward the people's petition to the Secretary of State for the Colonies for the removal of the Superintendent of Police and His Honour the Administrator before these depressed people, finding no relief from these disadvantages resort to desperation for relief". The amended motion read "Be it resolved that Government give such recognition to this body as required by law, and thus cause education along the lines to be given and thereby help Government to stamp out 'Shakerism'."[84] This was in keeping with the new strategy.

McIntosh argued that "any vagrant or criminal from America can come here and set up a religious body and is given recognition by Government, but when the people of St Vincent say we have a right as others to form a religion of our own, they are denied that right". He seemed bent on exposing and frustrating the administration. Given the official view that the Spiritual Baptists were Shakers under a new name, a decision was taken to change the name again – to "Christian Pilgrims". What he was finally seeking was to have the religion recognized through the grant of a marriage licence, and there was, he felt, no reason why the government should not be able to provide it. What was at stake was the right to worship and, under the new strategy, the name did not really matter.

One of the problems that the Labour Party faced at that time was a division within its ranks. It appeared, too, that the original motion did not have the support of all the members, for, indeed, when the representative for the Lee-ward constituency rose to second the motion, he said that, with the amendment of the motion, "I find myself one hundred percent in agreement with him", a reference to McIntosh. He questioned the denial of the Shakers' right to wor-ship in the way they wanted to and agreed with the mover of the motion that "most of the people are poverty-stricken, and since there is a certain amount of dissatisfaction, religion is the best means whereby these people can find a certain amount of comfort and satisfaction".

Support came from elected members for North Windward and Leeward. Opposition came from nominated members E.A.C. Hughes and O.D. Brisbane. The elected member for South Windward, Bonadie, who was at odds with his leader, reminded the administrator of the great trust he had in his hands in protecting the public morals. He wanted him to give serious consideration to the matter but warned that "as soon as you give recognition to bodies such as this, you will find hosts of applications coming in, and it may be that many will be from those who wish to indulge in practices".[85] He ended his contribution by warning the administrator to be cautious about any application "made by these people".

McIntosh remained firm. In rounding up the debate, he warned them, "I will come here a million times if necessary and I am going to come until we get what we want, and I tell you this much, if we don't get it in one way we will get it in another way." He saw no reason "why a lunatic of a Superintendent of Police should stop them". On being warned that his remark was out of order, he informed the president that he had already made the remark; moreover, he did not understand why the administrator had colluded with the superintendent of police.

McIntosh, in referring to a petition which he said the members of his "renamed" church were prepared to sign, said that if they were denied the right of religious freedom, he was prepared to repeat the words of the poem by the Jamaican Claude McKay, "If we must die, Oh let us nobly die so that the very monsters we defy shall be constrained to honour us, though dead." The council voted against the motion, with three persons supporting it, four against and one abstention.[86]

Following the defeat of the motion, the strategy decided on was to submit an application for the granting of a marriage licence. On 23 April 1951, McDonald Williams, who was the chief pastor of the Christian Pilgrim Church, submitted to Coutts an application for a licence to be a marriage officer. He informed him that there were three couples waiting to be married and hoped for a favourable response to his request.[87]

At an executive council meeting on 4 May 1951, Williams's application was considered. It was approved on condition that he could satisfy the Crown attorney and registrar that he had the capacity, educationally, to perform the duties involved. The licence, if granted, was to be reviewed from time to time. Williams was asked to arrange to be interviewed by the Crown attorney and registrar.[88]

Political and constitutional developments intervened at this point, because the country was beginning to prepare itself for the first elections under adult suffrage. The Labour Party was voted out of office at the elections held in 1951, and a new political constitution that enfranchised all adults over twenty-one years of age came into being. The struggle for the repeal of the ordinance and the role played by McIntosh and the members of the SWMA, both in the legislative council and outside, demonstrated the changed political circumstances, although constitutional constraints continued to block them. Even though the colonial constitution stifled the move to abolish the ordinance, colonial officials had begun to tread cautiously. The old arguments seemed out of place. It was, however, not until 1965 that the ordinance was finally revoked.

EDUCATION

One of the matters about which there was broad agreement with the colonial authorities was the necessity of pinning any reforms in education to an improvement in the social conditions of the people. The 1932 Commission on Education had made that link, but, up to the time of the release of the Moyne report, not much progress had been made in bettering the conditions that would have facilitated the growth of education. The Moyne Commission had referred to the efforts of that earlier commission on education "to point out in what respects the efficacy of even the best system of education is dependent on the social and economic environment from which the child comes and in which he will subsequently have to make his living".[89] In 1932, an official report from the Department of Education noted that "there is not a single school which cannot be regarded as over-crowded". The situation had not improved by 1943, "since only one school has been built in the past decade and the provision in relation to the number of children of school age is therefore growing worse year by year. Many of the existing schools, moreover, are in buildings which should be condemned."[90]

In its representation to the Moyne Commission, the St Vincent Teachers Association had dealt with the socioeconomic difficulties facing the people of the country, pointing to the absence of children from school because of poverty. One of its representatives, in calling for compulsory education, argued that it must mean "more building and furnishing and food, because it is impossible to try and educate children with empty heads and empty stomachs".[91] The representatives of the SWMA acknowledged that they had not included education in their memoranda since they knew that it was a substantial part of the submission of others, clearly a reference to the teachers' association, with whom they appear to have had strong links. They discussed, however, the question of the school-leaving age and of child labour, noting that the presence of naked children seen on the streets, which the members of the commission brought to their attention, was because of poverty.[92]

The SWMA had begun to demonstrate an interest in education even before it gained representation on the legislative council. The *Times* of 22 August 1936 reported that the SWMA was offering three scholarships to secondary schools. The association had then only been in existence for about five months.

At one of the early meetings of the legislative council, McIntosh pushed for the granting of an annual or biennial scholarship "of a value not exceeding one hundred and fifty pounds per annum and tenable at the Imperial College of Tropical Agriculture, Trinidad, on conditions similar to those governing the Saint Vincent Island Scholarship". The *Investigator* stated, "We watched with keen interest the introduction in the Legislature of a motion by the Hon. G.A. McIntosh for the establishment of an agricultural scholarship and it is to the great credit of His Honour, Mr. Wright, that he not only showed ready willingness to accept the proposal but pushed it to realisation with all possible speed."

Rupert John, in commenting on this, noted:

> In presenting the motion, the Honourable Member for Kingstown said that he did not consider it necessary to say much on the subject. St Vincent he pointed out was an agricultural country, and for a number of years efforts had been frequently made to obtain scholarships for boys of St Vincent to pursue studies in agriculture at the Imperial College of Tropical Agriculture in Trinidad for the upkeep of which the St Vincent Government made its regular contributions. The main difficulty that prevented young men from St Vincent availing themselves of the opportunity offered at the College was the high cost of living in Trinidad. McIntosh, therefore, proposed that Government should relieve this difficulty, by making the provision set out in the motion.[93]

This went along with a motion for the establishment of an agricultural school.[94] It was accepted by the administrator, and efforts were made to push it through, although other matters appear to have put it on the sideline.

The Moyne Commission noted that, with education, there was, until recently, a lack of "continuous inter-colonial cooperation" and stated that where it existed was through the appointment of education commissioners for the Windward and Leeward Islands. But, at an unofficial level, a degree of international cooperation was developing in the area of education and also in other areas, particularly as the regional labour movement was beginning to look even more seriously at regional integration. The conference of the CLC had brought this out clearly.

Its statement on education should be looked at carefully since, as with other matters, it was expected that members in their individual islands would have committed themselves to the programme agreed on. At the conference, McIntosh chaired the session on education, presumably because of his interest in it. With his leader as the chair, Bonadie, the SWMA's other representative, made a presentation for that body, touching on secondary education. He "advocated greater opportunities for secondary education for the vast masses of the people at the bottom of the social structure in order that their potential ability might not be lost to the state".[95]

A land settlement policy drawn up by the Land Settlement and Development Board and adopted by the legislative council in 1946 recognized that land settlement was unlikely to succeed unless accompanied by a change in the outlook towards education by the people and in the aims and methods of education and educators. The following are extracts from the land settlement policy:

> We . . . wish to place the strongest emphasis on the crying need for education in its widest sense. Education is the one consistent prerequisite to any practical measures which may be undertaken for the economic and social development of the island. The failure of education to prepare young people for happy and successful living in the communities of which they are a part is the most serious cause for dismay, whereas the inadequacy of the facilities for education is usually the cause for expression of the greatest concern. The reason for the perplexities which now face parents and pupils, government and educators and all concerned with the product of the present educational system, seems to lie in the failure to appreciate the real nature of the economic and social aspects of the problems of life as a whole.

It was expressing the view that education must be seen in its widest sense. It urged the establishment of vocational centres that were to be geared to the needs of rural communities: "There is a very urgent need for instruction in the practical application of scientific agriculture especially for training agricultural Instructor teachers, farm and estate overseers as well as prospective farmers. We strongly recommend that a suitable training institution be established for this purpose as early as possible."[96]

With an awareness of the critical place of agriculture in the lives of the working people and particularly because of the need to make a success of the land settlement scheme, McIntosh, at a meeting of the legislative council on 30 March 1950, gave notice of a question that he proposed to ask: "Will Government make provision for lectures on agriculture to be delivered to pupils of primary schools throughout the Colony by officers on the staff of the Agricultural Department?" In education, as with so many other things, McIntosh and his colleagues, operating from a position with little formal power, raised matters that were of benefit to the working people, hoping to push for action by the executive council.

At a meeting of the legislative council on Saturday, 13 May 1950, McIntosh argued, "It is time to get down to a real social order where we will care not only for ourselves, not only for our pockets, not only for our bank accounts and what we can accumulate; but for the general good of the masses and to bring them up physically, educationally and socially." Again, education was seen as being central to the betterment of the working people.

One of the areas to which the association paid a great deal of attention was compulsory education. This it saw in the context of discussions that were taking place about secondary education. As has been pointed out before, its struggles were carried out through any medium available and not limited to the halls of the legislative council. Again, McIntosh took the leading role in pushing its views, and he used the newspapers for this, responding to views expressed by the middle class. In a letter to the *Vincentian* on 11 June 1949, he jumped into the argument about education, accusing that section of the community of only looking after its own interests. He wrote, "So much piffle has been given out recently on the question of free or cheap Secondary Education by a section of the community whose interest in St Vincent appears to remain centred on just what concerns themselves, their families and their friends. Selfish interest seems to blind them and in any case if you touch their pockets you blow their brains and reason ceases to appeal to them."

While the SWMA advocated greater opportunities for secondary education, as was expressed by Bonadie at the conference of the CLC, its focus was clearly on people at "the bottom of the social structure", since it was felt that their potential should not be lost to the colony. In his letter to the *Vincentian*, referred to earlier, McIntosh felt that the emphasis should really be on compulsory education so that the children of poor parents would be in a position to benefit from secondary education. He was extremely concerned about the bias in the education system towards secondary education. This was seen in a question he asked at a meeting of the legislative council on 28 April 1949: "In view of the fact that there are at present six thousand children in this colony of school going age who do not attend school will Government examine the possibility of making primary education compulsory in this colony?"

The answer given was to the effect that compulsory education was not possible since there was insufficient accommodation for most of the children; in fact, only half of the children of school age could have been accommodated. McIntosh, in pressing his argument for greater emphasis to be placed on primary education, was counting on the support of "the parents of nineteen thousand hard working but poor Vincentians" in an effort to get the government to raise the standard of education for the benefit of all, as opposed to promoting the interest of four hundred children of middle-class parentage at secondary schools.[97] These parents on whose support he was depending were clearly not persons who were entitled to vote under the limited suffrage that existed at that time, but the policy of the SWMA was always to mobilize the voices outside the legislative council to exert pressure on those who had to make the final decision.

He tried to show clearly the bias in the education system. Four hundred children attended the existing secondary schools, while those who did not attend school at all amounted to six thousand who "are not considered at all; nobody cares for them, they remain the potential criminals of tomorrow". This, he suggested, should be the concern of the government.[98]

He argued that "without a good foundation in primary education, the money spent on secondary will have been completely lost". The strategy was to lift the consciousness of the working people and to get them to exert extra-parliamentary pressure, remembering that the riots of 1935 were still on the minds of the colonial authorities and planter elite who sat on the executive council.

The legislative council was used also to support the struggles of teachers. When the Moyne Commission visited St Vincent at the end of 1938, concerns were raised about clause 69 of the Education Code, which representatives of the Teachers Union stated was brought in after the riots, teachers having been singled out as among the ringleaders in the riots. H.E.A. Daisley, a member of the committee meeting with the commission, had been one of the persons targeted following the riots. The code stated:

> No teacher shall engage in any business or occupation that may interfere with his duty as a teacher. He shall not act as Editor of a newspaper, or take part directly or indirectly in the management thereof or contribute anonymously thereto, or be a member of an association organised mainly for political purposes or publish in any manner anything which may be properly regarded as of a political nature. He may, however, publish signed articles upon subjects of general interest.[99]

The Labour Party raised matters related to the political rights of teachers and had to fight some matters in council. The case of Ebenezer Duncan, who later became general secretary of the SWMA, stands out. Duncan, who was head teacher of the Kingstown Methodist School, was also editor of the *Investigator*, which he founded in 1929. He was, moreover, before the riots, a member of the RGA, serving at one time as its secretary. He was a staunch member of the Methodist Church and a lay preacher. The matter involving Duncan actually started before the riots.

On 21 April 1934, the inspector of schools, Theobalds, after a visit to the school, tabled what was considered a bad report through entries he made in the Visitors' Book. The report related to discrepancies in the recording of attendees at school on that day, the discipline of the children and their failure to answer adequately a test that he had given them. Duncan, whose school was outstanding in the performance of its students,[100] drew the attention of the school manager and the superintendent minister of the Methodist Church to the entry and questioned the truth of the allegations made. Later, it was found by the Board of Education that the entry had been altered by the inspector of schools.[101] The committee of management of the school, after investigating the matter, recommended to the Board of Education that Duncan be transferred to a school at Westwood, seventeen miles from Kingstown.

This was accepted by the board. The RGA made representation to the Board of Education on his behalf. Following the association's representation, the Board of Education backed away from accepting the church's recommendation, based on evidence presented that was not brought before it on its 14 July meeting. It urged the withdrawal of the transfer, pending the return to the colony of the manager of the school and the inspector of schools. They felt that there was not sufficient evidence to justify "the removal from his post".[102] The management committee disagreed.

Duncan, in any event, refused to accept the transfer since it would have created problems with the management of his newspaper. He refused to hand over the keys, citing the position of the board. He opened the school on the following Monday and worked without being challenged. On Tuesday, two members of the management committee went to the school and gave the teachers and children a holiday for the rest of the week. Their demand for the keys was again rejected, Duncan indicating that he was continuing to accept the board's notice on a legal point.

The management committee's recommendation for his dismissal was ultimately accepted by the board and taken through its necessary stages to the council and the governor-in-council. This, it would appear, caused divisions within the church. The newspapers took up the issue and raised strong protests, calling for payment of pension or other forms of compensation. One of the matters at issue here was the complex relation between the churches, in their capacity as managers of their denominational schools, and the education authorities. The Moyne Commission had later drawn attention to that relationship, acknowledging that criticisms were raised about the role of the church, with a recommendation that the government should assume full responsibility. It indicated that some of the complaints brought to them appeared justifiable. Among those levelling criticisms were representatives of the teachers' association. A note of caution was, however, issued by the commissioners. They felt that the denominational system had wide support, and its abolition was likely to create "serious opposition". They argued, too, that the West Indies lacked "those factors and traditions which elsewhere make for social cohesiveness and a sense of membership of a community". The role of the churches, under those circumstances, was considered to be important and critical. They stated, "Almost the sole integrating agency has been the religious influence exercised by the Churches. Religion plays an important part in the life of a large proportion of the population and if, as we hope, education is to perform its proper function of the creation and transmission and continual improvement of a social tradition, it would be most unwise to cut it completely adrift from the Churches."[103]

The RGA had taken to Duncan's defence, but there were no voices in the legislative council, at that time, that would have given Duncan and those who pushed his cause the needed support. The matter was brought to the legislative council in April 1939 in the form of a motion moved by the leader of the Labour Party. It is not clear why this was only done in 1939. By that time, the issue of his reinstatement would not have been a serious demand, so the emphasis was then on making sure he was adequately compensated for the time he served as head teacher. The motion read as follows:

> Whereas Mr. Ebenezer Duncan has served the Colony as Head Teacher with credit and satisfaction; And whereas there has not been found any cause to justify his being denied the rights, claims or privileges allowed Teachers under the provisions of the Head Teachers' Pension Ordinance; Be it therefore resolved that this Legislative Council of the Colony of St Vincent records its recognition of the efficient and satisfactory public service of Mr. Duncan as Head Teacher in the Colony and of his claim to the rights or privileges accorded all teachers under the provisions of the Head Teachers Ordinance; And be it further resolved that this Council recommends to the Government that Mr. Duncan be granted all considerations, rights or privileges as are justly his due under the provisions of the Head Teachers Pensions Ordinance, having regard to the period of 16 years he would have served had he been allowed to serve to the time for his retirement at 60 years of age.[104]

In introducing the motion, McIntosh related the circumstances that led to Duncan's dismissal and of the hardship imposed on him. The motion had the support of the elected members of the legislative council and one nominated member, Fraser. The executive council, at a meeting on 2 June 1939, agreed that

> Mr. Duncan be granted an ex-gratia payment equivalent to the gratuity for which he would have been eligible under the provisions of the Head Teachers' Pensions Ordinance, less a deduction of 5 percent as a penal measure, it being made clear to him that by dismissal he had forfeited his privileges under the Ordinance and that the gratuity was given purely as an act of grace in respect of his previous satisfactory service.

The governor gave his assent.[105]

Even before the case of Duncan, the Labour Party, through its leader, had, in 1938, made an intervention in the legislative council on behalf of another teacher, B.R. James, who was trying to secure a pension. James, who was a former head teacher of the Belair Anglican School, did not appear to have a particular problem with the establishment but seemed to have left before reaching the pensionable age. The motion moved by McIntosh was discussed at the next meeting of the executive council, when a decision was made to adhere to the council's last decision on the matter, "that Mr. James be given ex-gratia a modified gratuity amounting to £47.10, a decision to which His Excellency concurred".[106]

Duncan, as editor of a newspaper that was quite critical of the government, was obviously a target, especially due to the administration's view that members of the RGA were among the co-conspirators responsible for the riots. The issues involving the teachers were highlighted because of the important role teachers played in the Vincentian society, given the fact that, in 1931, only 41 per cent of the people were able to read or write and 2 per cent able to read only.[107] The SWMA kept the education system in focus and tried to monitor any changes that they felt might not be in the best interest of the people of the country. They organized a mass "monster" meeting at the market square on 9 May 1938 to make clear to the government their opposition to changes which the authorities appeared to have been contemplating. The main person behind the organization of the meeting was Cato, its secretary. Also speaking at the meeting, to a crowd which the newspapers estimated at two thousand, were other members of the association, Nanton and Bonadie. Two resolutions were passed at the meeting protesting against the appointment of a director or inspector of schools and any drastic alterations in the education system.[108]

In explaining the circumstances which led to the resolutions, they noted that changes suggested by H.W. Stokes, junior education commissioner, were likely to have ill effects on the colony. The *Times* had, earlier, in its editorial of 16 April 1938, strongly criticized the changes, under the caption "Suggestions of Alteration in Education a Farce – No Headmaster of the Grammar School, No Headmistress of the Girls High School, No Inspector of Schools". The *Times* explained its position:

> There is one unmistakable motive running through every suggestion and that is the appointment of a Superintendent or Director of Education who will be supposed to be an authority on Education and who will combine in his mighty self the post of Headmaster of the Grammar School, Headmistress of the Girls High School, Inspector of Schools, Trainer of Teachers etc. . . . . Who has ever heard of a School without a Headmaster or a Headmistress? The idea is preposterous.

The editorial described what was being contemplated as nonsensical. It argued that it would amount to a greater wastage of money, "while thousands of the very school children cannot obtain a solid midday meal. How many are given one or two cents to feed them during the day! The vital problem is to put parents in a better economic position; education will then adjust itself to suit."

The first part of the resolution focused on the views of W.H. Stokes, the junior education commissioner, on what should be the future of education in the country. The resolution in part stated, "And Whereas it is learnt that the Board of Education is now considering a scheme of educational reform proposed by Mr. Stokes; Be it therefore resolved that the inhabitants of the Colony that have assembled at this mass meeting do record their rejection of any scheme of Educational reform which is in conflict with their interests and to which they are opposed." Stokes had apparently made his views known at a public meeting, previously, at the Carnegie Hall.[109]

The *Times*, in its 7 May issue, made reference to the public's rejection of Stokes's views:

> Seldom has one seen such unanimity of public opinion as has been evinced by this community during the past few weeks in the matters of education. Every section of the local Press has voiced its disapproval in no uncertain manner, so that, it cannot be argued that the question is confined only to a given section of the community. . . . The name of Mr. Stokes is now a household name in the colony. It is as freely discussed at Government House as it is in the cottage of the poorest peasant.

The SWMA thus had public opinion on its side and was there to reflect the feelings of a wide cross-section of the public and to mobilize the working people in an effort to forestall the changes contemplated. This is another example of the association taking its struggle outside the legislative council to the people who did not meet the narrow franchise requirements of that period. Its second resolution spelled out the issue in some more detail:

> Whereas it is brought to the notice of the public of St Vincent that there is intention to appoint an officer over the Education Department to be known as Director or Superintendent of Education or Inspector of Schools such officer having to control the policy of Education both secondary and primary;
>
> And whereas such an arrangement has been previously proposed but was never put into effect by Government after wise objection by people of this Colony; And whereas either primary education or secondary education or both must be adversely effected [sic] under the management of a single individual;
>
> And whereas in the appointment of an officer to direct Secondary and Primary education would besides being detrimental to the colony's educational interests

entail expenditure which the colony cannot afford: Be it therefore resolved that this mass meeting of citizens of St Vincent held this 9th day of May 1938, solemnly protest against any proposal to appoint a Director or Superintendent or Inspector of Schools to supervise the secondary and primary systems of the colony.

The resolutions were to be sent to the secretary of state for the colonies, the governor, the administrator and "various sections of the West Indian Press".[110] It is not clear if any attempts were made to introduce the changes.

The association's mission was also to lift the political consciousness of the working people. In a letter to the *Times*, McIntosh had stated that he wanted "to broaden the intellectual horizon of our poor working people and to see a change in their lot". Education was, therefore, much more than what went on in the schools. One of the objectives of the SWMA was to help improve the living conditions of the working people and to prepare them to be active participants in that effort. Education, to them, was about living and involved a process that started at birth.

This was in keeping with the agreed position at the conference of the CLC. The conference stated firmly "that the school days of the citizen of a democracy are never ended and that the education of free men should begin in the antenatal clinic and end only at the grave. We therefore stress the need of education beyond the school age for all."[111] In light of his desire to lift the education of the masses, McIntosh paid particular attention to music and libraries. One of his motions in the legislative council in 1949 was a call on the government to appoint a director of music in order that a band be established and music taught in school. This he linked with the fact "that Government pays an amount annually for providing music to the inhabitants of this Colony" but that no band was available for public functions.[112]

The association built its own hall, the Association Hall, in which it sponsored debates, held concerts, discussions and dances and provided a venue for bands to practise, for music to be taught and concerts held. Indeed, the political education of Vincentians was high on its agenda. In 1947, at a meeting of the legislative council, one of the questions asked by McIntosh was centred on the need for government to take action and speed up adult education.[113] This also fitted in with the CLC's statement on education. One of its main tasks was the re-education of the people to rid themselves of the misconception that "some are born to possess and others to serve the possessors" and to come to an understanding that "everyone is born with a right to an equal opportunity to develop his talents and at the same time to serve the community". It called on its "constituent members" "to use every means already available or that can be devised of educating public opinion to accept this conception not merely intellectually but also as part of their way of life, in order that the home, the school, the workshop, the club, the office and the university may be pervaded by its influence".[114]

The SWMA's hall was used as a venue for highlighting and encouraging the development of the talents of working people. At a concert organized on 13 July 1938 by Evelyn Clarke, a social worker, working people were given prominence. The secretary of the SWMA, in outlining the objectives of what he called social performances, indicated that they were "to relieve the workers of the continual drudgery of their existence and to develop what latent dramatic and musical talent they possess".[115]

McIntosh and his colleagues decried the level of illiteracy in the country. He argued that in the West Indies, the masses bought and read newspapers. In St Vincent, however, he said, "we can never have a daily newspaper and in fact the non-publication of a newspaper in St Vincent as happened recently seems to matter very little because the masses have not been educated".[116] This was of concern to him because it was known that the introduction of adult suffrage was not far away and because, as part of the labour movement, they were engaged in the process of drafting a road map to federation of the colonies. The statement on education by the CLC saw education as critical in their aim of creating "a self-governing federation of the British territories in the Caribbean under a democratic government". The statement also expressed the conference's view that "the citizen of a democracy must be educated to think and form sound opinions from the critical examination of accurate information". The focus was, therefore, on "the development of all our people into educated West Indian citizens".[117]

The years from 1945 to 1951 were to see a greater focus on the move to adult suffrage and a federation of the colonies. Education was going to be critical to the success of these two goals. The representatives of the Labour Party did not have political control. Their aim was to keep these matters on the agenda and to advocate on their behalf, both in council and outside. The initial official position about the attainment of adult suffrage was that there should be a literacy test involved in the right of any adult to exercise the franchise. McIntosh strongly opposed this, as did the Colonial Office later.

The issues addressed in this chapter were ones critical to the working people, and the SWMA, in their work both in the legislative council and outside, tried to bring them to the government's attention. In doing so, they educated and, at the same time, mobilized the support of the working people who did not qualify to meet the franchise requirements that were then available. Selwyn Grier's observation at the time of the riots that there were significant numbers of people who were not represented in the legislative council was obviously still in the consciousness of the colonial officials and political elite as they contemplated constitutional changes.

CHAPTER 7

THE MOVE TO ADULT SUFFRAGE

IN THIS CHAPTER, THE MOVE TO ADULT SUFFRAGE is highlighted, as well as the search for a path to a federation of the colonies, issues that the Labour Party considered essential to the causes they were pushing. These were part of the colonial programme that was informed by the Closer Union and Moyne Commissions and forwarded to the colonies by the secretary of state. The dynamics of the interplay between the labour movement in the colonies, the unofficial Dominica conference of 1932, the internal politics of St Vincent and the other colonies, and their reaction to initiatives of the Colonial Office in turn shaped and refined the process leading to adult suffrage. A federation of the colonies was seen as a step that was "the goal of the political development"[1] of the colonies when "the old order changeth yielding place to new".[2]

In examining the situation in the Caribbean following the riots of the 1930s, Arthur Lewis argued that "the major issues today no longer revolve round the aspirations of the middle classes, but are set by working class demands. Federation and elective control are still in the forefront, but they are now desired in the interest of the masses and side by side with them are new issues." He identified these new issues as "slum clearance, social services, land settlement, extension of the franchise", among others that he said were not often discussed before.[3] As shown in the earlier chapters, matters relevant to labour, land settlement, education and religion, as it pertained to the Shakers, were at the top of the SWMA's agenda, but it has to be pointed out that that body also pushed for programmes related to housing, health, slum clearance, prison reform and water supply, which were part of the social welfare package recommended by the 1945 Royal Commission.[4]

During the campaign for the 1946 elections, one of the main issues on their platform was a federation of the British Caribbean colonies. Closely connected to this was the matter of adult suffrage. The editorial in the *Times* of 13 July 1946, while commenting on "Elections in Trinidad", used the opportunity to raise the issue of adult suffrage:

> As strong advocates of West Indian Federation we see in the introduction of Universal Adult Suffrage in all these islands the greatest political move towards the eventual realization of this great goal. It cannot be doubted for one moment that the curse of insularism that has kept the islands from coming together has been due greatly to the lack of sympathy of vested interests. With the introduction of Adult Suffrage there is great likelihood of an introduction in the island's Legislatures of men with broader sympathies for poorer neighbours.[5]

This was also the position of the SWMA and its political arm, since they saw themselves best positioned to represent the working people. Adult suffrage was a constitutional matter, but it had broad implications that went beyond the mere constitutional and political. It was equally central to the issue of political union, which was becoming the focus of attention among the labour movement and the politicians who had emerged following the lowering of the franchise in 1937. Many of the political activists in the region felt that constitutional advancement would have been limited without the larger entity that political union would have brought into the calculations. Federation was, therefore, tied in with further constitutional advance.

Colonial policies, as they were played out between 1946 and 1951, have also to be seen within the context of World War II and post-war developments. Secretary of state Lord Moyne gave an indication of the importance of this when he stated, "when I took office the prime minister told me that in his opinion the close connection with the Americans made it even more important than it was before to press on with the rehabilitation of social conditions in the West Indies".[6] This obviously arose from the nature of the relationship forged with the Americans during the war and their interest in what was happening in the British colonies of the Caribbean – in their backyard, as some perceived it. Certainly, to the Americans, it was a "geopolitical imperative".

The protests of the 1930s provided the context for social and constitutional development. The Moyne Commission was strongly of this view and made its recommendations with this in mind. The commission argued, "It is doubtful whether any schemes of social reform, however wisely conceived and efficiently conducted, would be completely successful unless they were accompanied by the largest measure of constitutional development which is thought to be judicious in existing circumstances."[7]

That conclusion was based on its reading of public opinion in the region. For all of that reform and development to be possible, it was necessary to have "greater participation of the people in the business of government". The demand for providing a larger voice for the people in managing their affairs the commission regarded as a "genuine sentiment and reflects a growing political consciousness" that was widespread. The commission, although seeing adult suffrage as inevitable, was cautious about its timing. It was strongly against proposals for the granting of "immediate and complete self-government based on universal suffrage". It restated its view, "More, and not less participation by the people in the work of government is a real necessity for lasting social advancement", but felt that what was important as a starting point was to have a "truly representative character of the Legislative Councils". It was not prepared to recommend "any drastic change in their functions".[8]

This was the atmosphere in which the SWMA continued to highlight matters of concern to the working people. It became part of a growing call for change that was advocated by the labour movement in the region. The Moyne Commission had drawn attention to this, arguing that "it is evident that throughout the B.W.I. contact is being maintained between those in each Colony who are most interested in securing rapid political progress and constitutional developments such as the widening of the franchise, in any area may be found to reinforce the strength of the movement for federation of the whole group".[9]

This can be seen by the participation of the SWMA in meetings of the CLC and by the contact maintained by McIntosh with Marryshow, president of the CLC, and with Arthur Cipriani of Trinidad, who led the Trinidad Working-men's Association, later renamed the Trinidad Labour Party.

In responding to the report of a conference of delegates from the Windward Islands that was held in Grenada on 17 and 18 January 1945 and whose purpose was to examine the Moyne Commission's recommendations on "Constitutional and Closer Union", the secretary of state was of the view that priority was being given to constitutional reform over the issue of federation. Based on his review of the conference report, he concluded that "local opinion in the Windward Islands will expect that constitutional reform should be granted before consideration is given to the possibilities of federation". He was against that position, arguing that it might result in the "necessity of preparing and putting in force two sets of instruments effecting constitutional changes within a comparatively short period and so lead to misunderstanding and confusion".[10]

There were certainly differences, as some persons regarded constitutional reform as urgently needed and felt, too, that it was a means of achieving the goal of federation. At the Windward Islands conference to which the secretary of state referred, H.A. Davis, one of St Vincent's delegates, moved a motion requesting that the franchise be extended to universal adult suffrage, though at that time, paradoxically, advocating a literacy test. The other Vincentian delegate moved a resolution calling for federation but suggested that a practical test of the advantages of federation would manifest itself by having first a closer union of the Leeward and Windward Islands.[11] But an earlier part of the resolution moved and seconded by the Dominican delegates stated, "The Constitutional Reform foreshadowed in the foregoing Resolutions is a condition precedent to Federation in terms of subsection (f) of section 28 of the Royal Commission Recommendations or any other form of West Indian Federation."[12]

At the 1945 conference of the CLC, McIntosh indicated that "he was in favour of a federal government that allowed the greatest measure of autonomy in each colony with adult suffrage and single chamber legislatures".[13] He saw federation as a step they needed to take immediately. In fact, as far as he was concerned, they did not have to wait until all the colonies were ready for it. Canada, after all, he stated, started with "two provinces [sic]". The conference's statement on political education indicated that they favoured the granting, to all units, of "wholly elected legislatures" founded on universal adult suffrage, "with policy making executive councils responsible to the legislatures and of wholly elected local government authorities".[14] With regard to a federation, its position was that "the development of the Caribbean area as an economic entity is the only way of creating a stable and self supporting economy and that this is possible only if such a programme of development and expansion is conceived and directed by West Indians in the Caribbean under the unified control obtainable under a federal constitution with responsible government".

The conference also endorsed the secretary of state's call for a meeting of the legislatures of the region to obtain their opinion and for the convening of a conference of West Indian delegates.[15] It supported his view that federation with self-government was the ultimate aim of the policy of His Majesty's Government for those colonies.[16]

Among many of the leaders of the labour movement and of the legislatures, there was no distinction between their call for constitutional reform and that for federation. Where there was disagreement, it had largely to do with the form of universal suffrage, some seeing it as involving a literacy test, even though the idea of a literacy test was incompatible with the concept of universal suffrage, and on the matter of whether the colonies should enter federation as separate units or as a single amalgamated body constituting the Windward and Leeward Islands. At another labour conference in Jamaica in 1947, attended by McIntosh and Duncan, the support was for a federation with Dominion status, patterning themselves after constitutional developments in Canada, Australia and India. Marryshow, the president of the CLC, indicated, on his way to the conference, that federation was not going to be possible without representative government since they cannot be "half slave and half free".[17] Duncan admitted to the difficulty involved in convincing the gathering that each unit should be autonomous and represented as individual units with allotments of representatives on "an arranged population basis". The St Vincent delegation, with other colleagues, succeeded in having that position adopted.[18]

The secretary of state's call for a meeting of the legislatures of the region and for the convening of a conference of West Indian delegates that was accepted by the CLC resulted, in 1947, in the convening delegates of the Leeward and Windward Islands and a broader conference of delegates to discuss the issue of closer association of the British West Indian colonies. The Windwards/Leewards conference that was held in St Kitts in January 1947 proposed a federation of the Leeward and Windward Islands with a central government. The general understanding was that the colonies of the Windward and Leeward Islands would meet as one unit at the proposed conference on closer union. They were of the view that such an arrangement would be a practical test of the advantages of federation of the British West Indies but realized that they must move on and that, given the interest in the broader meeting for closer association, they should join their other colleagues before their proposal could be implemented.[19]

The object of the conference on closer union was to allow individual governments and legislatures to view collectively the matters at hand. Arthur Creech Jones, then secretary of state for the colonies, hoped "that the delegates will enjoy a freedom of action which will admit of attainment of such collective views in the course of the debates and after full consideration of all the relevant factors".[20] Prior to the convening of the Closer Union Conference at Montego

Bay, Jamaica, in 1947, the Labour conference, referred to earlier, was also held in Jamaica and opted for a federation with Dominion status.

The idea of a union of the Windward and Leeward Islands was rejected, most likely based on the position of the Labour conference. As stated by Patrick Emmanuel, "The declaration at Montego Bay that local reform should proceed on its own and not tied to progress on the federal plane put paid to the earlier British insistence that agreement on the federation of the smaller territories was the sine qua non for their own constitutional progress."[21] There was an agreement on the principle of political federation and on the setting up of a committee to move the idea of a federation further along and to draft a federal constitution.

These matters pertaining to federation and constitutional reform were played out in the legislative council in St Vincent and in the broader Vincentian society, as happened elsewhere. In St Vincent, it exposed problems within the SWMA and Labour Party. The secretary of state's proposals on amalgamation that had been sent to the colonies created quite a bit of excitement and controversy within the Vincentian society. A statement sent in 1946 to media houses in the region by an unknown group that called itself the St Vincent Constitution Committee gave, as the critics stated, what was considered a false impression that St Vincent had rejected the secretary of state's proposals. The *Times*, whose editor, Bonadie, was one of the leading proponents of the position declared by the secretary of state, reacted strongly. The paper argued that the proposals had not yet been discussed by "any competent body".[22]

The secretary of state's approach was influenced by the Moyne Commission's report, which had favoured the amalgamation of the Windward and Leeward Islands as constituting "a practical test of the advantage of Federation". Given the position taken by the 1945 Conference of Delegates from the Windward Islands, he suggested that "an agreement for the unification of the Leeward and Windward Islands would not, however, prejudice the grant of constitutional reform" and felt that "it would naturally be convenient if the two matters were discussed side by side".[23]

The release sent to the foreign press by, as the *Times* described it, this "unrecognised body", the St Vincent Constitutional Reform Committee, declared that St Vincent had rejected the secretary of state's proposals. The controversy was heightened by the appearances of pieces in the *Barbados Advocate*, the *Trinidad Guardian* and the Grenadian *West Indian* that responded to the release. The *Times* reproduced the article from the *Barbados Advocate* under the caption "Barbados Press Attacks St Vincent's Crude Rejection of Closer Union Proposals". The *Barbados Advocate* admitted that it was not as yet privy to the "details of the rejection but felt that it was most likely to set back the scheme for federation". It speculated falsely that the issue of the location of the seat of government for the amalgamated body might have been the bone of contention.[24]

Spurred on by the pieces in the West Indian press on the issue, a section of the Vincentian public, led by Bonadie, stepped into action. The *Times* editorial of 6 April emphasized the point that the secretary of state's despatch had not yet been discussed by any organized body. The editor was optimistic that the colony would accept the proposals with necessary amendments and, where possible, counterproposals. It stated, too, in response to what it considered a misleading impression, that "it is precisely the thing that will always happen in any country when intelligent people keep aloof and allow all sorts of politicians and incompetents to meddle too far with such weighty affairs of the Island". The paper, in fact, felt that the secretary of state for the colonies had fallen into their laps "when he suggests that the unification of the Windward and Leeward Islands should be discussed side by side".

Stung by the reaction of the West Indian press, the defenders of the secretary of state's proposals continued to act. An ad hoc committee meeting was held at the Carnegie Library on Saturday, 6 April 1946. The committee was described as a grouping of people of "St Vincent's higher intelligence". The chairman of the meeting was Marryshow of Grenada, whose visit to the colony was for a discussion with the governor on "urgent matters" and for assisting in designing a strategy to deal with the fallout from the message falsely claiming that St Vincent had rejected the secretary of state's proposals.

On the following Monday, messages were sent to the *Trinidad Guardian* and *Barbados Advocate* to correct the "false impression" that had been created about St Vincent's position. The message was sent by the editor of the *Times* and appeared to have been a decision taken by the ad hoc committee at its meeting. The message stated that the "misleading message concerning blunt, discourteous rejection originated from small, ill-formed group, not connected with the Workingmen's Association or any other recognised political organisation".[25]

Other meetings were called on the issue. On Monday evening, a meeting was held to justify the message sent out earlier that day, following the ad hoc committee's meeting. T.A. Marryshow's address at that meeting was described as most impassioned. He was critical of the "indecent haste" of the small, unrecognized group that had placed the colony on the spot. The meeting, however, broke up in disarray.[26] The *Vincentian* of 13 April 1946 was critical of the organizers of the meeting which "reflected no credit whatsoever on the promoters". It was evident to that paper that "there was no premeditated course to be followed and the conflicting views were infuriating".

No details about the meeting were given by the newspaer, but a notice appeared for another meeting to be held on 15 April. The organizers were Bonadie, Davis and Brisbane, elected members of the legislative council and members of the SWMA. A resolution that was passed at the meeting was printed in the *Vincentian* of 20 April with no comment. The resolution emphasized what it described as the consciousness of the people about the many benefits of a closer union and reaffirmed that their ultimate goal was a federation of the colonies "into one unit with self-government". That reference to a federation of the colonies was to the issue of amalgamation of the Windward and Leeward Islands. The "ultimate" goal of federation was likely to be "facilitated rather than retarded by the process of group federation". The meeting was to resolve that "this body of representative citizens of St Vincent in meeting assembled in the town of Kingstown this 15th day of April 1946, accept in principle, though not in detail, the proposals of the Secretary of State for the Colonies subject to such amendments as may be agreed upon by the Colonies concerned". The resolution also called for the election of an ad hoc committee of twelve persons "with power to co-opt others". Its task was to consider the proposals and submit such amendments or counterproposals as it found necessary.[27]

That was certainly not the end of the issue, for another meeting was convened on Saturday, 25 April, at the Carnegie Library. The reason for calling that meeting was not clear, but it unearthed some information about the apparent conflict within the Labour Party and SWMA. The first thing that was strange about the meeting was that it was held under the auspices of the SWMA and St Vincent Constitutional Reform Committee.[28] This was the same committee that was supposed to have been ill-informed and "not connected with the Workingmen's Association or any other recognised organisation".[29] Even more surprisingly, that meeting approved counterproposals relating to the federation issue, along with a petition to the king. These were put forward by McIntosh and Duncan.

The *Times* of 4 May, under the caption "Unknown St Vincent Correspondent Sends Out More Messages", quoted from the report of that meeting that was sent out by the unknown source but only commented on its reference to Bonadie who was singled out as "the lone figure . . . sponsoring the Colonial

Office amalgamation scheme". Bonadie took exception to the view that no one else had seen the benefits of amalgamation. He responded in the 4 May edition, "The truth is that the most responsible and Unselfish persons in the Community are already admitting that the Pros Outweigh the Cons in the projected Amalgamation of the Windwards and Leewards." What was becoming quite clear was that there were divisions within the SWMA and its political arm. These divisions became even more obvious during the parliamentary debate on the secretary of state's despatch and the resolution to accept the contents of the proposals.

The governor addressed the legislative council on 18 April 1946. The focus of his address was on the despatch of the secretary of state for the colonies on the issue of a Windwards-Leewards federation.[30] This address was to be broadcast to the other colonies that were supposedly part of the amalgamation effort. This was to be followed by a debate in the legislative council, held subsequently on 2 May. Three of the four elected members of the Labour Party appeared to be in unison and strongly supported amalgamation, while the party's leader declared clearly that he could not support his colleagues on that issue. The majority, however, voted to accept the principle of amalgamation "as a basis for the discussion of the details of the recent Federation Despatch from the Secretary of State for the Colonies". A committee made up of unofficial members of the legislative council was selected to work on the details of the proposals.[31]

The resolution was moved by the Crown attorney, P.C. Lewis, and seconded by the colonial treasurer, Cools Lartigue, without comments. Leading the debate on the resolution was Bonadie. He was hesitant about the advisability of having the debate at that time because the matter had not been as widely discussed as it needed to. He was, however, aware that any agreements in the legislative council did not preclude any memoranda from any individual or group.

As one of the representatives at the 1945 Grenada conference, Bonadie found it necessary to justify some of the proposals made. The central point of his presentation was the view that unity was strength. Davis, the other delegate to the Grenada conference, supported his position. He raised an issue that was taken up later by McIntosh. He declared that there was confusion about the words "Amalgamation" and "Federation". He presumed that the select committee would use their dictionaries to clarify the differences.

Other speakers supported the resolution. Punnett, one of the nominated members of the council, took a very strange position. He supported the resolution but was not in favour of amalgamation. He was sure that amalgamation would do no good for the island but was not sure that it would be harmful. He hoped it would not be. He felt that there were some good points in the resolution which, when carefully studied, might work.

McIntosh made it clear from the beginning that he was unable to join his colleagues in supporting the resolution. He even felt that the resolution should have come not from the government but from unofficial members, who should have consulted their constituencies. He praised the position taken by Punnett but reacted strongly to a part of Davis's presentation. He said, "It is peculiar that members should come here to sit down and advocate for something that they are totally ignorant of and to ask for dictionaries to find out what is the meaning of words."[32] He was all for full freedom and made reference to the 1945 despatch from the then colonial secretary, Oliver Stanley, whose intention was to provide for a federation with responsible self-government.[33] He was critical of the Grenada conference and looked on the delegates as "political babes" who were asking for constitutional reform and leaving out federation. To that end, the Grenada conference had, he felt, turned back "the hands of the clock".

He also drew the council's attention to the conference of the CLC held in Barbados in 1945. The conference had federation as its goal for political development. Delegates wanted a strong federal constitution and favoured giving all units wholly elected legislatures based on universal adult suffrage "with policy making Executive Councils responsible to their legislatures and of wholly elected government authorities".

He pledged his loyalty to the recommendations of that conference, to which he felt bound, and was surprised that the other delegate to that conference, Bonadie, did not support its view. He provided an explanation of the differences between "Amalgamation" and "Federation". Amalgamation, he argued, was an old issue that dated back, in St Vincent, to 1885, when an attempt was made to amalgamate St Vincent and other islands, which was rejected by the people of St Vincent. He said that he was told that they must not be selfish and should give up all insularity, but how was it supposed to work practically, he asked.[34] He was opting for federation, not amalgamation. He stated further, "Do not be fooled into believing that Amalgamation is a step to Federation, because we will be told that we are not individual colonies but one Colony."[35]

Clearly, something was wrong within the Labour Party. McIntosh's language during the debate did not demonstrate any sign of collegiality. Even more telling had been the party's rejection of Bonadie, Davis and Brisbane as candidates for the October elections. Did their rejection by the party have anything to do with the position they took on the issue of amalgamation? It is hard to imagine that it was pure coincidence. Whether or not this was the initial cause of the rift is not clear.

It appeared that McIntosh's position on the debate might have had strong support within the SWMA, though not from the elected members of the party. Bonadie had vowed earlier to get his party to discipline employees of the SWMA who were part of the St Vincent Constitutional Reform Committee. These employees were not identified, but opposition to the proposals of the secretary of state for the colonies must have involved others who were members of the association. It is significant, too, that, as indicated earlier, the SWMA had joined the Constitutional Reform Committee in convening a meeting to discuss the proposals.

The conflict, which was clearly out in the open, did affect the standing of McIntosh and the party. Fortunately, there were no serious challengers, for their main opponents were representatives of the planter class, who appeared out of place at that time. In a report on the upcoming elections, a writer in the *Times* of 1 June 1946, under the caption "Highlights of the Coming General Elections", described the situation in the Kingstown district but noted that "although Mr. McIntosh has lost some ground through his recent political activities the people of St Vincent appreciate and know what they owe him". He also expressed the concern felt by some "that something will happen before this workers' legacy is squandered beyond recovery". McIntosh and his group were seen as representatives of the workers in battle against the planters.[36] In another piece on 28 September, the writer, who seemed to have been covering the elections for the *Times*, said, about the rifts within the party, "recent action in attempting to oust or as they more crudely describe it to 'kick' men of sterling characters like Davis, Bonadie and Brisbane out of the Council, have caused the people of the island to place the character of the President of the Workingmen's Association and his limpets under the microscope. It is a serious and uncomfortable thing when the public start to become so critical."[37]

Even though, at that time, there was no official announcement about the introduction of adult suffrage, this was very much in the air. The newspapers expected that it was high on the Colonial Office's agenda. The atmosphere was also heightened by developments within the town boards and village councils. After the elections of 1946, legislation was being put in place for the establishment of village councils. This was part of the general movement towards constitutional change and owed little to the activity of the Labour Party. Changes in the constitution of the Kingstown Board, established in 1897, were being considered, to mark the board's fiftieth anniversary in 1947. The board was to be made a "wholly elected body". Before 1946, it was partly nominated and partly elected. For the "small towns", the governor had the authority to appoint town wardens for each of them.[38] Persons were nominated, and the superintendent of public works was to serve as *ex officio* chairman. In 1948, the establishment of the Kingstown Board as a wholly elected body was made official. In 1949, the small town boards and village councils were inaugurated under the Small Towns and Village Councils Ordinances. The small town boards and village councils had a combination of elected and nominated members. For the small town boards there were to be four elected and two nominated members, and for the village councils four elected and three nominated members.[39]

The impact of the legislation ushering in changes to the composition of the town boards and village councils was recognized. It was highlighted by the *Vincentian*, which saw it as "a political awakening for this colony, a step which will lead to great things, a training for bigger things which are to come, the bud from which will eventually blossom forth a West Indian nationhood with Federation and Self-Government". The paper looked at it with the expectation of constitutional reforms leading to adult suffrage and the move towards the establishment of a federation. It welcomed "the extended system of Local Government through the recently enacted 'Small Towns and Village Councils Ordinances'. It allows the towns and villages to have a say in their own administration."[40] To be an elector, an individual had to be a British subject "of full age, able to read and write the English language and . . . be resident in the district in which he votes or seeks election".[41] The political impact of this could be clearly seen, since some of the persons who served as town wardens before 1949 and who became chairmen and members of the different boards and councils had either been sitting in the legislative council or were members of the town boards and village councils. Some became candidates for the first elections under adult suffrage in 1951. This happened in just about every district.[42]

There was general excitement in December 1950 when elections to the local bodies were held. Voters, and the public generally, anxiously awaited the results. Among the successful candidates were E.A. Joachim, who was the representative for the North Leeward area; Herman Young, who was to contest the 1951 elections for South Leeward; and St Aubyn Cato and C.W. Prescod, who were candidates for the North Windward and Central Windward areas.

In Kingstown were persons such as McIntosh and Bonadie, sitting members of the legislative council.

The announcement in 1949 that adult suffrage was to be introduced further lit up the political scene and created excitement among the people who were going to be voting for the first time. A notice in the *Government Gazette* informed that a "simple literacy test" was required for adults who had attained the age of twenty-one. The secretary of state indicated that property qualifications for candidates were to be removed. The issue of wholly elected legislatures had not, the secretary of state for the colonies noted, been discussed.[43]

The *Vincentian*, the only paper then in production, stated in its editorial that the call for wholly elected legislatures was widespread.[44] It, however, supported the literacy test that was to be used to determine one's ability to vote. It quoted from John Stuart Mills to the effect that "suffrage should not be granted to anyone who could not read, write or perform a sum in the rule of three. If they do not know on what the simple literacy test will be based, the simplest way is to find out if the person can sign his/her name."[45]

At a meeting of the legislative council, the question of the literacy test was considered and was agreed on by a majority of members, but McIntosh refused to support it. He had already made his position on the literacy test quite clear at the meeting of the legislative council on 13 May 1950 that commemorated the silver jubilee of elected representation in the colony:

> Manhood suffrage could be nothing more than every man of 21 years going forward and exercising his right to vote; but some want to attach a literacy test. It is not manhood suffrage if we are going to hang on a literacy test. The man who can't read and write needs representation more. We should not hamper him if he has not been taught to read and write; and I am going to oppose that literacy test which is not true manhood suffrage. The man who can't read and write has greater need to have manhood suffrage than the man who can read and write and see about himself; and so when this does come up, whatever I may be asking for, I want to see the widest scope of democracy which will give every man his chance. It is the only way we are going to bring him up. He will never learn to swim if we do not give him a chance to get into the water. Give them every opportunity to rise.[46]

At an earlier meeting of the legislative council, in the latter part of 1949, at which the matter of the literacy test was raised, there was discussion on the property and income qualifications to vote and to be candidates. Again, a majority of members recommended that income and property qualifications be reduced by 50 per cent and the deposit remain at the current level. All but two members disagreed with the entire abolition of income and property qualifications, McIntosh being one of the two. There was unanimity, however, on increasing the number of elected members from five to eight.⁴⁷ At a later meeting, all representatives of the Labour Party favoured a complete removal of property and income qualifications for persons seeking to stand as candidates.

The final package for constitutional reform that was agreed upon by the secretary of state for the four colonies of the Windward Islands was outlined at a meeting of the Legislative Council of St Lucia on 24 July 1950. The matter of adult suffrage was reviewed following a report of the Standing Closer Association Committee. It had been recommended in that report that election for the proposed federal legislature be by universal adult suffrage. The colonies of the Windwards "in Committee" then agreed that elections to the legislatures be on the same basis and no literacy test be introduced, as McIntosh wanted. Resident qualifications for candidates were to remain at twelve months; property and income qualifications were to be removed and replaced by a deposit of $120.

For the legislative councils, the administrator was to be president of the legislative committee, and the councils were to consist of fourteen members: the president, three *ex officio* members, three nominated and eight elected members. The memoranda from the secretary of state explained that the composition agreed upon "gives effect unanimously to the desire for a clear elected majority". The power to define electoral districts was to remain with the governor in executive council.

The *ex officio* members were to retain their right to vote until a ministerial system was introduced. The role of the *ex officio* members was highlighted since it was felt that they "must necessarily play an important part in the Council, and it would be invidious and a source of weakness rather than strength to deprive them of their voting right".

The governor's reserve powers remained unchanged, central as they were to continued British control. As Denis Benn notes, "concessions towards representative government were seen as a means of accommodating local demands for a measure of representative government rather than a surrender of the substance of imperial control".⁴⁸

The term of existence of the legislative council was to be three years. It was given the right to select three members to serve on the executive council, but this was not to be limited to elected members, and all members were allowed to vote in making the selection. The legislative council also had the right to remove an elected member from the executive council by a two-thirds majority. The official members of the executive council were the administrator, the attorney general or Crown attorney, the financial secretary or treasurer, and one other official member.

When the governor was present in any of the islands, he was to preside over the executive council, and "the constitutional status of the Executive Council as advisor to the Governor was to remain".[49] The constitutional framework that was to govern the first elections under adult suffrage had thus been set up. An Order in Council of 28 July 1949 declared that the existing legislature was to be extended beyond its normal limit to facilitate the next general elections being held under adult suffrage.[50]

Although the focus was then on the first elections under adult suffrage, and the constitutional methods that were to facilitate this, it did not remove the issue of federation from people's attention. Voluntary organizations within the colony had been facilitating public discussions on the two issues of federation and adult suffrage.[51] Some persons still saw federation as the key to the future development of the colony. For McIntosh, as he indicated at the special jubilee meeting of the legislative council, if the colony was to progress, "we no longer can consider St Vincent only; we want to move on where we will consider the West Indies as a new nation taking her place in the world". In doing so, he recognized, there would need to be an entire change in the constitutional set-up.[52]

An Order in Council dated 1 August 1951 provided for the redefinition of electoral districts "on a population basis". Provision was made through the Legislative Council (Elections) Ordinance for the registration of voters and the procedure that had to be followed. This provided for elections based on universal adult suffrage.[53]

A few individuals began to express an interest in contesting the elections scheduled for 1951. One of the earliest expressions of interest came from dentist Frank Ellis who, in a letter to the *Vincentian* on 29 July 1950, stated, "I beg through your weekly periodical to place my name before the electorate at the next election to contest a seat for the local legislature as things are not what they seem."

B.R. James, a schoolteacher, stated his intention to the public and launched a manifesto. A.C. Allen, in expressing his desire to be a candidate, pledged "to support equal laws for all classes regardless of position, race or creed and for the protection of all that is right". In a commentary in the latter part of 1950, F.A. Simmons noted that the political scene was "showing signs of animation".

He seemed to have been making fun of James's fifteen-point manifesto, which was one up on the fourteen-point statement of President Wilson (of the United States). For the Grenadines, Simmons noted that "certain elimination bouts were proceeding at a pace and style characteristic of the tempestuous seas that wash the shores of those emerald isles". He seemed, at that point, to have had no doubt that the Labour Party would prevail, since their "roots are firmly fixed in the masses". He made reference to their slogan, "For the cause that lacks assistance, for the wrongs that need resistance and the good that we can do."[54]

The Labour Party was off to a quick start, declaring its candidates quite early, on 22 September 1950, at its Association Hall, although there were changes later to the final slate.[55] An announcement came shortly after, noting the formation of a new party. The party, named the New Era Party, was under the leadership of Frank Ellis, who had earlier declared his intention of contesting the next general election. Little was heard later about that party. The leader did contest the election, but as an independent. Some of the other members had declared their intention to contest as independents before finding accommodation later with a new party.[56]

LAUNCHING OF THE UNITED WORKERS PEASANTS AND RATEPAYERS UNION

Real excitement and expectation were generated with news about the launching of a new union on May Day, 1 May 1951. This was to take the form of a march from the King George V Playing Field at Arnos Vale to Victoria Park, a distance of three-and-a-half miles. On that memorable Tuesday, some two thousand workers marched, "all wearing a black cross which incidentally represented those who made the necessary sacrifice so that labour may gain the measure of power which they now enjoy".[57] Changes to the trade union legislation that were introduced in 1950 provided a new climate for the organization of trade unions. The Trades Union and Trade Disputes Ordinance 1950 updated existing legislation based on a model from the Colonial Office.[58] The president, George Charles, wore "evening dress with a six-inch scarlet red sarong across his shoulders" and carried a wooden sword. The members and well-wishers sang "patriotic songs", accompanied by two brass bands.

Charles was about thirty years old. He had done some small farming in St Vincent before migrating to Trinidad, where he worked on a farm belonging to

businessman George Huggins. He became associated with Butler's trade union
and also served for three years as a member of one of the county councils.[59]
He claimed to have been inspired by Uriah Butler and, after his return to St
Vincent in 1950, set about forming a union.[60]

At Victoria Park, a joint Methodist-Anglican church service was held. This
was followed by addresses by union members and government and Kingstown
Town Board officials. Among the speakers were Evans Morgan, the union's
grievance officer; Herman Young, also a union member; the chairman of the
Kingstown Board, St Clair Bonadie; the administrator; the labour commissioner; Charles; Robert DaBreo, identified as a "prominent garage owner and
member of Kingstown Corporation", who moved the vote of thanks; and D.A.
McNamara, registrar of the Supreme Court, who was in charge of trade union
registration.

The registrar delivered the different paraphernalia that were necessary to
the union's registration. He also drew the public's attention to something that
was to transform the political climate. He did so while expressing his concerns
and reservations. He indicated that he was informed "from hearsay" that the
president had promised his members that the union would contest the upcoming general elections and "fill all eight seats on the Legislature". Although he
was unsure about the names of the union's candidates, he was not impressed
with the quality of members whom he saw. He felt that, while the country
needed "men of sober calculating ability", the members would not have been
able to cope with the demands of the federal council and were likely to be mere
spectators. Looking at the procession, he felt that few of them were "capable
of holding their own in a fair-to-middling debate and on questions of any
technical significance, nearly all will be completely at sea". He urged capable
persons who were concerned about the future of the colony to come forward
and offer their support, hoping that they would have been able to convince the
union's management to select them as their candidates.

The bearded Charles "in very dramatic style . . . took a bible and swore to be
faithful to the Union promising never to let them down. Continuing, he said, he
was prepared to fight constitutionally until all the wrongs of the workers were
righted."[61] This apparent entry of the union into the contest for the 1951 elections
brought a new factor into the equation and was to drastically transform and
enliven the political atmosphere.

THE ELECTION CAMPAIGN

It is not clear when the decision was made for the newly formed union to contest the general elections. On 10 March 1951, one individual who later became a candidate for the union, Samuel Slater, placed a message in the *Vincentian* declaring his desire to contest the forthcoming elections. He promised to issue a manifesto later. Evans Morgan, the union's grievance officer, posed some questions that he felt voters should keep in mind before voting. He suggested they look at what the individual had contributed to the political field, that they find out if he had a commendable character and was able to represent them politically and constitutionally to government.[62]

There was nothing to indicate that they were going to be part of any political party. When Bonadie, a member of the legislative council and executive member of the Labour Party spoke at the May Day rally, he was doing so as the chairman of the Kingstown Board. His focus was on the union "as union". He urged that they remain united so they could play a part in the development of the country. Once they were divided, they "became the helpless victims of those who are merely out to exploit [them] and [their] labour for their personal benefit". If he was aware of their political agenda, he certainly gave no indication that it was of any significance.

The union-cum-political-party was soon on the campaign trail. Its first political meeting was held on the evening of Tuesday, 22 May, at the market square. Speakers included Charles, Young and Morgan, who spoke at their May Day rally. Two additional speakers addressed the audience: Julian Baynes, who was to contest one of the seats, and Ebenezer Joshua. Joshua, who was based in Trinidad, arrived in the colony on 18 May and was described as a "visiting member of the Butler party of Trinidad". The forty-three-year-old Joshua was the son of Mr and Mrs J.E. Joshua, who lived at McKie's Hill overlooking the market square.[63] He was a teacher in St Vincent before migrating to Trinidad in 1941. After a stay of about two years, he went to Guyana and spent two years there before returning to Trinidad, where he took up work as a teacher. He became involved with Butler when he volunteered to proofread his newspaper, the *People*. Joshua became involved in Butler's union and went into full political activity, contesting a legislative council seat against Roy Joseph, mayor of San Fernando. A delegation from St Vincent had, it appeared, journeyed to Trinidad and invited him home, where he took up the position of treasurer of Charles's United Workers Peasants and Ratepayers Union.

A lot of this was not known and he was simply regarded as a visiting member of Butler's party from Trinidad. The "radical sounding rhetoric" of some of the speakers was new to a people who were going to be voting for the first time. Charles promised the audience "a political fight in underpants" for the eight seats that were going to be contested. Joshua, on the other hand, presented "a sample of the good, old rabble rousing oratory" that excited the crowd during his address, which was longer than an hour. He let them know that "political spring is here".[64]

F.J.V. Patterson, who reported on the meeting for the *Vincentian*, was certainly impressed. He wrote, "Whatever their shortcomings these men cannot be treated with indifference. They feel that they have a message and a mission. They are a sort of reflection of the tremendous changes that have been taking place in society in the whole world for many years now, in that sense, these men are moving with the times." Their rhetoric was considered to be socialistic, with the complaint that, like all socialist leaders, they suffered "from the same prejudices which they justifiably attack in the 'capitalist' and that is, intolerance and lack of sweet reasonableness". He, nevertheless, did not want to see Charles's union fail. The president had done a tremendous job in building his union, but Patterson cautioned that if he and other leaders did not have "sanity, sincerity and tolerance" characterizing their "every public utterance, there would come a quick day when even their own followers would find them out and look for another leader".

He was particularly impressed with Baynes's "indelicate wit", but more so with Joshua, who had evidently "achieved a high place in Mr. Butler's party in Trinidad". Joshua spoke highly of Butler and informed the gathering that, on one occasion, he had "pronounced a curse on England (Perfidious Albion) at Trafalgar Square to the extent that old women wept, tears streamed from the eyes of young men and Scotland Yard was stricken with panic".[65] That kind of political talk seems to have been well received by the excited crowd.

A news item in the *Vincentian* of 26 May 1951 reported that Eric Gairy, president general of the Grenada Manual and Mental Workers' Union, addressed a meeting at the market square "last Friday evening", which would have been 25 May. Joshua was said to have been one of the speakers. There is certainly a problem with that information. Gairy had, prior to this, been declared a prohibited immigrant, a decision taken by the executive council on 24 April 1951. The administrator informed members at a meeting of the council, later in 1951, that protests against their decision had been received from the People's

National Party of Jamaica and the St Kitts Union. "Council noted the protests with interest."⁶⁶

Not much had been heard of the Labour Party since it declared its candidates in 1950. A letter from its political leader appeared, after the fact, in the *Vincentian* of 16 June 1951. He informed the public that he was leaving the colony on 7 June to attend the Festival of Britain. He took the opportunity to remind them of what the SWMA had achieved. He warned against those whom he called new "misleaders" with "no outstanding characteristics, no personality, no education and no knowledge of policy". He was obviously pointing at the new persons appearing as part of Charles's union team. He called on persons with greater knowledge and better intelligence to rally around his organization.⁶⁷

The *Vincentian* continued to monitor other meetings of the new body. Its reporter, who covered a meeting held at the market square to present Rudolph Baynes as the union's candidate for Kingstown, argued that nothing new was said. He saw room for "much improvement" and urged a reshuffling of candidates since he was of the view that "there are better political materials in the Union that [*sic*] they are offering".⁶⁸

At another meeting held at the market square, the *Vincentian* remarked that Baynes "was far above the mentality of most of the audience". Joshua, who was at that same meeting, was described as brilliant "as usual" and worthy of a place on council. It had, however, some questions and concerns about the electoral constituency in which he was running, fearing his ability to succeed in that one. It preferred to see him in St Georges, "because it would be a pity if he is left out". Other meetings had continued in other districts.

One of the puzzling issues was the inactivity of the Labour Party. The lone newspaper, the *Vincentian*, would obviously have reported on any of their meetings, but they seemed to have been relying on statements to the newspaper, particularly to voters in Kingstown, the district held by McIntosh. In the 29 July issue of the *Vincentian*, electors in Kingstown were reminded that McIntosh was in England. They again urged the voters to be careful with those who were putting themselves forward, whom they described as "blustering political rankers" who had "noisiness" as their chief recommendation. Their lack of "verbal equipment" they considered to be "painfully evident". "Our Councillors must be men able to talk, but to talk not nonsense but good sense all the time."

Another message addressed to the electors of Kingstown urged them to look out for the return of McIntosh at the end of the month and for the first meeting. They were reminded that he had championed their cause for the past fourteen years. The party had, over the years, placed emphasis on improving their social and economic conditions and, by extension, the general welfare of the community. Their policies remained the same[69] and would be reaffirmed at a meeting when their leader returned. He was expected to inform them about the efforts he made on their behalf while in England. They were reminded that voting was their solemn duty. They were to choose the right man to look after their interests in the legislative council, "and the best you can do at the coming election is to choose the man who by experience, intelligence, practical knowledge – his general ability – and willingness to serve is the best suited to represent you".[70]

Subsequently, on 6 September, there was a meeting of the Labour Party at the market square. It was not what the party and its supporters were expecting. McIntosh, who was then sixty-five, spent a great deal of his address defending his age. Age savoured of experience. He was not going to be perturbed by the "cheap criticism". His mission was to serve his people. Age, he argued, should not be measured by the number of days but by the ability to serve. The meeting, at some stage, appeared to have got out of hand, although the reporter did not give details of what happened. He was, however, surprised that there had been no arrests.

The *Vincentian*'s editorial of 25 August 1951 had been expressing concerns about the persons who were being put forward as candidates. It had no faith in any of them, "and the people should have less as they are asking them to be traitors by casting their votes in the wrong direction". It accused both the union and the association of deliberately "offering men who are hopelessly unqualified to cope with the duties they would be called upon to perform". It feared that they would open the colony to ridicule and become "the laughing stock of their fellow Vincentians".

Despite stating their lack of confidence in all the persons being put forward as candidates, as late as 1 September 1951, the paper was appealing to voters to vote for responsible people, and it continued its call on capable men to come forward. It continued its lament in its issue of 22 September and admitted the failure of its appeals. It had hoped that they could have attracted men "of the calibre of Mr O.W. Forde", prominent lawyer and estate owner.[71] The paper claimed that its heart and those of like minds were bleeding for the common man. They were deserted by their more able brothers, who had "left them to their fate". The only thing left for them to do was "to ask Almighty God to guide and direct you so that on Election Day, the 15th October, you may cast your vote rightly". If you followed the paper's own logic, this was an impossible task, for there was no one among the list of candidates capable of steering them "through all the dangerous half-hidden political shoals which are so numerous today".[72]

Nominees for the 1951 elections were known by 29 September. The nominees represented the two existing parties and a number of independents. The Labour Party's candidates were listed under the "Workers Association" and those of Charles's union under the "Workers Union" (see table 9).

Table 9. Nominees for 1951 General Elections

Electoral Districts	Names	Party
North Windward	C.W. Prescod	Workers Association
	J.P. Henry (Georgetown)	Independent
	E.T. Joshua (Sion Hill)	Workers Union
Central Windward	St Aubyn Cato	Workers Association
	George Lewis	Independent
	George Charles	Workers Union
St George	St Clair Bonadie	Workers Association
	B.R. James	Independent
	J.A. Baynes	Workers Union
South Windward	Ronald Brisbane	Workers Association
	Jonathan Deane	Independent
	Evans Morgan	Workers Union
Kingstown	George McIntosh	Workers Association
	Dr Frank Ellis	Independent
	Rudolph Baynes	Workers Union
South Leeward	Claude M. Richards	Workers Association
	S.O. Jack	Independent
	Herman Young	Workers Union
North Leewards	E.A. Joachim	Workers Association
	Sam Slater	Workers Union
The Grenadines	C.L. Tannis	Workers Union
	C.V. Banyan	Independent
	C.B. Wallace	Independent

Source: *Vincentian*, 9 September 1951.

ELECTION DAY, 15 OCTOBER 1951

Two things stood out: the number of independents who were nominated and the absence of any candidates for the Labour Party in the Grenadines. From 1937, it had been unable to gain a foothold there, but it had always either run a candidate there or supported one on the slate. After fourteen years in control of the legislative council, their failure to select a candidate for that constituency might have reflected the state of the party. The party's nominee for South Leeward, Claude M. Richards, had ultimately to withdraw from the electoral contest because of ill health.[73]

Election day was Monday, 15 October. Of the registered voters, 69.7 per cent cast their ballots for twenty-two candidates nominated to contest the eight constituencies.[74] The day was one of excitement and expectation, influenced to some extent by the town board and village council elections that had been held in December 1950. Voters were keen and ensured that the sick and the blind were taken to the polling booths.[75] The masses of people had been kept in the political wilderness for long. Now their time had come.[76]

The headlines of the colony's single newspaper summed up what had happened: "Colony Embarks New Constitution Adult Suffrage"; "Union Workers Create Political Landslide Captured Eight Seats". Charles's Union Party, as it was listed on the official election stationery and later dubbed the Eighth Army of Liberation, won overwhelmingly, with the closest contest being in Kingstown, contested by McIntosh. In that constituency, the combined opposition votes were larger than those of the winning candidate, Baynes. There were 1,298 rejected votes.[77] Six candidates lost their deposits.[78] They were Lewis of the Central Windward Constituency, Brisbane and Deane of the South Windward Constituency, Ellis of Kingstown, James of St George, and Jack of South Leeward.[79]

The reaction of the *Vincentian* was to be expected. It suggested that, based on those who were elected, "we may be making progress physically but certainly not intellectually". Despite the paper's criticisms of the quality of persons who had put themselves forward as candidates, it praised the efforts of the Workers Union, stating that their performance showed what could be accomplished by hard work, especially given the short time that the union was in existence and it called on the community to support them.[80]

The performance of the Labour Party was quite surprising, even shocking, for a party that had dominated the legislative council since 1937. It had been completely swamped by Charles's union, which only came into existence a few months prior to the election. As noted before, the Workingmen's Association–cum–Labour Party had been facing divisions within its ranks, and this was manifested in the internal differences on federation and constitutional change. There might have been more to the divisions, particularly when three of the sitting members of the legislature were denied the right to represent the party at the 1946 general elections. The fact that one of these members, Bonadie, the vice-president, was selected to contest the 1951 election did not necessarily mean that the differences were mended. The registrar's statement at the launching of Charles's union might have said something about the state of the Labour Party. As indicated before, he said he learned from hearsay that the president of the union had promised to contest the next election and to win all eight seats. He was concerned that, with adult suffrage, that was possible. What is striking about this is that the party that had, up to that time, dominated the legislative council seemed not to have featured in his thinking on the matter.

Although the Labour Party had given strong support in the legislative council for the upgrading of the colony's trade union legislation and the association was instrumental in the formation of a number of labour unions, more of its attention seems to have been focused on political work within the legislative council than on the organization of workers. Its team for the 1951 elections was selected in 1950, but the party seems to have lain dormant, if one was to judge by the lack of information on any possible activities. With the formation of the new union, they appeared to have gone on the defensive, using mainly the newspapers to denounce the "misleaders" who had "sprung up to traverse the road prepared" by them and to appeal to the voters to remember the contribution they had made.[81]

McIntosh, who left the colony on 7 June to attend the Festival of Britain, spent an extended period of time there and did not return until the end of August. The reason for his long absence at such a critical time was never really given. Voters had been asked to await his appearance at a meeting at the market square, where he was expected to "reaffirm the party's policies" and to speak about "his efforts and achievement on behalf of the Colony while he was in England".[82] This meeting, as indicated earlier, did not go the way they expected.

Clearly, McIntosh and his Labour Party could not be judged on their achievements or failures, for, under the Crown colony system at that time, they were more advocates than legislators. The final decisions on matters raised and passed in the legislative council rested with the governor and executive council.

This was seen clearly with the repeal of the Shaker ordinance that was passed by the legislative council but went no further. Their impact, really, was in forcing items onto the agenda and mobilizing support outside the legislative council.

The United Workers Peasants and Ratepayers Union had some momentum from its launching at its May Day rally only four months earlier. Charles had, with the rest of his team, put a lot of emphasis on organizing workers in the rural areas through village committees that they had set up.[83] Many of the heads of these committees were shopkeepers, who played leading roles. They were literate and had access to information through the weekly newspapers. Persons in the communities would congregate at these shops and listen to the shopkeeper read from the newspaper. They thus became key political players in those communities. Charles and Joshua had gained valuable experience with trade unions and in political work through their association with Uriah Butler in Trinidad and their involvement in local council elections there.

Adult suffrage brought a broader constituency of voters onto the political scene, and this demanded a new style and approach. The union speakers appealed to the voters' religious orientation with hymns and biblical references and, as in the case of Joshua, references to classical literature and ancient history. Adult suffrage had been achieved, so that when the Labour Party talked about reaffirming its policies, it seemed out of step with the challenges that the new political climate presented.

Joshua was the candidate who seems to have most attracted the attention of voters, as he focused his attacks on colonialism and the evils in society. A columnist in the *Vincentian* of 26 May 1951 described the group as "moving with the times". Their anti-colonial and socialistic tone and attacks on the plantocracy might, however, have been more rhetoric than anything else, for, as one political scientist suggested, Joshua was never a socialist "either of the Marxist or Fabian variety". His was "a brand of populism which incorporated a genuflection to socialist ideas and concern for the betterment of the workers and peasants in their struggle against the plantocracy".[84]

Their style and rhetoric seemed to have had a profound impact on a people who saw the political kingdom as the key to solving their problems, lifting them from the depths of poverty and deprivation.[85] All of this reflected changes taking place in other colonies, particularly in the Windward Islands. Patrick Emmanuel made the point that, in Grenada, Marryshow's style was valid and productive within "the politics and political expectations of Crown Colony politics. The mass political involvement of the 1950s was conducive to the style of Gairy."[86] A similar kind of argument could be applied to St Vincent, with McIntosh's political style being more conducive to Crown colony politics, while Joshua and Charles, the leading members of the new party, appeared better suited to the challenges of adult suffrage.

Before 1951, the masses were kept out of the formal political arena but participated in protests and in petitioning for land and for better working conditions. Those working people who made presentations to the 1897 West India Commission had, even at that time, expressed the need for elected representation. The 1935 riots created a different environment. The working people who participated in the riots made the connection between what went on in the court yard on 21 October and the governor's response in recognizing the validity of some of their demands and in purporting to accede.

The year of 1951 was an important landmark in the history of the country. This was seen clearly in O.W. Forde's letter to the *Vincentian*, a month before the election, that appeared to have been addressed to his fellow planters.

> We must accept the view that trade unions are here to stay, if some cannot even accept they are good. . . . We must also accept and be resigned to the fact that adult suffrage is also here to stay. We must adopt a change of heart and win the cooperation of those who work for us if we cannot get accustomed to the idea that the pendulum of time has swung the other way.[87]

The disturbances throughout the region during the 1930s were key factors in the pace with which the constitutional and political changes leading to adult suffrage came about. These were accompanied by other social changes that were meant to address some of the needs of working people. Local circumstances, as in St Vincent, would have unearthed the colony's own players and highlighted matters that were relevant to them.

NOTES

INTRODUCTION

1. This chapter is a reworking of a paper, "Towards a Re-examination of the 1935 Riots", presented at the St Vincent Country Conference, sponsored by the University of West Indies School of Continuing Studies, St Vincent, 24 May 2003.

2. O. Nigel Bolland, *On the March: Labour Rebellions in the British Caribbean 1934–1939* (Kingston: Ian Randle, 1995); O. Nigel Bolland, *The Politics of Labour in the British Caribbean: The Social Origins of Authoritarianism and Democracy in the Labour Movement* (Kingston: Ian Randle, 2001); Richard Hart, "Origin and Development of the Working Class in the English-Speaking Caribbean Area, 1897–1937", in *Labour in the Caribbean: From Emancipation to Independence*, ed. Malcolm Cross and Gad Heuman (London: Macmillan, 1988), 43–79; Ralph Gonsalves, "The Role of Labour in the Political Process of St Vincent, 1935–70" (master's thesis, University of the West Indies, 1971); Ralph Gonsalves, *The 1935 Labour Riots in St Vincent and Their Political Significance* (Kingstown: Yulimo, 1966); Ralph Gonsalves, *The McIntosh Trial and the 1935 Uprising*, Educational Pamphlet no. 9 of the Movement for National Unity (Kingstown: Movement for National Unity, 1985); Adrian Fraser, "Peasants and Agricultural Labourers in St Vincent and the Grenadines 1899–1951" (PhD diss., University of Western Ontario, 1986); Kenneth John and Oswald Peters, "1935 Revisited", in *Search for Identity: Essays on St Vincent and the Grenadines*, ed. Baldwin King, Kenneth John and Cheryl King (Kingstown: Kings-SVG Press, 2006) 267–73; Lorna DeBique, "The 1935 Riots in St Vincent and the Grenadines" (Caribbean Studies Project in partial fulfilment of requirements for BA degree, University of the West Indies, Barbados), 1–13.

3. Bolland, *Politics of Labour*; Hart, "Origin and Development".

4. Fraser, "Peasants and Agricultural Labourers".

5. Bolland, *Politics of Labour*, 248; Governor Grier to Malcolm MacDonald, 12 November 1935, Confidential file (hereafter cited as Conf.) 97/1935 (57), no. 189, St Vincent Archives (hereafter SVA).

6.   Bolland, *Politics of Labour*, 362.
7.   Ibid., 357.

CHAPTER I

1.   Bolland (*Politics of Labour*, 212) argues that the series of disturbances that rocked the Caribbean started in Belize, Trinidad and Guyana in 1934.
2.   The other two islands were Dominica and St Lucia.
3.   Ebenezer Duncan, *Kingstown* (Kingstown: Model Printery, 1965), 10–14.
4.   See figure 1.
5.   Great Britain, *Report of the West India Royal Commission 1897*, British Parliamentary Papers (Dublin: Irish University Press, 1970), 7:48.
6.   Fraser, "Peasants and Agricultural Labourers", 102–4.
7.   The issue of land settlement as essential to the well-being of the working people had been widely discussed in the newspapers and raised by members of the SWMA at public meetings and in the legislative council, for those who were members of the council. See editorial of the *Times,* 10 September 1938, "Is Land Settlement Needed in St Vincent?" The *Investigator* of 8 February 1938 argued that the welfare of the colony depends largely on the extension of Peasant Land Settlement. McIntosh argued for land settlement in an article in the *Times,* 26 March 1938.
8.   *Colonial Office Annual Report, St Vincent* (London: HMSO, 1935), St Vincent Archives; *Agricultural Department Annual Report*, 1938, table 2, SVA. The Belair estate was purchased in 1912 but was not ready for allotment until 1914.
9.   All references to the *Times*, in text as well as notes, are to the Kingstown (St Vincent) edition.
10. *Agricultural Department Annual Report*, 1938, table 2, SVA.
11. Grimble to Grier, 22 July 1935, Minute Papers (hereafter cited as MP), SVA; Fraser, "Peasants and Agricultural Labourers", 118.
12. Grimble to Grier, 22 July 1935, MP, SVA.
13. Administrator Grimble to Governor Grier, 22 July 1935, "Land Tenure", MP, SVA.
14. Ibid.
15. "Editorial Notes: Land Settlement for Bequia", *Times*, 23 February 1935.
16. C.Y. Shephard, *Survey of Peasant Agriculture in the Leewards and Windwards* (Port of Spain: Imperial College of Tropical Agriculture, 1945), 44; A.S. Fraser, "Development of a Peasantry in St Vincent 1846–1912" (MPhil thesis, University of the West Indies, Cave Hill, Barbados, 1980).
17. Maurice St Pierre, "West Indian Cricket: A Socio-historical Appraisal", *Caribbean Quarterly* 19, no. 2 (June 1973), 7–27.

18. *Times*, 25 November 1935.

19. Rupert John, *Pioneers in Nation-Building in a Caribbean Mini-State* (New York: UNITAR, 1979), 58.

20. *Times*, 3 January 1935.

21. *Vincentian*, 22 June 1935.

22. *Investigator*, 2 October 1935.

23. "From Whence We Came", National Broadcasting Company, St Vincent, no. 326, 1 February 1999, prepared and presented by Adrian Fraser.

24. *Agricultural Department Annual Report* (1935), SVA.

25. *Agricultural Department Annual Report* (1906-7 and 1907-8), SVA.

26. Report of the West Indian Sugar Commission, London, 1929-30, Cmd. 3517, 39, SVA.

27. Great Britain, *Annual Administration Report*, 1934, SVA.

28. G. Wright, "Economic Conditions in St Vincent, British West Indies", *Economic Geography* 5, no. 3 (1929): 254.

29. S.G. Stephens, "Cotton Growing in the West Indies during the 18th and 19th Centuries", *Tropical Agriculture* 21, no. 2 (February 1944): 26-29.

30. Wright, "Economic Conditions in St Vincent", 170.

31. C.K. Robinson, "Government Cotton Ginnery", appendix P in *A Plan of Development for the Colony of St Vincent*, compiled by Bernard Gibbs, adopted by the St Vincent Development Committee, 1947, 374, SVA.

32. Frederick Walker, "Economic Progress of St Vincent, B.W.I. since 1927", *Economic Geography* 13, no. 3 (1937): 217-34.

33. "Report of Commission of Inquiry into the Arrowroot Industry", *Vincentian*, 12 November 1949; *Colonial Office Annual Report, St Vincent* (London: HMSO, 1946), SVA.

34. "Report of Commission of Inquiry", *Vincentian*, 12 November 1949.

35. *Agricultural Department Annual Report*, 1935, SVA.

36. Fraser, "Peasants and Agricultural Labourers", 186.

37. Walker, "Economic Progress of St Vincent", 232.

38. Douglas Hall, *Free Jamaica 1838-1865* (New Haven: Yale University Press, 1959), 158.

39. Fraser, "Peasants and Agricultural Labourers", 155-57; Orde Brown had drawn attention to the involvement of the independent cultivator in the market economy.

40. Report from the Select Committee on West Indian Colonies, 1842: Evidence of Hay MacDowall Grant, British Parliamentary Papers.

41. *Colonial Office Annual Report, St Vincent* (London: HMSO, 1898), SVA.

42. Fraser, "Peasants and Agricultural Labourers", 188.

43. *Annual Administration Report*, 1934, SVA.

44. Walker, "Economic Progress of St Vincent", 231; *Annual Administration Report*, 1935, SVA.

45. *Investigator*, 4 August 1935.

46. *Report of the West India Royal Commission, 1944–45 (Moyne Commission)* (London: 1945; repr., Barbados, Government Printing Department, 2000), 8 (hereafter cited as *Moyne Commission Report*).

47. *Colonial Office Annual Report, St Vincent* (London: HMSO, 1936), SVA.

48. G. St J. Orde Brown, *Labour Conditions in the West Indies* (London: HMSO, 1939), Cmnd. 6070, 155.

49. Roger Abrahams, *The Man-of-Words in the West Indies: Performance and the Emergence of Creole Culture* (Baltimore: Johns Hopkins University Press, 1983), 140.

50. *Moyne Commission Report*, 174.

51. Orde Brown, *Labour Conditions in the West Indies*, 155.

52. *Moyne Commission Report*, 92.

53. *Times*, 28 February 1935.

54. *Vincentian*, 8 June 1935.

55. *Annual Report on Primary Education in St Vincent* (1935) (Kingstown: Government Printing Office, 1936).

56. Colony of Saint Vincent, *Annual Blue Book* (St Vincent: 1935), SVA.

57. C.V.D. Hadley, "Personality Patterns, Social Class, and Aggression in the British West Indies", *Human Relations* 2, no. 4 (1949): 351.

58. Ibid., 360.

59. *Times*, 14 January 1939.

60. I have included in the proletariat section agricultural labourers, general labourers, domestic servants, boatmen and fishermen, clerks and shopmen; in the unestablished emergent or lower middle class, junior public officers (the census does not differentiate between junior and senior public servants), police, nurses, shopkeepers/hucksters, mechanics and handicraft men, mariners, laundresses and seamstresses; and in the established upper middle class, members of the legal and medical profession, civil engineers and surveyors, merchants, agents and dealers, hotelkeepers, proprietors, lessees, managers of plantations and persons living on private means.

61. *St Vincent: Report and General Abstracts of the Census of 1931*, prepared by Walter Grant (Kingstown: Government Printing Office, 1931), 7–8, SVA.

62. They called themselves "the Wilderness People". For more information, see Adrian Fraser, *From Shakers to Spiritual Baptists: The Struggle of the Shakers of St Vincent and the Grenadines* (Madison: Kings-SVG Publishers, 2011).

63. Sheena Boa, "Walking in the Highway to Heaven: Religious Influences and

Attitudes Relating to the Freed Population of St Vincent 1834–1884", *Journal of Caribbean History* 35, no. 2 (2001): 192.

64. Ibid.

65. S.F. Branch to West India Royal Commission, memo, 1897, SVA.

66. Boa, "Walking in the Highway", 194.

67. Griffith, chief of police, report, 1905, file on Shakerism, SVA.

68. Minutes of Legislative Council Meetings, 1909–1915, CO 263-33, SVA; Minutes of Legislative Council Meeting, 8 July 1912.

69. *Times*, 11 July 1912.

70. *Sentry*, 12 July 1912.

71. Fraser, *From Shakers to Spiritual Baptists*, 30.

72. Report on Certain Convictions for Shakerism, CO 321/273, XC 11723, 21 February 1913.

73. See Edward L. Cox, "Religious Intolerance and Persecution: The Case of the Shakers in St Vincent, 1900–1934", *Journal of Caribbean History* 28, no. 2 (1994): 23–24.

74. George Dundas (to Strahan), report accompanying the Blue Book for 1877, 10 May 1878, no. 69, SVA.

75. Ann Spackman, *Constitutional Development of the West Indies, 1922–68: A Selection of Major Documents* (Essex: Caribbean University Press, 1975), 25.

76. *Moyne Commission Report*, 379.

77. *Vincentian*, 23 December 1933.

78. John, *Pioneers in Nation-Building*, 158–60, 169, 183.

79. *Blue Book of Statistics*, 1936.

80. The RGA was established in 1919 to struggle for the reintroduction of electoral representation.

81. Great Britain, Report of the Closer Union Commission, April 1933, Cmnd. 4383/1932-33, 1078.

82. *Colonial Office Annual Report, St Vincent* (London: HMSO, 1946), SVA.

83. *Colonial Office Annual Report, St Vincent* (London: HMSO, 1951), SVA.

84. Patrick Emmanuel, *Crown Colony Politics in Grenada, 1917–1951* (Barbados: ISER, 1978), 73–74; Gordon K. Lewis, *The Growth of the Modern West Indies* (New York: Monthly Review Press, 1968), 156.

85. Emmanuel, *Crown Colony Politics*, 91.

86. Ebenezer Duncan, *A Brief History of St Vincent: With Studies in Citizenship*, 4th ed. (Kingstown: Model Printery, 1967), 52.

87. *Investigator*, 16 December 1936.

88. Gonsalves, *1935 Labour Riots*, 5–6.

CHAPTER 2

1. Bolland highlights the salt ponds in Belize. He has consistently in his work on the labour rebellions in the 1930s made a case for the inclusion of Belize as one of the first colonies to have had disturbances.
2. The administrator assumed the position of colonial secretary whenever the governor was present.
3. Minutes of Legislative Council Meeting, St Vincent, 18 October 1935, CO 263/51, XC 11792; see also *Times*, 31 October 1935.
4. *Vincentian*, 26 October 1935.
5. Minutes of the Meeting of the Finance Committee held on 2 May 1935, Conf., 1935, SVA.
6. "Governor's Address to the Representative Government Association", *Vincentian*, 22 June 1935.
7. Minutes of Legislative Council Meeting, 18 October 1935, SVA.
8. Matches, clearly, were not a luxury item and were widely used by the working people.
9. John, *Pioneers in Nation-Building*, 4.
10. Ibid., 3.
11. Evidence of Laois MacMaster, policeman who patrolled Middle Street on 19 October, given at the preliminary trial of George McIntosh. "Proceedings of the Preliminary Trials of George McIntosh", *Port of Spain Gazette* (government publication), December 1935. (The *Gazette* was given the sole rights of publication of the preliminary trials.)
12. McIntosh to the *Times*, 1 April 1939.
13. *Investigator*, 26 October 1935.
14. Minutes of Legislative Council Meeting, 21 October 1935, SVA.
15. Evidence of Donald Romeo at preliminary trial of McIntosh. "Proceedings", *Port of Spain Gazette*, December 1935, SVA.
16. Administrator Grimble to Governor Grier, 20 January 1936, Memo no. 1, SVA (including McIntosh's statement on his arrest). McIntosh was arrested at 11:30 p.m. on 23 November 1935, at his residence at Paul's Lot, by Alexander Haywood, sergeant of police. Grier, 21 October 1935.
17. Grier to MacDonald, 12 November 1935, SVA.
18. *Times*, 24 October 1935.
19. News reports from the *Times* and *Vincentian*, 24 October 1935; Evidence of Donald Romeo, "Proceedings", *Port of Spain Gazette*, December 1935; Interviews of Sheriff Lewis in John and Peters, "1935 Revisited", 267–73. Governor Grier did estimate the crowd that confronted him to be about three hundred.

20. Caspar London, "Samuel Lewis and the 1935 Revolt", n.d. (unpublished based on interviews of Samuel "Sheriff" Lewis in 1970s), 1–6; John and Peters, "1935 Revisited", 270.

21. London, "Samuel Lewis and the 1935 Revolt".

22. McIntosh's statement on his arrest, Grimble to Grier, memo, 20 January 1936, SVA.

23. In Grier's report to MacDonald, 12 November 1935, he noted, "The man who had sent the letter asking for an interview, had obtained a bell and by ringing it, at last managed to enable me to speak to those who were near me." Conf. 97/1935 (57), SVA.

24. Report of Administrator Grimble, 31 October 1935, Conf. 97/1935, SVA.

25. McIntosh's statement on his arrest, Grimble to Grier, memo, 20 January 1936, SVA.

26. Grier to MacDonald, 12 November 1935, SVA.

27. *Times*, 24 October 1935.

28. Clement Cato, interview by author, New Montrose, 7 March 1989. Clement Cato was one of the policemen at the courthouse at the time of the riots and was normally stationed at the police headquarters in Kingstown.

29. Grier to MacDonald, 12 November 1935, SVA.

30. The following were broken – three boxes, two presses, two tables, one desk, one chair, one tool chest, two clocks, one bell and a scale. Eight handcuffs and some keys were taken away; three pots of rice were broken, and one bucket and cup taken away from the bakery; glass windows were smashed; the main gate, the male dormitory door and the female prison door were broken down. The chief warder's bicycle was smashed as the door to his quarters was broken. Ten male and twenty-six female prisoners were released, with sixteen taken away. Of the sixteen prisoners who had gone away with the crowd, thirteen returned voluntarily, two were brought back by the police and one remained at large up to the end of October. Letter from Chief Warder J. Joshua to Administrator, 31 October 1935, SVA.

31. N. Quammie, Warder, to Acting Chief of Police, 3 March 1936, Conf. 97/1935 (126a), SVA. Two of the prisoners who had helped to restrain the others and withstand the prompting of the crowd were given a three-month remission of their term, and a third was given extra marks, which were equivalent to one month's remission of sentence. The three prisoners were identified as Mapp, Todd and Browne.

32. Evidence of police constables Alexander Roberts and Frederick John, "Proceedings", *Port of Spain Gazette*, December 1935; Donald Romeo, statement at police headquarters, 21 November 1935, included in despatch from administrator to governor; Conf. 97/1935, 20 January 1936, Re. Charges against Mr G.A McIntosh;

Administrator Grimble, Report of the Disturbances in St Vincent, 31 October 1935, Conf. 97/1935, SVA.

33.   Reports on the incident did not mention Fred Hazell by name, but it was widely known that he was the merchant involved. On his return after receiving medical attention, he shot and killed someone known as John Bull, who, he was informed, was responsible for the damage he received (Robert Ogarro and Norman Williams, interview by author, 28 November 1990, New Montrose). The governor reported on the incident as follows: "Before the firing actually began the police had been joined by a prominent merchant of Kingstown who is a lieutenant in the local Volunteer Force. This man who is well known and popular in the community, had earlier on made an attempt to disperse the crowd in front of the Court House by speaking to them, but he had been attacked and struck on the head by a man armed with a heavy stick. He was saved from further injury by some members of the crowd who knew him and got him away from his assailant. After having his head dressed at the hospital he had obtained a rifle and took up his position with the volunteer forces." St Lucia, Grier to Mac Donald, no. 189, Conf. 97/1935 (57), 12 November 1935.

34.   *Port of Spain Gazette*, 25 October 1935; Grier to MacDonald, 12 November 1935, SVA; Cato, interview by author.

35.   Grier to MacDonald, 12 November 1935, SVA.

36.   Grimble, Report of the Disturbances, 31 October 1935, SVA; Alum Jones, Commanding Officer, HMS *Challenger*, at St George's, Grenada, to Commander-in-Charge American and West Indies Station, Conf. Report on the Disturbances at Kingstown on 21 October 1935, 29 October 1936, 1304/7, SVA.

37.   Jones, Conf. Report on the Disturbances, 29 October 1936, SVA.

38.   Disposition of Police before and after the reading of the Riot Act – 21 October 1935; and casualties suffered by the Force before Firing commissioned, Conf. 97/1935 (45b), 8 November 1935, SVA.

39.   Grier to MacDonald, 12 November 1935, SVA; Cato, interview by author.

40.   Grier to MacDonald, 12 November 1935, SVA. Clement Cato was able to show me the mark on his finger where it had been broken.

41.   Osment "Mento" Williams, when interviewed fifty-five years after the incident, still harboured the view that Corea and other members of the elite in the society were the architects of the measures introduced in the legislative council.

42.   The *Port of Spain Gazette* on 23 October 1935 did mention the looting of the dry goods stores of Richards Brothers and McConnie Gill and Company, although the local newspapers were silent on this. These would have been relatively minor, since claims that were submitted to the authorities for damages included an amount for the trade stock of persons other than Corea, but the claim was for

£15.1, as opposed to Corea's for £2,100. Summary of damages and losses caused by the riots, enclosure in St Vincent despatch no. 74, 21 November 1935.

43. Grimble, Report of the Disturbances, 31 October 1935, SVA.

44. Norman Williams, Robert Ogarro and Baha Lawrence, interviews by author. Norman Williams was a bystander at the time of the Kingstown riots; an attendant at a store in Kingstown then, he was on lunch break and on his way home when the commotion at the court yard attracted him there.

45. "A Resident's Account", *Port of Spain Gazette*, 29 October 1935. The reference to the ship is to the HMS *Challenger*; Persons interviewed – Norman Williams, Robert Ogarro and Clement Cato – also made references to seeing persons walking with bolts of cloth.

46. Market "place" and "square" were used interchangeably.

47. Grimble, Report of the Disturbances, 31 October 1935, SVA.

48. There is no indication that he had originally arranged to meet with them at 10:00 a.m.

49. *Times*, 1 April 1939. Part of this story was corroborated by Donald Romeo in a statement he gave at the police headquarters on 21 November 1935: "I met a crowd of people gathered opposite the Court House Yard. I heard them saying that they are going to the Governor-in-Chief. Soon after I saw Mr. McIntosh came out from the Court House on his bicycle, the crowd of people went around him and they tell him they want to see the Governor. Mr. McIntosh told them if they want to see the Governor don't go to him with any noise, it is much better to get a letter and carry it to him. Mr. McIntosh started for his drug store and the crowd followed him. When we got at Mr. McIntosh store he told us to wait on him and he will give us a letter to take to H.E. [His Excellency, the governor], he then start to type the letter. While typing he said to the crowd of people you all go back to the Court House and wait me. Most of us went back to the Court House and wait Mr. McIntosh's arrival. About 15 minutes later he came up from his drug store and all the people rush towards him. Mr. McIntosh told the people to wait on him and give him a chance. Mr. McIntosh went upstairs the Court House with a letter to H.E he returned back and told the crowd that the Governor-in-Chief says to wait until 5:00 p.m. he will be going at the library, the crowd started to shout saying that they cannot wait."

50. Grimble, Report of the Disturbances, 31 October 1935, SVA.

51. Grier to MacDonald, 12 November 1935, SVA.

52. McIntosh's statement on his arrest, Grimble to Grier, memo, 20 January 1936, SVA.

53. Report from Lt H.J. Hughes to the Colonial Secretary, 31 October 1935, Conf. 97/1935 (25a), SVA.

54. *Times*, 24 October 1935.

55. There was, however, no indication that his house was attacked.

56. Report from Lt H.J. Hughes, 31 October 1935, SVA.

57. Report by Lance Corporal A. Baynes, St Vincent Volunteers, 31 October 1935; among reports forwarded by Lieutenant Alfred Hazell to the Hon. Colonial Secretary, 31 October 1935: Conf. 94/1935.

58. Baha Lawrence, interview by author, 18 January 1990. At the time of the interview, Lawrence was the manager of a gas station on Granby Street, where the interview took place.

59. Jones, Conf. Report on the Disturbances, 29 October 1936, SVA.

60. Lucas Layne, interview by author, 28 April 1989. At the time of the interview, Layne worked as a security guard. During the riots, he was one of two policemen stationed at the Georgetown police station; Vincentian surgeon A. Cecil Cyrus remembers being a six-year-old student at the Layou Primary School (Layou is eight miles away from Kingstown) when, at about 3 p.m., the launch *Veda S* arrived from Kingstown and brought news of the riots that had taken place. Although not fully aware of what it meant, the reaction of the teachers on hearing the news suggested to him that something serious had happened. *A Dream Come True: The Autobiography of a Caribbean Surgeon* (Charleston: Hobo Jungle Press, 2015), 84.

61. Layne, interview.

62. Report from Captain Alban Da Santos in connection with the Mission entrusted to him to the Windward District, to the Hon. Colonial Secretary, 31 October 1935, Conf. 94/1935, SVA.

63. Osment Williams, Ronald Paris and Kathleen Sardine, interviews by author, Campden Park, 1990. Osment Williams was injured during the riots at Camden Park; Ronald Paris was among the rioting crowd in Campden Park; and Kathleen Sardine was a young girl during the riots, living in the same house as her uncle DeSouza.

64. Captain Conrad Hazell's report to the Colonial Secretary, Conf. 97/1935, SVA.

65. *Vincentian*, 26 October 1935; Grimble, Report of the Disturbances, 31 October 1935, SVA.

66. Summary of damages and losses caused by the riots, Conf. 97/1935 (45d), SVA. Most of the claims submitted by officials had to do with damages to their vehicles that were parked at the yard of the courthouse on 21 October.

67. "Notice", 24 October 1935, signed by Arthur Grimble, Government Office, 24 October 1935; *Vincentian*, 26 October 1935.

68. Grier to Rear Admiral J. Edgell, Hydrogapher of the Navy, Admiralty, Whitehall, 30 October 1935, SVA; Jones, Conf. Report on the Disturbances, 29 October 1936, SVA.

CHAPTER 3

1.   These were considered areas with significant slum populations.
2.   Grier to MacDonald, 12 November 1935, SVA.
3.   Ibid.; *Colonial Annual Report for St Vincent 1935*, SVA.
4.   Governor Grier to Rt Honourable J.H. Thomas, 20 January 1936, MP, Conf. 97/1935 (121), SVA.
5.   Grier to Commander-in-Chief, America and West Indies Station, telegram, 6 November 1935, Conf. 97/1935 (60) telegram no. 239, SVA.
6.   Grier to Sir Cosmo Parkinson, 20 January 1936, SVA; "Double Tragedy in St Vincent: Chauffeur Hacks Employer Then Takes Arsenic", *Port of Spain Gazette*, 1 January 1936.
7.   It was believed that clubs were formed to get around the liquor licensing regulations, "They are the resort of undesirables [*sic*] subject to no rules as to membership and as there is at present no legislation pertaining to them, the proprietor of the licensed premises connected with them observes practically no closing hours." H. O'Reilly to Grimble, 20 January 1936, "Report on the Closing of Shops in Kingstown on the Night of 21 December 1935", Conf. 97/1935 (112a), SVA.
8.   Ibid. The club in question, it was noted, was the scene of revelry following the outcome of the case against McIntosh.
9.   This will be developed in chapter 4.
10. *West Indian Crusader*, 2 November 1935, reprinted extracts of the governor's speech to the RGA on October that were carried in the *Times*, 31 October 1935. A copy of the speech was included in the despatch with Grier's report to MacDonald on 12 November 1935, St Lucia 189, Conf. 97/1935 (57).
11. Minutes of Legislative Council Meeting, 28 October 1935, CO 263/51, 72297; *Investigator*, editorial, 1 February 1936.
12. The *Investigator* and *Times* were owned by persons who were members of the RGA and, later, of the SWMA.
13. MP, 143/1935 no. 246, SVA.
14. Notice, *Government Gazette*, 25 October 1935.
15. Administrator, Grenada, to Governor, St Vincent, telegram, no. 19, Conf. 97/1935.
16. "Censoring of News", editorial, *Times*, 24 November 1935.
17. Alfred Clement DeBique was a solicitor and journalist and a critic of the colonial administration. He was a founding father of the St Vincent RGA and was present at the courthouse on 21 October when the riots began.
18. Grimble to Grier, 29 January 1936, Conf. 97/1935 (120).
19. Administration, St Vincent, to Canapress, Halifax, telegram, 3 February 1936.
20. Canapress to Administration, St Vincent, telegram, received 4 February 1936;

St Vincent to Canapress, telegram, 4 February 1936; Canapress to St Vincent, telegram, received 5 February 1936; Conf. 10 February 1936 (in file of 1935 riots among despatches between administrator and governor)

21. Marryshow to Wright, 5 August 1936 (copy included in file on the 1935 riots)
22. *Times*, 6 February 1936.
23. *Investigator*, 2 November 1936.
24. Governor Grier to J.H. Thomas about the visit of Susan Lawrence, Government House, 10 February 1936, 71091/36 Windward Islands, in "Miss Lawrence and Seditious Propaganda" (MP-1936), SVA.
25. See chapter 1.
26. Notice, *Government Gazette*, 28 October 1935, SVA.
27. *Times*, 2 January 1936.
28. Reproduced in *Port of Spain Gazette*, 15 December 1936.
29. Grimble to Grier, "Closing of Certain Shops", 24 January 1936, SVA.
30. "State of Emergency", Minutes of Executive Council Meeting, 29 January 1936, MP 143/1935 no. 10, SVA.
31. Grimble to Grier, "Closing of Certain Shops", 24 January 1936, SVA.
32. Ibid.
33. Telegram from Grier to the Secretary of State for the Colonies, 31 January 1935, Conf. 97/1935 (122), SVA; Grimble to Grier, 29 January 1936, SVA.
34. "State of Emergency", Minutes of Executive Council Meeting, MP, SVA; *Government Gazette*, 1 February 1936.
35. "Sir Selwyn Grier and the People: The Reflections and Opinions of John Citizen", *Times*, 19 March 1936.
36. Minutes of the (Adjourned) Meeting of the Legislative Council of St Vincent, 16 November 1935, CO 263/51, XC 11792.
37. *Vincentian*, 16 November 1935, quoting from minutes of the legislative council of 14 November.
38. Minutes of Legislative Council Meeting, 14 November 1935, CO 263/51, XC 11792.
39. "An Ordinance to provide for the punishment of seditious acts and seditious libel, to facilitate the suppression of seditious publications, and to provide for the temporary suspension of newspapers containing seditious matter", assented to by Grier on 27 November 1935, no. 47 of 1935, SVA.
40. Extract from Note of Interview with Susan Lawrence, 71901/36 Windward Islands; Grier to Thomas, 10 February 1936, SVA.
41. British Parliamentary Debates, House of Commons Sessions 1935–1936, 20 May 1936, 312: 1182–83.
42. "Sir Selwyn Grier and the People".
43. "The Seditious Publications Ordinance", *Times*, 7 May 1936.

44. Labour Organisation file 64320/36; CO 321/396, McIntosh's speech at Rally in Georgetown; *Times*, 22 and 29 August 1936; enclosure in despatch, St Vincent, 8 September 1936; Grimble to Grier, 2 September 1936, SVA.

45. SVA 71091/36 Windward Islands. Grier to Thomas, 10 February 1936, SVA.

46. Grimble to Grier, "Closing of Certain Shops", 24 January 1936, SVA.

47. "Seditious Publications Ordinance to Be Amended", *Times*, 22 May 1937.

48. This would have been the Negro Welfare, Cultural and Social Association of which Vincentian-born Elma Francois was a member. Elma was an acquaintance of George McIntosh before she migrated to Trinidad.

49. Harold Moody, President, League of Coloured Peoples (Memorial Hall, Farringdon Street, London EC4) to J.H. Thomas, Secretary of State for the Colonies, 11 February 1936, SVA.

50. Ibid.

51. *Times*, 7 May 1936: The *Times* commented on correspondence from the secretary as published in the League of Coloured Peoples organ, the *Keys*.

52. *Vincentian*, 26 October 1935, quoted in the *West Indian Crusader*, 2 November 1935.

53. *Times*, 20 February 1936.

54. *Times*, 24 October 1935.

55. *Vincentian*, 16 November 1935; *Investigator*, 6 November 1935.

56. Governor Grier's speech to members of the RGA at the Library, 28 October 1935, in *Vincentian*, 2 November 1935, SVA.

57. Minutes of the Kingstown Board, 29 October 1935.

58. Governor's address to the RGA, 28 October 1935.

59. Will be discussed later.

60. "Reaction to the Riots", Methodist Church (Mission House, Kingstown) to Sir Selwyn McGregor Grier, Conf. 97/1935 (58), 14 November 1935, SVA.

61. "Supreme Court of Judicature: Hearing of the Suit Nanton vs Frederick", *Vincentian*, 2 November 1935.

62. Ibid.

63. Randolph Williams to Sir Algeron Aspinall, 27 November 1935, Letter from Richmond Hill, SVA.

64. RGA to Sir John Maffey, 17 February 1936, presented to him on his visit to St Vincent, SVA.

65. Resolution of the Grenada Labour Party, sent through Administrator to Governor Grier, 6 March 1936 (in file on the 1935 riots).

66. CO 32/363, XC 11792, SVA.

67. W. Ormsby Gore (Downing Street) to Grier, 16 June 1936, Conf. 97/1935 (145), SVA.

68. Grier to the Secretary of State, Conf. telegram, 31 October 1935, SVA.

69. "Question by Honourable Member for Kingstown", file on the 1935 riots, 13 October 1941, SVA.
70. "Arrest of McIntosh", coded telegram sent to Governor, Grenada, at 5:05 p.m., 22 November 1935, Conf. 97/1935 (66), SVA.
71. Grimble to Grier, memo, 20 January 1936, SVA.
72. Report of the Visit of E.F.L. Wood (known as the Wood Commission), MP, to the West Indies and British Guiana, 1921–22, London, 1922, Cmnd. 1679, 6.
73. Ken Post, *Arise Ye Starvelings: The Jamaican Labour Rebellion of 1938 and Its Aftermath* (The Hague: Martinus Nijhoff, 1978), 286.
74. Governor's address to the RGA, 28 October 1935.
75. Governor Grier to Sir Cosmo Parkinson, 17 November 1935, Conf. 92/1935, SVA.
76. Ibid.
77. C.C. Ross, Memorandum relating to the Prosecution of Mr G.A. McIntosh for Treason-Felony, Conf. 97/1935 (81), AG 2/12/35, SVA. Grimble to Grier, memo, Conf. 97/1935 (82), 20 January 1936, SVA.
78. C.C. Ross, memo.
79. Ibid.
80. Ibid.
81. "Arrest of McIntosh", telegram, SVA.
82. "Proceedings", *Port of Spain Gazette*, December 1935.
83. The last witness referred to here is Sybil Powers, wife of the auditor of the Windward Islands, for whom arrangements had to be made to come from Grenada to give evidence. Mrs Powers was present at the sitting of the legislative council on 21 October; she claimed to have followed McIntosh out of the legislative council hall and heard certain words being spoken by him: "The time has passed to ask favours"; "take it, take it, take it".
84. "Proceedings", *Port of Spain Gazette*, December 1935.
85. "Arrest of McIntosh", telegram, SVA.
86. Grimble to Grier, "G.A. McIntosh, Re Charge Against", 20 January 1936, Conf. 97/1935, SVA.
87. Evidence of George Thomas, "Proceedings", *Port of Spain Gazette*, December 1935.
88. Statement of Leonard Mayers. Grimble to Grier, memo, 20 January 1936, SVA.
89. Ibid.
90. I have not been able to identify Gonsalves.
91. Grimble to Grier, 24 December 1935, Conf. 97/1935 (104).
92. Ibid.
93. Sub-inspector from Trinidad and Tobago. Grimble to Grier, 24 December 1935, Conf. 97/1935 (104), SVA.

94.   Attorney General Ross was transferred to Grenada. Grimble to Grier, 24 December 1935, Conf. 97/1935 (104), SVA.
95.   Grier to Parkinson, 17 November 1935, SVA.
96.   Daisley had also been charged for Treason-Felony. McIntosh's reflections in *Demerara Tribune*, 5 January 1936, quoted in *Times*, 4 February 1939.
97.   Grier to Thomas, 28 March 1936, Conf. 17/1935 (140), SVA.
98.   Grier, Notes on Observation of Susan Lawrence, 71901/36, SVA.
99.   C.D. Milbourne's report re Don Morgan, enclosed in Grimble to Grier, 22 January 1936, SVA.
100.   Grimble to Grier, 22 January 1936; *Demerara Tribune*, 5 January 1936, quoted in *Times*, 4 February 1939; *Times*, 26 December 1935.
101.   *Times*, 16 January 1936; O'Reilly, memo, 19 March 1936, Conf. 97/935 (13)a.
102.   Grimble to Grier, 27 January 1936, Conf. 97/1935 (115), SVA.
103.   Grimble to Grier, 2 December 1935, SVA.
104.   Grimble to Grier, 31 January 1936, Conf. 97/1935 (122), SVA.
105.   Ibid.
106.   O'Reilly, memo, 19 March 1936. The *Times*, in its issues of 16 and 23 January, carried updates on the trial but with little comment, possibly because of the state of emergency.
107.   *Times*, 30 January 1936.
108.   Grier, Notes on Observations.
109.   Administrator to Chief of Police, query, 24 January 1936; H. Grist, Chief of Police, to Administrator, reply, 25 January 1936, Conf. 97/1935 (115), SVA.
110.   Grier to Thomas, 28 March 1936, SVA.
111.   London, "Samuel Lewis and the 1935 Revolt".
112.   Grier to Parkinson, 15 March 1936, SVA.
113.   Grimble to Grier, 16 April 1936, SVA.
114.   Grier to Parkinson, 15 March 1936, SVA.

CHAPTER 4

1.   L. Toney, Comment on the Governor's Official Report, 12 November 1935, file no. 189 on the 1935 riots, SVA.
2.   J. Broome also represented the *Barbados Journal* and *Daily Mail* (of England).
3.   27 February 1936.
4.   Grier to Secretary of State, telegram, St Vincent, 22 October 1935, SVA.
5.   Governor Grier to Sir Cosmo Parkinson, 26 October 1935, St Vincent, CO 32/362, XC 11792, C 86/35; Government's report, 12 November 1935, Conf. 97/1935 (57), no. 189, SVA. The persons were not identified, nor were the criminal charges indicated.

6.   Grier to Parkinson, 26 October 1935.

7.   Minutes of Legislative Council Meeting, 28 October 1935, SVA.

8.   Will be discussed later.

9.   *Vincentian*, 2 November 1935.

10. Grier to MacDonald, 12 November 1935, SVA.

11. *Moyne Commission Report*, 8.

12. Ibid., 197.

13. "Sir Selwyn Grier and the People".

14. *Vincentian*, 26 October 1935 (carried in the *West Indian Crusader*, 2 November 1935), 7.

15. *Sentry*, 17 January 1930.

16. Grier to MacDonald, 12 November 1935, SVA.

17. Ibid.

18. F.L. Engledow, *Report on Agriculture, Foresty and Veterinary Matters for the 1938/39 West Indian Royal Commission*, Cmd. 6608, HMSO, June 1945.

19. *Moyne Commission Report*, 7.

20. Fraser, "Peasants and Agricultural Labourers", 111–17.

21. Grimble to Grier, 22 July 1935, SVA.

22. Petition from Barrouallie, 27 January 1936, Conf. 70/1935, SVA.

23. This is taken up in chapter 5.

24. *Times*, 17 August 1940.

25. Clement Cato and Lucas Layne, interviews by author. There is no other available evidence that supports this.

26. Report from Captain Alban Da Santos, 31 October 1935, SVA.

27. *Government Gazette*, 1 October 1919, St Vincent, SVA.

28. *Times*, 2 March 1922.

29. Ibid.; Fraser, "Peasants and Agricultural Labourers", 298.

30. *Times*, 8 and 15 August 1935.

31. *Times*, 15 August 1935.

32. Arthur Grimble, Notes on Investigations Subsequent to the Riots, 8 November 1935, Conf. 97/1935 (45), SVA.

33. *Vincentian*, 26 October 1935.

34. *Times*, 28 November 1935. See also Robert G. Weisbord, "British West Indian Reaction to the Italian-Ethiopian War: An Episode in Pan-Americanism", *Caribbean Studies* 10, no. 1 (1970): 34–41.

35. Grier to Thomas, 28 March 1936, Conf. 17/1935 (140), SVA.

36. CO 32/363, XC 11792–C86/35, 26 October 1935, SVA.

37. *Vincentian*, 26 October 1935.

38. CO 32/363 no. 189, SVA.

39. Letter to the editor, 11 January 1936, SVA.
40. Information about these coloured Vincentians is difficult to find. The governor had mentioned a wealthy African whose house was attacked but did not disclose the name.
41. "West Indian Outbreaks", editorial, a Grenada newspaper.
42. John, *Pioneers in Nation-Building*, 159–70, 183.
43. Gonsalves, *1935 Labour Riots*, 5–6.
44. Evidence of Donald Romeo, "Proceedings", *Port of Spain Gazette*, December 1935.
45. Grier to MacDonald, 12 November 1935, CO 32/363.
46. *Times*, 31 October 1935.
47. Grier to MacDonald, 12 November 1935, SVA.
48. Grier to Parkinson, 17 November 1935, SVA.
49. Grier to MacDonald, 12 November 1935, SVA.
50. Ibid.
51. McIntosh sold items used by the working people that were not limited to medicinal items.
52. See Hart, "Origin and Development".
53. The severest sentence, ten years' hard labour, was given to Martin Durham, who was the alleged leader of the rioters at Cane Garden; *Times*, 30 January 1936.
54. *Flambeau* (organ of the Kingstown study group) no. 8, September 1967, 32. There might have been some exaggeration about the role Sheriff ascribed to himself, but the fact that he was one of those who took control in the court yard is recognized.
55. This applies to the outbreak of violence at the yard of the courthouse.
56. "Mento" Williams, interview by author.
57. Fraser, "Peasants and Agricultural Labourers", 318.
58. The state of communication has to be taken into account in understanding the time when the Georgetown riots occurred. There would have been limited telephone communication, under regular circumstances, but telephone wires were cut. A. Cecil Cyrus, who lived in Layou, explains that, in Layou, which was eight miles from Kingstown, news of the riots only reached them when the motor launch *Veda S* arrived at 3:00 p.m. on its way further north to Chateaubelair. See Cyrus, *Dream Come True*, 84.

CHAPTER 5

1. These will be dealt with in chapter 6.
2. Bolland, *Politics of Labour*, 356.
3. Ralph Gonsalves, *The October 1935 Uprising in Saint Vincent (Youlou) and the October 1917 Revolution of the Soviet Union* (Kingstown: Yulimo, 1977), 15.

4.   Minutes of Legislative Council Meeting, 12 December 1949, SVA.

5.   Bolland, *Politics of Labour*, 356.

6.   The St Vincent riots followed those of St Kitts earlier in the year and were therefore the second to have taken place in the Caribbean region during the period of the 1930s. The St Kitts riots were traditionally accepted as the beginning of the series of disturbances that rocked the Caribbean in the 1930s, but Bolland (ibid.) has argued that the disturbances actually started in Belize in 1934.

7.   *Times*, 12 December 1935.

8.   Fraser, "Peasants and Agricultural Labourers", 373.

9.   Ibid.

10.   *Times*, 31 October 1936.

11.   Quiz, "Comments and Criticism: Our Little World": Impact of Riots on Consciousness", *Times*, 31 October 1936.

12.   Ibid.

13.   Kenneth John, "St Vincent: A Political Kaleidoscope", *Flambeau*, no. 5 (July 1966), reprinted in *The Aftermath of Sovereignty: West Indian Perspectives*, ed. D. Lowenthal and Lambros Comitas (New York: Anchor Press, 1973), 83.

14.   *Proceedings of the West Indian Conference Held at Roseau, Dominica, B.W.I., October–November 1932* (Castries, St Lucia: Voice Printery, 1932).

15.   Ibid., 24, 58–9.

16.   Ibid., 16, 43.

17.   This was the gut reaction of the middle class, but, in the case of McIntosh, the fact that he was under suspicion and investigation might have influenced his immediate reaction.

18.   F.R. Augier et al., *The Making of the West Indies* (London: Longmans, 1960), 276.

19.   *Proceedings of the West Indian Conference*, 2.

20.   Great Britain, Report of the Closer Union Commission, 1078; Fraser, "Peasants and Agricultural Labourers", 59.

21.   Augier et al., *Making of the West Indies*, 276–77.

22.   Robert Anderson, the St Vincent delegate to the 1932 conference, stated that "any political achievement in the constitution may reasonably be attributed to this conference". See R.M. Anderson, ed., *The St Vincent Handbook* (Kingstown: Office of the Vincentian, 1938), 222.

23.   Ibid.

24.   *Investigator*, 16 December 1936.

25.   *Times*, 8 March 1934.

26.   Garvey delivered two addresses during his visits to St Vincent on his way to and from Halifax, Nova Scotia. The first was on 19 October and the second on 27 October 1937. McIntosh's association actually hosted Garvey during his two visits,

as did Cipriani's Trinidad Labour Party (previously called Trinidad Workingmen's Association) on his visits to Trinidad.

27. *Times*, 5 March 1936.
28. The fact that the paper said that there was some talk of a new association suggests that its formation was at first not widely known.
29. *Times*, 5 March 1936; *Investigator*, 4 March 1936.
30. *Times*, 4 June 1936.
31. *Investigator*, 1 April 1936. It seemed to have been modelled on the Trinidad Workingmen's Association that was later renamed the Trinidad Labour Party.
32. *Investigator*, 4 April 1936.
33. Referred to sometimes simply as "the Association".
34. *Times*, 31 December 1938.
35. *Investigator*, 13 May 1936; *Investigator*, 13 June 1936.
36. *Investigator*, 27 July 1936.
37. The first Monday in August was celebrated as Emancipation Day.
38. *Times*, 8 August 1936.
39. Ibid. A similar pattern was seen at the 1932 Unofficial West Indian Conference, when the first official act of the conference was to pass a resolution of loyalty to the Crown. At the closing ceremony, too, the chairman, Rawle, asked the audience "to demonstrate your unswerving loyalty to the Throne and Person of His Majesty by joining in the National Anthem".
40. Administrator Wright to Governor Grier, Secret Enclosure to Despatch, 2 September 1936, SVA.
41. *Times*, 8 May 1936.
42. Labour Organisation file 64320/36, SVA; CO 321/369.
43. *Vincentian*, 27 March 1937.
44. Lewis, *Growth of the Modern West Indies*, 159.
45. Labour Organisation file, SVA.
46. Gonsalves, *1935 Labour Riots*, 6.
47. *Investigator*, 4 January 1936.
48. *Investigator*, 1 February 1936.
49. Quiz, "Our Future Legislators", *Times*, 12 December 1935.
50. McIntosh to Hannays, 1935 riots (conf.), 27 January 1936, SVA; *Times*, 28 January 1939; Frankie McIntosh (grandson of George McIntosh) to author, 6 February 2013.
51. Anderson, *St Vincent Handbook*, 222.
52. *Investigator*, 16 December 1936.
53. Ibid.
54. *Times*, 31 December 1936.

55.   *Times*, 9 January 1937.

56.   Quiz, "Comment and Criticism: Our World", *Times*, 16 January 1937.

57.   I was unable to locate the petition, which was only referred to but not cited. It might be that what McIntosh was actually referring to was a petition against the extension of the franchise.

58.   *Times*, 20 March 1937.

59.   Ibid.

60.   "Labour Party" was an unofficial name. Even in 1951, the name registered on the ballot was "Workers Association".

61.   *Times*, 20 March 1937.

62.   *Times*, 20 February 1937.

63.   *Times*, 20 March 1937.

64.   These were really not officially "parties". The SWMA was a political arm. The planters were, at that time, a group running as independents who decided to group themselves together to meet the challenge of the new organization that was seeking to enter the legislative council which they had long dominated.

65.   *Times*, 27 March 1937.

66.   Ibid.

67.   Ibid.

68.   Ibid.

69.   In 1938, electors in St Vincent numbered 1598 – that is, 2.78 per cent of the population. Franklyn Knight, "The Caribbean in the 1930s", in *General History of the Caribbean*, vol. 5, edited by Bridget Brereton (London: UNESCO, 2004), 46.

70.   *Investigator*, 27 March 1937.

71.   *Times*, 27 March 1937.

72.   *Vincentian*, 27 March 1937.

73.   *Times*, 3 April 1937.

74.   Ibid.

75.   Ibid.

76.   *Times*, 2 March 1940.

77.   *Times*, 20 April 1940.

78.   Ibid.

79.   *Times*, 16 March 1940.

80.   In 1942, an Order in Council had extended the life of the legislative council because of the war.

81.   *Times*, 1 June 1946.

82.   *Times*, 6 July 1946.

83.   *Times*, 20 July 1946.

84.   "Highlights of the Coming General Elections", *Times*, 29 June 1946.

85. "Highlights of the Coming General Elections", *Times*, 28 September 1946.
86. *Times*, 14 September 1946.
87. *Times*, 1 February 1946.
88. Ibid.
89. *Times*, 10 August 1946
90. *Times*, 22 December 1945; *Times*, 2 February 1946.
91. *Times*, 2 February 1946.
92. *Times*, 17 August 1946.
93. John, *Pioneers in Nation-Building*, 95.
94. *Vincentian*, 29 February 1936.
95. *Times*, 15 June 1946.
96. *Times*, 27 July 1946.
97. Ibid.
98. At the first meeting of the legislative council, St Clair Bonadie was chosen as representative for South Windward, following a motion by the Crown attorney that the council exercise its right according to the Letters Patent to serve (*Government Gazette*, 23 November 1946). At that meeting, the issue of who was entitled to vote arose following a motion by McIntosh. A ruling from the governor and secretary of state dictated that the whole house was entitled to vote, rather than being limited to elected members. Bonadie won by a single vote, 5–4 (*Vincentian*, 23 November 1946).

CHAPTER 6

1. Knight, "Caribbean in the 1930s", 43.
2. *Moyne Commission Report*, 8.
3. "The Moyne Commission and the West Indian Intelligentsia, 1938–39", *Journal of Commonwealth Political Studies* 9, no. 2 (July 1971): 135.
4. Grimble, Report of the Disturbances, 31 October 1935, SVA.
5. *Times*, 27 February 1937.
6. *Moyne Commission Report*, 321.
7. Grier to MacDonald, 12 November 1935, SVA.
8. *Investigator*, 19 December 1936. The speech was reported in an article headlined "Land Settlement and Wages".
9. See, for example, *Times*, 26 March 1938, 10 September 1938; *Investigator*, 3 April 1937, 22 April 1939.
10. Minutes of Legislative Council Meeting, 9 December 1912, SVA.
11. C.C. Skeete to the Commissioner of Agriculture, Report on a Visit to St Vincent 17 March–2 April 1936 to investigate the suitability of the Leeward District of St

Vincent for Peasant Settlement, Land Settlement File 1936, no. 64310, CO 321/368, Conf. 5/6/36, SVA.

12. Letter dated 11 March 1939 from Fraser agreeing to rent 50 acres, Provision of lands for Small Towns and Villages: Rental of land from Honourable A.M. Fraser, Conf. 5/1939, MP, SVA.

13. Fraser already had 60–100 acres occupied by his own workers.

14. Administrator before the Finance Committee, Conf. 5/1939 (5) 1.3.39, SVA.

15. Conf. 5/1939 (8), SVA.

16. Administrator to Secretary of State, 3 July 1939, SVA.

17. *Times,* 11 February 1939.

18. Acting Governor to Malcolm McDonald, 3 July 1939, St Vincent 131, SVA.

19. *Times*, 17 August 1940.

20. *Times*, 11 February 1939.

21. Ibid.

22. "Government Land Settlement Policy", 1943, Land Settlement File, SVA.

23. Minutes of Legislative Council Meeting, 28 June 1945, SVA.

24. This included the colonial treasurer, the social welfare officer and director of agriculture of the Windward Islands

25. *Times*, 15 December 1945.

26. *Times*, 19 October 1946.

27. F.A. Casson was formerly F.A. Corea, who had been a nominated member of the legislative council during the 1935 riots.

28. *Agricultural Department Annual Report*, 1946, SVA.

29. Gibbs, *Plan of Development*, 22.

30. Orde Brown, *Labour Conditions in the West Indies*, 157.

31. Augier et al., *Making of the West Indies*, 271.

32. *Times*, 21 January 1939.

33. Bolland, *Politics of Labour*, 360.

34. MP 3/1940, SVA.

35. Susan Craig, "The Germs of an Idea", afterword to *Labour in the West Indies: The Birth of a Workers Movement*, by W. Arthur Lewis (London: New Beacon Books, 1977), 63.

36. Arthur Grimble, *A Review of Matters Affecting the Windward Islands during 1946*, presented to the Legislative Councils of the Windwards (Kingstown: Government Printing Office, 1946), SVA.

37. Anderson, *St Vincent Handbook*, 355.

38. *Investigator*, 12 February 1938.

39. *Times*, 26 October 1940.

40. *St Vincent Gazette*, 1939, SVA; *Times*, 7 October 1939.

41. *Times*, 19 October 1940.
42. *Vincentian*, 10 March 1945.
43. *Colonial Office Annual Report, St Vincent* (London: HMSO, 1947), SVA.
44. *Colonial Office Annual Report, St Vincent* (London: HMSO, 1948), SVA. The Labour Party/SWMA seemed to have been paying more attention to their political role than to the organization of workers.
45. Minutes of Executive Council Meeting, 19 February 1937, SVA.
46. Ibid.
47. *Investigator*, 21 August 1937. The administrator had been making the point about the paternalist policies of estate management. This was seen in the case of Richards at Mount Bentinck but was not generally the case, especially after the passage of certain pieces of labour legislation.
48. It was, of course, easier to organize workers on large plantations where numbers mattered. The emphasis was, however, on their work in the legislative council, something which obviously influenced their defeat at the polls in 1951.
49. *Colonial Office Annual Report, St Vincent* (London: HMSO, 1947).
50. *Vincentian*, 8 April 1950.
51. *Colonial Office Annual Report, St Vincent* (London: HMSO, 1949), SVA.
52. *Times*, 23 November 1940, SVA.
53. Orde Brown, *Labour Conditions in the West Indies*, 43.
54. Patricia Stephens, *The Spiritual Baptist Faith: African New World Religious History, Identity and Testimony* (London: Karnak, 1999), 58–59; C.M. Jacobs, *Joy Comes in the Morning: Elton George Griffith and the Shouter Baptists* (Trinidad: Caribbean Historical Society, 1996), 282; Melville Herskovits and Frances Herskovits, *Trinidad Village* (New York: Knopf, 1947), 343–44.
55. "The Shakers of St Vincent: A Stable Religion", in *Religion, Altered States of Consciousness and Social Change*, ed. Erika Bourguignon (Columbus: Ohio State University Press, 1973), 219.
56. Ibid.
57. It was difficult preventing the practice in the remote areas where prayer houses were located, but, in Kingstown, it was easy to exercise authority over the religion, whose practice was generally forbidden.
58. Minutes of Executive Council Meeting, 3 April 1939, SVA.
59. Minutes of Legislative Council Meeting, 13 April 1939, SVA.
60. "McIntosh on Shakerism", *Times*, 28 October 1939, SVA.
61. Duncan, editor of the *Investigator*, seemed to have formally joined the association and, in fact, became secretary in 1941.
62. *Vincentian*, 2 September 1939, SVA.
63. File on Shakerism, SVA.

64. McIntosh to S.C. Connell, Clerk of the Legislative Council, 23 June 1939, Kingstown, J. 29/1939 (5), file on Shakerism, SVA.
65. Minutes of Executive Council Meeting, 3 April 1939, SVA.
66. Ibid., 24 June 1939, SVA.
67. Ibid., 29 September 1939, J. 29/1939 (9), SVA.
68. Administrator Bain Gray to Governor Sir Henry Popham, 16 October 1939, Conf. 29/1939 (11), SVA.
69. Malcolm MacDonald to the Governor, Downing Street, 29 January 1940, file on Shakerism, SVA.
70. Chief of Police's report to the Administrator on two Shaker meetings held in Kingstown, 6 October 1939, Conf. J. 29, SVA.
71. *Times*, 15 June 1940.
72. Minutes of Legislative Council Meeting, 5 October 1950, SVA.
73. Bishop of the Windward Islands to the Administrator, 14 January 1945, file on Shakerism, SVA.
74. Administrator W.F. Coutts to the Clergy, strictly conf., 16 September 1949, file on Shakerism, SVA.
75. Reverend Pitt, memo, enclosed in letter from Ernest Higman, 14 October 1949, SVA.
76. The clergy's report noted that there were at least thirty-five known centres of Shakerism, including a Praise House and "Cult" House.
77. Letter from the clergy, 14 October 1949, file on Shakerism, SVA.
78. Coutts to the SMO, pers. and conf., Government House, 19 October 1949, file on Shakerism, SVA; SMO to Coutts, pers. and conf. , 8 November 1949, file on Shakerism, SVA; Dr Macmillan to SMO, pers. and conf., 8 November 1949, file on Shakerism, SVA.
79. Dasent to Administrator, 6 February 1950, Conf. 39/41 (27), file on Shakerism, SVA; see also Conf. 39/41 (28), SVA.
80. Colonial Office to Governor R.D.H. Arundell, 22 April 1950, Shakerism, Suppression of, 64427/50, Conf. 1949-391, MP, SVA.
81. McIntosh realized the serious handicap that existed because of the constitutional provisions at that time and, therefore, was taking the struggle in other directions. The permission given to hold a "patronal" process in Georgetown in 1949 had given them some hope, but the position taken in 1950 forced McIntosh back to the legislative council, where his strategy seemed to be to embarrass the authorities.
82. Superintendent of Police to the Administrator, "Questions asked in Council 17 July 1950", 29 July 1950, Conf. C39/49(H)(3), file on Shakerism, SVA.
83. "Notice of Questions to be asked by the member for Kingstown", Conf. C39/49(H), file on Shakerism, SVA.

84. The body referred to was the new name that was adopted, the Spiritual Baptists.

85. Ths is in reference to the way in which the Shakers practised their religion.

86. Extract from Minutes of Legislative Council Meeting, 5 October 1950, C39/49A(6), file on Shakerism, SVA.

87. Conf. 39/49A(81), file on Shakerism, SVA.

88. C39/49(A)(9), file on Shakerism, SVA; Bernard Gibbs to McDonald Williams, 11 May 1951, C39/49A(10), file on Shakerism, SVA. There was no indication that he was granted the licence.

89. *Moyne Commission Report*, 107.

90. Gibbs, *Plan of Development*, 67. Gibbs was quoting from "Education in St Vincent", produced in 1943 by the educational adviser to the Comptroller for Development and Welfare in the West Indies.

91. *Times*, 28 January 1939.

92. *Times*, 9 January 1939.

93. John, *Pioneers in Nation-Building*, 10–11; *Investigator*, 19 February 1938.

94. *Times*, 24 June 1939.

95. Official report of the conference, 34, SVA.

96. Gibbs, "Land Settlement Policy", *A Plan of Development for the Colony of St Vincent*, appendix K, "Agricultural Policy for St Vincent", as presented by the Land Settlement and Development Board and adopted by the Legislative Council, 1946, SVA.

97. "McIntosh on Education", *Vincentian*, 11 June 1949, SVA.

98. Ibid.

99. *Times*, 28 January 1939.

100. John, *Pioneers in Nation-Building*, 44.

101. Ibid.; "The Methodist School Controversy: Facts about the Case", *Times*, 20 September 1934.

102. Reverend Richards, manager of the school, left the island the day after his committee had requested Duncan's transfer to the board; the inspector of schools was also out of the colony. *Times*, 20 September 1934.

103. *Moyne Commission Report*, 93–94.

104. John, *Pioneers in Nation-Building*, 44–47; *Vincentian*, 15 April 1939.

105. Minutes of Executive Council Meeting, 2 June 1939, SVA.

106. Minutes of Executive Council Meeting, 13 January 1939, AA1.15.5, SVA. It is not clear why the council's "last decision" was not carried out.

107. *St Vincent: Report and General Abstracts of the Census of 1931*, SVA.

108. *Times*, 14 May 1938.

109. Ibid.; see also letter captioned "A Criticism by Junius: 'The Educational Mess'", *Times*, 2 April 1938.

110. *Times*, 14 May 1938.
111. Official report of the conference, 57.
112. *Vincentian*, 30 April 1949.
113. *Vincentian*, 26 April 1947.
114. Official report of the conference, 57.
115. *Times*, 16 July 1938.
116. *Vincentian*, 11 June 1949. The reference to the non-publication of a newspaper has not been identified.
117. Official report of the conference, 57.

CHAPTER 7

1.   *Caribbean Labour Congress: Official Report of Conference* (Bridgetown: Advocate Co., 1945), 49.
2.   *Proceedings of the West Indian Conference*, 7.
3.   Lewis, *Labour in the West Indies*, 42.
4.   At a meeting of the legislative council in 1945, while speaking about the pressing matter of an adequate water supply for Kingstown, the party's leader reminded the administrator that he had said previously that the board would soon be recipients of money from the Colonial Development and Welfare Fund. He would have been glad if it had been spent long ago. Minutes of Legislative Council Meeting, 13 September 1945, SVA; see questions raised in the legislative council on 12 December 1949, *Vincentian*, 10 December 1949, and *Minutes of Legislative Council for the year ended 1949* (Kingstown: Government Printing Office, 1950).
5.   *Times*, 13 July 1946.
6.   Rafael Cox Aloma, *Revisiting the Transatlantic Triangle: The Constitutional Decolonization of the Eastern Caribbean* (Kingston: Ian Randle, 2009), 19.
7.   *Moyne Commission Report*, 373.
8.   Ibid., 449.
9.   Ibid., 326–27.
10. "Despatch from the Secretary of State for the Colonies to the Governors of the Leeward Islands and the Windward Islands, dated 14th March 1946", supplement to the *Leeward Islands Gazette*, 4 April 1946, in Spackman, *Constitutional Development*.
11. "Windward Islands Conference on Constitutional Reform: Official Communiqué", *Government Gazette*, 1945–46, 15.
12. The "foregoing resolutions" dealt with matters relating to official representation in the legislative council, universal adult suffrage, the governor's reserve power, and margin of qualification between voters and members of the legislative council.

Government Notice, "Windward Islands Conference on Constitutional Reform", by Government Secretary Bernard Gibbs, Government Office, 20 January 1945, SVA.

13. *Caribbean Labour Congress*, 23.
14. Ibid., 49.
15. Ibid., 23–24.
16. Ibid., 48.
17. *Vincentian*, 13 September 1947.
18. *Vincentian*, 4 October 1947.
19. Government Notice, 11 April 1947, *Government Gazette*, 1947.
20. Government Notice, 19 August 1947, *Government Gazette*, 1947.
21. Emmanuel, *Crown Colony Politics*, 137, 144.
22. *Times*, 13 April 1946.
23. *Government Gazette*, 1946, SVA.
24. *Times*, 13 April 1946.
25. Ibid.
26. Ibid.
27. *Vincentian*, 20 April 1946.
28. *Times*, 14 May 1946.
29. *Times*, 13 April 1946.
30. They seemed to have been using the words "amalgamation" and "federation" interchangeably, but the focus was definitely on the secretary of state's despatch that called for amalgamation.
31. *Times*, 4 May 1946.
32. Ibid.
33. Stanley's 1945 despatch: "I consider it important (therefore) that the more immediate purpose of developing self-governing institutions in the individual British Caribbean colonies should keep in view the larger project of their political federation as being the end to which, in view of the Royal Commission policy should be directed..." Colonial Office, Despatch from the Secretary of State for the Colonies, appendix 1, *Closer Association of the British West Indian Colonies* (London: HMSO, 1947), Cmnd. 7120, quoted in Emmanuel, *Crown Colony Politics*, 130.
34. *Times*, 25 May 1946.
35. *Times*, 1 June 1946.
36. *Times*, 28 September 1946.
37. Ibid.
38. *Colonial Office Annual Report, St Vincent* (London: HMSO, 1946), SVA.
39. *Vincentian*, 8 January 1949.
40. Ibid.

41. *Colonial Office Annual Report, St Vincent, 1950/51* (London: HMSO, 1951), SVA.

42. *An Economic Survey of the Colonial Territories*, vol. 4, *1951* (London: HMSO, 1953); *Vincentian*, 6 December 1947, 9 December 1950.

43. *Government Gazette*, 1949, SVA.

44. *Vincentian*, 9 April 1949.

45. This was most likely taken from Mill's *Consideration on Representative Government*.

46. Minutes of Special Meeting of the Legislative Council, 13 May 1950, SVA. It is to be assumed that, based on his stated position on adult suffrage, this referred also to women.

47. Minutes of Legislative Council Meetings of St Vincent, for the half-year ending 31 December 1949, SVA.

48. Denis Benn, *The Caribbean: An Intellectual History, 1774–2003* (Kingston: Ian Randle, 2004), 56.

49. Minutes of Legislative Council Meeting, St Lucia, 24 July 1950, SVA; "Extracts from Royal Instructions to the Governor of the Windward Islands", 10 August 1951, in Spackman, *Constitutional Development*.

50. *Vincentian*, 17 September 1949.

51. For example, there was a discussion on federation organized by the Edinboro Community Circle and one on the forthcoming general elections by the Grammar School Old Boys Association. *Vincentian*, 14 October 1950.

52. Minutes of Legislative Council Meeting, 13 May 1950.

53. *Colonial Office Report on St Vincent for 1950 and 1951* (London: HMSO, 1953), 29, SVA.

54. F.A. Simmons, "The Political Scene in 1950", *Vincentian*, 28 November 1950; see also *Vincentian*, 4 and 18 November 1950.

55. *Vincentian*, 7 October 1950.

56. *Vincentian*, 21 October 1950. The party had identified eight candidates, among them S. Slater, Herman Young, C. McRichards and Julian Baynes, who contested for other parties.

57. *Vincentian*, 5 and 12 May 1951.

58. *Colonial Office Report for St Vincent for 1950 and 1951* (London: HMSO, 1953), SVA.

59. *Vincentian*, 12 March 1951.

60. Cecil Ryan and Cecil "Blazer" Williams, "From Charles to Mitchell: Part 1" (Kingstown: Projects Promotion, n.d.).

61. *Vincentian*, 5 and 12 May 1951.

62. *Vincentian*, 10 and 24 March 1951.

63. Joshua was the chief warder at the prisons at the time of the riots.

64. *Vincentian*, 26 May 1951.

65. Ibid.
66. Minutes of Executive Council Meeting, no. 259, 1951, SVA.
67. It should have appeared in the issue of 9 June.
68. *Vincentian*, 30 June 1951.
69. The party seemed oblivious to the great expectations and new atmosphere that was emerging.
70. *Vincentian*, 18 August 1951. There seemed to have been no public meetings in Kingstown during McIntosh's absence. One is left to assume, however, that other candidates were working in their particular constituencies.
71. It was felt at one time that he would be a candidate for the Labour Party.
72. *Vincentian*, 22 September 1951.
73. *Vincentian*, 6 October 1951.
74. *Compendium of the Electoral Statistics: St Vincent and the Grenadines (1951–1998)*, Permanent Mission of St Vincent and the Grenadines, for the Organisation of American States, 2001.
75. *Vincentian*, 20 October 1951.
76. Discussions held with elderly persons at different forums.
77. The marking of an X for the respective candidate was somewhat complicated, with the marks having to fit clearly between the lines. Once an X went over the line, the vote was often rejected.
78. This meant that they did not receive a certain percentage of the votes that had been predetermined.
79. *Vincentian*, 20 October 1951.
80. Ibid.
81. *Vincentian*, 16 June 1951.
82. *Vincentian*, 18 August 1951.
83. Evans Morgan, interview by author, Toronto, Canada, 29 October 1985. Morgan was one of the candidates of Charles's party. He was the union's grievance officer and won his seat in 1951 but resigned shortly after.
84. Ralph Gonsalves, "E. Joshua, Hero or Traitor", *Beacon* 1, no. 3 (1976): 6.
85. Kenneth John, "Politics in a Small Colonial Territory, St Vincent 1950–70" (PhD diss., University of Manchester, 1971), 38.
86. Emmanuel, *Crown Colony Politics*, 184–85.
87. "Letter from O.W. Forde dated 12 September 1951", *Vincentian*, 15 September 1951.

SELECTED BIBLIOGRAPHY

PRIMARY SOURCES

Official Documents and Reports

Great Britain. Report of the Closer Union Commission. April 1933. Cmnd. 4383/1932–33.

Great Britain. *Report of the West India Royal Commission 1897*. British Parliamentary Papers, vol. 7. Dublin: Irish University Press, 1970.

Noble, Robert E. "The Shakerism Prohibition Ordinance, 1912". 7 September 1912. PRO CO 327/209, XC 11723.

Orde Brown, G. St J. *Labour Conditions in the West Indies*. London: HMSO, 1939. Cmnd. 6070.

Report of the Visit of E.F.L. Wood, MP to the West Indies and British Guiana, 1921–22. London. 1922. Cmnd. 1679.

Report of the West India Royal Commission, 1938–39. London: HMSO, 1945.

Report of the West India Royal Commission, 1944–45 (Moyne Commission). London: 1945; repr., Barbados, Government Printing Department, 2000.

West India Royal Commission. *Report on Agriculture, Fisheries, Forestry and Veterinary Matters*, by F.L. Engledow, 1944–45. Cmnd. 6608. London: 1945.

St Vincent Archives

Agricultural Department Annual Reports. 1935–1950.

Annual Administration Reports. 1931–37, 1947–51.

Blue Books. 1935–1951.

Chief of Police to Administrator. 22 October 1912. CO 321/209, XC 11723.

Colonial Office Annual Reports, St Vincent. 1935–1951. London: HMSO.

File on Shakerism: Minute Papers and Confidential Documents with extracts from newspapers and official correspondence.

Grimble, Arthur. *A Review of Matters Affecting the Windward Islands during 1946.*

Presented to the Legislative Councils of the Windwards. Kingstown: Government Printing Office, 1946.

Government Gazettes, 1912, 1919, 1935, 1936, 1939, 1945, 1946, 1947, 1949, 1950.

Minute Papers. 1935 riots.

Minute Papers. Administrator's records, including reports and records of daily transactions 1935–1951.

Minute Papers. Shakerism, Suppression of. Confidential 39/1949: 391.

Minutes of Executive Council Meetings. 1936, 1937, 1939, 1946, 1949, 1950, 1951.

Minutes of Legislative Council Meetings. 1909–15, 1935, 1939, 1945, 1946, 1949, 1950.

Hansard. Parliamentary Debates, 22 March 1965, Kingstown, St Vincent.

Report and General Abstracts of the Census of 1931. Prepared by Walter Grant. Kingstown: Government Printing Office, 1931.

Report on Certain Convictions for Shakerism. 21 February 1913. CO 321/273, XC 11723.

Resolution Passed at the Kingstown Methodist Circuit Quarterly Meeting. 24 July 1912. CO 321/209, XC 11723.

Public Documents

Anderson, R.M., ed. *The St Vincent Handbook.* Kingstown: Office of the Vincentian, 1938.

Archer, A.J. *Guide Book to St Vincent.* 7th ed. Kingstown: Government Printing Office, 1932.

Caribbean Labour Congress: Official Report of Conference. Bridgetown: Advocate Co., 1945.

Gibbs, Bernard. *A Plan of Development for the Colony of St Vincent.* Adopted by the St Vincent Development Committee. Port of Spain: Guardian Comercial Printery, 1947.

Proceedings of the West Indian Conference Held at Roseau, Dominica, B.W.I., October–November 1932. Castries, St Lucia: Voice Printery, 1932.

Newspapers

Agricultural Reporter (Barbados), 9 August 1912.

Investigator (Kingstown), 1935–40.

Port of Spain Gazette (Trinidad), 29 September 1912, October 1935–January 1936.

Rambler (St Vincent), 22 July 1912.

Sentry (Kingstown), 1912–14, 1930.

Times (Kingstown), 1912, 1922, 1932–46.

Vincentian (Kingstown), 1932–51.

SECONDARY SOURCES

Books

Abrahams, Roger, D. *The Man-of-Words in the West Indies: Performance and the Emergence of Creole Culture.* Baltimore: Johns Hopkins University Press, 1983.

Aloma, Rafael Cox. *Revisiting the Transatlantic Triangle: The Constitutional Decolonization of the Eastern Caribbean.* Kingston: Ian Randle, 2009.

Augier, F.R., S.C. Gordon, D.G. Hall, and M. Reckord. *The Making of the West Indies.* London: Longmans, 1960.

Benn, Denis. *The Caribbean: An Intellectual History, 1774–2003.* Kingston: Ian Randle, 2004.

Bolland, O.N. *The Politics of Labour in the British Caribbean: The Social Origins of Authoritarianism and Democracy in the Labour Movement.* Kingston: Ian Randle, 2001.

Brereton, Bridget. *A History of Modern Trinidad, 1783–1962.* London: Heineman, 1981.

Comitas, Lambros, and D. Lowenthal, eds. *The Aftermath of Sovereignty: West Indian Perspectives.* New York: Anchor Press, 1973.

Cyrus, A.C. *A Dream Come True: The Autobiography of a Caribbean Surgeon.* Charleston: Hobo Jungle Press, 2015.

Duncan, Ebenezer. *A Brief History of St Vincent: With Studies in Citizenship.* 4th ed. Kingstown: Model Printery, 1967.

———. *Kingstown.* Kingstown: Model Printery, 1965.

Emmanuel, Patrick. *Crown Colony Politics in Grenada, 1917–1951.* Barbados: ISER, 1978.

Fraser, Adrian. *From Shakers to Spiritual Baptists: The Struggle of the Shakers of St Vincent and the Grenadines.* Madison: Kings-SVG Publishers, 2011.

Gonsalves, Ralph. *The McIntosh Trial and the 1935 Uprising.* Educational Pamphlet no. 9 of the Movement for National Unity. Kingstown: Movement for National Unity, 1985.

———. *The 1935 Labour Riots in St Vincent and Their Political Significance.* Kingstown: Yulimo, 1966.

———. *The October 1935 Uprising in Saint Vincent (Youlou) and the October 1917 Revolution of the Soviet Union.* Kingstown: Yulimo, 1977.

Hart, Richard. *Towards Decolonisation: Political, Labour and Economic Development in Jamaica, 1938–1945.* Kingston: Canoe Press, 1999.

Herskovits, Melville, and Frances Herskovits. *Trinidad Village.* New York: Knopf, 1947.

Hill, Robert, ed. *Marcus Garvey and the Universal Negro Improvement Association Papers.* 2 vols. Los Angeles: University of California Press, 1983.

Jacobs, C.M. *Joy Comes in the Morning: Elton George Griffith and the Shouter Baptists.* Trinidad: Caribbean Historical Society, 1996.

John, Karl. *Land Reform in Small Island Developing States: A Case Study on St Vincent, West Indies, 1890–2000*. College Station, TX: Virtualbookworm Publishing, 2006.

John, Rupert. *Pioneers in Nation-Building in a Caribbean Mini-State*. New York: UNITAR, 1979.

Lewis, W. Arthur. *Labour in the West Indies: The Birth of a Workers Movement*. 1938. Reprinted with afterword by Susan E. Craig. London: New Beacon Books, 1977. Citations refer to the 1977 edition.

Lewis, Gordon K. *The Growth of the Modern West Indies*. New York: Monthly Review Press, 1968.

Macmillan, W.H. *Warning from the West Indies*. Harmondsworth: Penguin Books, 1936.

Parry, J., and P.M. Sherlock. *A Short History of the West Indies*. London: McMillan, 1956.

Post, Ken. *Arise Ye Starvelings: The Jamaican Labour Rebellion of 1938 and Its Aftermath*. The Hague: Martinus Nijhoff, 1978.

Reddock, Rhoda. *Elma Francois: The NWCSA and the Workers Struggle for Change in the Caribbean in the 1930s*. London: New Beacon Books, 1988.

Rubin, Vera. *Caribbean Studies: A Symposium*. Seattle: The University of Washington Press, 1960.

Rude, George. *The Crowd in History, 1730–1848*. New York: Wiley and Sons, 1964.

Ryan, Selwyn. *Race and Nationalism in Trinidad and Tobago: A Study of Decolonization in a Multiracial Society*. Toronto: University of Toronto Press, 1972.

Shephard, Charles. *An Historical Account of the Island of St Vincent*. London: Cass, 1997. First published 1831 by Nicol.

Shepherd, C.Y. *Survey of Peasant Agriculture in the Leewards and Windwards*. Trinidad: Imperial College of Tropical Agriculture, 1945.

Singham, A.W. *The Hero and the Crowd in a Colonial Polity*. New Haven: Yale University Press, 1967.

Spackman, Ann. *Constitutional Development of the West Indies, 1922–68: A Selection of Major Documents*. Essex: Caribbean University Press, 1975.

Stephens, Patricia. *The Spiritual Baptist Faith: African New World Religious History, Identity and Testimony*. London: Karnak, 1999.

Stockdale, Frank. *Development and Welfare in the West Indies, 1940–1942: A Report*. London: HMSO, 1943.

Thomas, Roy, ed. *The Trinidad Labour Riots of 1937: Perspectives 50 Years Later*. Port of Spain: Extra-Mural Studies Unit, University of the West Indies, 1987.

Articles

Abbott, George. "The Collapse of the Sea Island Cotton Industry in the West Indies". *Social and Economic Studies* 13, no. 1 (March 1964).

Boa, Sheena. "Walking in the Highway to Heaven: Religious Influences and Attitudes Relating to the Freed Population of St Vincent 1834–1884". *Journal of Caribbean History* 35, no. 2 (2001).

Cox, Edward L. "Religious Intolerance and Persecution: The Case of the Shakers in St Vincent, 1900–1934". *Journal of Caribbean History* 28, no. 2 (1994).

Craig, Susan. "The Germs of an Idea". Afterword to *Labour in the West Indies: The Birth of a Workers Movement*, by W. Arthur Lewis. London: New Beacon Books, 1977.

Elkins, W.F. "Marcus Garvey, the Negro World and the British West Indies: 1919–20". *Science and Society* 36 (Spring 1972).

Hadley, C.V.D. "Personality Patterns, Social Class, and Aggression in the British West Indies". *Human Relations* 2, no. 4 (1949).

Handley, J.S. "The History of Arrowroot and the Origin of Peasantries in the British West Indies". *Journal of Caribbean History* 2 (May 1971).

Harris, Coleridge. "The Constitutional History of the Windwards". *Caribbean Quarterly* 6, nos. 2 and 3 (May 1960).

Hart, Richard. "Origin and Development of the Working Class in the English-Speaking Caribbean Area, 1897–1937". In *Labour in the Caribbean: From Emancipation to Independence*, edited by Malcolm Cross and Gad Heuman, 43–79. London: Macmillan, 1988.

Henney, Jeannette. "The Shakers of St Vincent: A Stable Religion". In *Religion, Altered States of Consciousness and Social Change*, edited by Erika Bourguignon, 219–61. Columbia: Ohio State University Press, 1973.

Hills, Theo. "Land Settlement Schemes: Lessons from the British Caribbean". *Revisita Geografica* 63 (July/December 1965).

John, Kenneth. "St Vincent: A Political Kaleidoscope". *Flambeau*, no. 5 (July 1966). Reprinted in *The Aftermath of Sovereignty: West Indian Perspectives*, edited by D. Lowenthal and Lambros Comitas. New York: Anchor Press, 1973.

John, Kenneth, and Oswald Peters. "1935 Revisited". In *Search for Identity: Essays on St Vincent and the Grenadines*, edited by Baldwin King, Kenneth John and Cheryl King, 267–73. Kingstown: Kings-SVG Press, 2006.

Keizer, Norma. "A Short History of Education in St Vincent during the 19th Century". *Flambeau* (1966).

Knight, Franklyn. "The Caribbean in the 1930s". In *General History of the Caribbean*, vol. 5, edited by Bridget Brereton, 42–81. London: UNESCO, 2004.

La Guerre, John. "The Moyne Commission and the West Indian Intelligentsia, 1938–39". *Journal of Commonwealth Political Studies* 9, no. 2 (July 1971).

Lewis, W.A. "Issues in Land Settlement Policy". *Caribbean Economic Review* 111 (1951).

Manning, Frank. "Celebrating Cricket: The Symbolic Construction of Caribbean Politics". *American Ethnologist* 616 (1981).

Marshall, W.K. "Vox Populi: The St Vincent Riots and Disturbances of 1862". In *Trade, Government and Society in Caribbean History, 1700–1920*, edited by B.W. Higman, 84–115. Jamaica: Heinemann Educational Books Caribbean, 1983.

Nanton, Philip. "The Changing Pattern of State Control in St Vincent and the Grenadines". In *Crisis in the Caribbean*, by F. Ambursley and R. Cohen, 223–46. London: Heineman, 1983.

Rubenstein, Hymie. "The Utilization of Arable Land in an Eastern Caribbean Valley". *Canadian Journal of Sociology* 1, no. 2 (1975).

St Pierre, Maurice. "West Indian Cricket: A Socio-historical Appraisal". *Caribbean Quarterly* 19, no. 2 (June 1973).

Samaroo, Brinsley. "The Trinidad Workingmen's Association and the Origins of Popular Protest in a Crown Colony". *Social and Economic Studies* 21, no. 2 (June 1972).

Stephens, S.G. "Cotton Growing in the West Indies during the 18th and 19th Centuries". *Tropical Agriculture* 21, no. 2 (February 1944).

Wright, S. "Economic Conditions in St Vincent, British West Indies". *Economic Geography* 5, no. 3 (1929).

Theses and Papers

Fraser, Adrian. Fraser, A. "The Constitutional History of St Vincent and the Grenadines to 1951". Paper presented to the Constitutional Reform Commission, Kingstown, St Vincent, 2004.

——. "From Whence We Came". National Broadcasting Company, St Vincent, no. 326, 1 February 1999. Prepared and presented by Adrian Fraser.

——. "Development of a Peasantry in St Vincent 1846–1912". MPhil thesis, University of the West Indies, Cave Hill, Barbados, 1980.

——. "Peasants and Agricultural Labourers in St Vincent and the Grenadines 1899–1951". PhD dissertation, University of Western Ontario, 1986.

Gonsalves, Ralph. "The Role of Labour in the Political Process of St Vincent, 1935–70". Master's thesis, University of the West Indies, 1971.

Hourihan, John Joseph. "Rule in Hairoun: A Study of the Politics of Power". PhD dissertation, University of Massachusetts, 1975.

John, Karl. "Policies of Programmes of Intervention into the Agrarian Structure of St Vincent, 1890–1974". Master's thesis, University of Waterloo, 1974.

John, Kenneth. "Politics in a Small Colonial Territory, St Vincent 1950–70". PhD dissertation, University of Manchester, 1971.

London, Caspar. "Samuel Lewis and the 1935 Revolt". Based on interviews of Lewis by London, Kingstown in the 1970s. N.d.

Ryan, Cecil, and Cecil "Blazer" Williams. "From Charles to Mitchell: Part 1". Projects Promotion, Kingstown. N.d.

Spinelli, Joseph. "Land Use and Population in St Vincent, 1763–1960: A Contribution to the Study of the Patterns of Economic and Demographic Change in a Small West Indian Society". PhD dissertation, University of Florida, 1973.

Interviews by Author

Cato, Clement, policeman in Kingstown at the time of the 1935 riots. New Montrose, 7 March 1989.

Lawrence, Baha, taxi driver in 1935. Granby Street gas station, 24 January 1990.

Layne, Lucas (Canute), policeman in Georgetown in 1935. 28 April 1989.

Morgan, Evans, former grievance officer of the United Workers and Ratepayers Union. Toronto, 29 October 1985.

Williams, Osment, Ronald Paris and Kathleen Sardine. Camden Park, November 1990.

Williams, Norman, bystander and witness at the court yard during the 1935 riots. New Montrose, 28 November 1990. (He was a bystander at the time of the Kingstown riots: he was on lunch break as an attendant at a store in Kingstown and was on his way home when the commotion at the court yard attracted him there.)

INDEX

leadership of riot, 94–95, 203n54

Licences (Amendment) Ordinance 1935, 30, 32, 33, 83

literary association, 20

Literary Digest, 89–90

looting, 38–39, 40, 194–95n42; Camden Park-Chauncey, 46; Cane Garden, 42; recovery of stolen goods, 50

Lovelace, Adolphus, 47

luxury tax, Customs Duties (Amendment no. 4) Ordinance 1935, 31–32

MacDonald, Malcolm (secretary of state), 126, 36; on repeal of Shakerism Prohibition Ordinance, 141

MacDonald, Sheila, 106–7

MacMaster, Laois, 33, 192n11

Maffey, Sir John, 67

Mangin, Charles, 87

Maran, Rane, 87

Marryshow, Albert T., 162, 166; commission of inquiry, 67–68; criticism of education system, 27; and Crown colony politics, 184–85; lecture on Italian invasion of Abyssinia, 26, 34, 88; on representative government, 164; as special guest at SWMA rally, 106–7; Workers Day address, censorship of, 55–56

matches, tax on, 31, 32, 49, 51, 86, 93, 192n8

Maxwell, Archdeacon R.S., 143

Mayers, Leonard, 72

Mayreau, 4

McCarter, Henry, 76

McCaulay, Samuel, 76

McDonald, Donald, 42

McDonald, T.M., 126, 128

McDowall, Cyril, 65

McDowall, Peter, 73, 74

McIntosh, D.C., 116

McIntosh, George, 97, 116; 1937 general election, 113, 114; 1940 general election, 117, 118; 1950 general election, 172; 1951 general election, 179–80, 181, 183, 215n70; arrest of as riot instigator, 49, 57, 69–70; bell-ringing, 34–35, 193n23; case against as riot instigator, 49, 57, 66; case dismissal, 71–73, 98–99, 200n83; as champion of the poorer class, 32–33, 124; compulsory education, 150–51; as conspirator in government conspiracy theory, 93–94, 203n51; education of the masses, 157–58; estate workers grievances, 134; federation, 168–69; on function of SWMA, 105; land settlement board, 128; letter to the governor, 33–34, 195n49; meeting at Carnegie Public Library, 40–41; patronal festival, advocacy for, 144–45, 210n81; reaction to riot, 66; recognition of Spiritual Baptists/Christian Pilgrims, 145, 146–47; removal from legislative council, 119; on Seditious Publications Ordinance, 62; and Shakerism Prohibition Ordinance, 137–39; on St Vincent riot, 40; and the SWMA, 103; SWMA agenda, 106; as SWMA candidate, 109, 112, 113; SWMA scholarships, 148–49; treason-felony charge, 70–71; trial of, 68–69; on uneven distribution of land, 126–27; universal adult suffrage, and federation, 163

McIntosh, Sydney, 118, 120, 121

McKay, Claude, 146

McMillan, W.M., *Warning from the West Indies*, 127

www.ingramcontent.com/pod-product-compliance
Lightning Source LLC
Chambersburg PA
CBHW022352280326
41935CB00007B/167